And Reality Be Damned...

Undoing America: What media didn't tell you about the end of the Cold War and the fall of communism in Europe.

Robert Buchar

Eloquent Books

Eloquent Books
An imprint of Strategic Book Group
P.O. Box 333
Durham CT 06422
www.StrategicBookGroup.com

ISBN: 978-1-60911-166-3

Printed in the United States of America

Book Design: Suzanne Kelly

Praise for
And Reality Be Damned . . .

"Robert Buchar's book fills a vacuum: it sheds welcome daylight on the KGB's secret ways of embellishing Communism and its tyrants. Most people now realize that telling lies in order to change minds is what Communism was all about, but they are still unable to fully explain how such a bankrupt system was able to trick hundreds and hundreds of millions into believing that it was the way of the future. Changing minds is what the KGB did best, and Mr. Buchar's book allows the inner workings of the machine running its disinformation operations to lie spread out on the table for all to see."

Lt.Gen.ION MIHAI PACEPA

CONTENTS

PREFACE

In December 1961 a KGB major named Golitsyn defected to the United States with information about a Soviet long-range strategy. He provided the CIA with a package of documents, including one that described a new KGB directorate of disinformation (Department "D"). The document said that catching American spies was not the KGB's primary concern. Better to create an elaborate web of disinformation "to negate and discredit authentic information the enemy has obtained." The KGB's tactic was to feed the CIA a steady diet of pleasing falsehoods. Eventually, the CIA would only believe stories tailored by the KGB. This, in turn, would allow Soviet agents to penetrate more easily into the heart of U.S. intelligence. Golitsyn warned the CIA that Soviet disinformation was carefully devised to support a long-range plan in which the balance of power would be inconspicuously shifted in favor of the communist bloc. With the exception of the CIA's James Angleton, few credited Golitsyn's warning. Having been disbelieved and cast aside, Golitsyn submitted a top-secret manuscript to the CIA in 1982. According to this manuscript, by 1986 the Soviet Union would be led by a man "with a more liberal image." This man would initiate "changes that would have been beyond the imagination of Marx or the practical reach of Lenin and unthinkable to Stalin." The Soviet system would be liberalized, and the liberalization "would be spectacular and impressive. Formal pronouncements might be made about a reduction in the Communist Party's role; its monopoly would be apparently curtailed.... The KGB would be reformed. Dissidents at home would be amnestied; those in exile abroad would be allowed to take up positions in the government.... Political clubs would be opened to nonmembers of the Communist Party. Leading dissidents might form one or more alternative political parties. Censorship would be relaxed; controversial books, plays, films, and art would be published, performed, and exhibited."

The CIA did not take Golitsyn's manuscript seriously, and gave Golitsyn permission to publish it as a book, titled New Lies for Old, which appeared in 1984. It included 148 falsifiable predictions. According to researcher Mark Riebling "139 out of 148" of Golitsyn's predictions "were fulfilled by the end of 1993–an accuracy rate of nearly 94 percent." Did anyone agree with Golitsyn's analysis, or approve his predictions at the time? Leading pundits and CIA analysts mocked Golitsyn's work. "Unfortunate is the only term for this book," wrote a CIA analyst in 1985. There were no apologies or compliments given to Golitsyn when 139 of his predictions came true. By that time Golitsyn's critics were busy congratulating themselves on winning the Cold War. The success of Soviet disinformation was total. From that point forward the world would only understand what the KGB wanted them to understand.

According to the 1982 memoirs of a high-level Czechoslovakian defector named Jan Sejna, "One of the basic problems of the West is its frequent failure to recognize the existence of any Soviet 'grand design' at all. Those rejecting this concept unwittingly serve Soviet efforts to conceal their objectives and further complicate the process of determining such objectives." As a leading official, Sejna worked directly for the top level of the Czech communist government. In 1967 Sejna and his colleagues were briefed on Moscow's strategy. "It had always been made clear that the Plan's objectives were firm but the means and methods of achieving them were flexible," wrote Sejna in his memoirs. "This flexibility often serves to confound Western political analysts, who tend to confuse a change in tactics with a profound change in ... thinking." Therefore, Khrushchev's denunciation of Stalin in 1956 was a tactic and not a change of heart. According to Sejna, even though Khrushchev denounced Stalin's crimes, the Kremlin had not abandoned Stalin's objectives.

While addressing Western ambassadors during a reception at the Polish Embassy in Moscow on 18 November 1956, Khrushchev publicly stated: "Whether you like it or not, history is on our side. We will bury you!" ("Мы вас похороним!") On 24 July 1959 Khrushchev told visiting U.S. Vice President Richard Nixon that his grandchildren would live under communism. Two months later Khrushchev visited the United States where he made the exact same boast to U.S. Agriculture Secretary Ezra Taft Benson. When Benson assured him the opposite, Khrushchev reportedly said: "You Americans are so gullible. No, you won't accept communism outright, but we'll keep feeding you small doses of socialism until you'll finally wake up and find you already have communism. We won't have to fight you. We'll so weaken your economy until you'll fall like overripe fruit into our hands." Khrushchev's intention was recently explained by the former deputy chief of Romania's foreign intelligence service, Ion Pacepa, who made the following observation to Robert Buchar: "The whole foreign policy of the Soviet bloc states, indeed its whole economic and military might, revolved around the larger Soviet objective of destroying America from within through the use of lies. The Soviets saw disinformation as a vital tool in the dialectical advance of world communism. KGB priority number one was to damage American power, judgment, and credibility."

It is noteworthy that Khrushchev did not say, "You will live under communism." He also did not say, "Your children will live under communism." He told his American opposites that their grandchildren "would live under communism." Khrushchev was admitting that Moscow's plan was a long-range plan, involving decades of work. Starting in February 1967 the Warsaw Pact countries received regular directives detailing their part in the overall Plan. "When my friends and I studied the Strategic Plan," wrote Sejna, "our initial reactions were identical: we considered it quite unrealistic, especially in its timing, which we thought wildly optimistic." Only after Sejna defected to the West did he change this opinion. "I could find no unity, no consistent objective or strategy among Western countries. It is not possible to fight the Soviet system and strategy with small tactical steps. For the first time I began to believe that the Soviet Union would be able to achieve her goals–something I had not believed in Czechoslovakia."

The Kremlin strategists envisioned that sometime after 1990 an economic and political sequence would unfold, leading to the collapse of the American economy and "the advent to power in Washington of a transitional liberal and progressive government." In September 1967 the Secretary of the Soviet Central Committee, Konstantin Katushev, arrived in Prague to orally brief the Czech communist leaders. The Czechs feared that an economic crisis in America would lead to the emergence of a right-wing regime. The United States could move to "either extreme," Katushev admitted, "as ... in the McCarthy period and the Vietnam War. If we can impose on the U.S.A. the external restraints proposed in our Plan, and seriously disrupt the American economy, the working and lower middle classes will suffer the consequences and they will turn on the society that has failed them. They will be ready for revolution."

The Russian strategists foresaw that the American workforce would be facing a difficult situation in twenty to forty years. America's enormous progress in technology, said Katushev, was a destabilizing influence because it led to underemployment by unskilled workers. "This phenomenon," Katushev noted, "is one I consider the United States cannot deal with." Though American workers could turn to the right, he added, "It's more likely ... that a progressive regime will emerge because, in spite of their power, the governing bureaucratic elite and industrial elite, and the media, are fundamentally liberal in their outlook and ashamed of their failure to solve basic national problems."

In 1967 Soviet Marshal Matvei Zhakarov visited Prague to encourage the recruitment of "high-level agents of influence" in the rising elite of America's universities, media and government. Moscow perceived that power was passing from the hands of the "old industrial plutocracy." If the Soviet bloc could penetrate the U.S. media and academia, it would be easier to manipulate the society as a whole. While the Strategic Plan called for disrupting the U.S. economy and encouraging the election of a progressive presidential candidate, it also aimed at splitting the United States from Europe. According to Sejna, "The Russians planned to play upon the nationalist, bourgeois prejudices of the leading European countries in order to convince them that Europe must strive to become a distinct entity, separate from the United States."

In order to gain technology and money from the West, Moscow also planned to launch an unprecedented peace offensive, which would involve the liquidation of the communist bloc. About this plan, Sejna wrote: "The erosion of NATO begun in Phase Two [of the Plan] would be completed by the withdrawal of the United States from its commitment to the defense of Europe, and by European hostility to military expenditure, generated by economic recession and fanned by the efforts of the 'progressive' movements. To this end we envisaged that it might be necessary to dissolve the Warsaw Pact, in which event we had already prepared a web of bilateral defense arrangements, to be supervised by secret committees of Comecon."

In terms of operational details, the Plan relied on future sabotage and terrorist operations. These would benefit from the infiltration of organized crime and Soviet-sponsored drug trafficking. The Russian planners believed that the American economy could be sabotaged, that the CIA was effectively blind, and that drug trafficking could open a back door to America's financial centers and geographical heartland. Sejna's testimony on this subject was published in 1990 in a book titled Red Cocaine, written by Joseph D. Douglass, Jr., with an introduction by Ray S. Cline, former Deputy Director for Intelligence at the CIA. The role of terrorism was especially important to the thrust of the Strategic Plan. When Robert Buchar asked Russian historian Vladimir Bukovsky whether the Soviets fathered modern terrorism, Bukovsky replied: "Oh definitely. I can show you hundreds of documents proving that. I mean how they supplied, trained, created and … control almost every terrorist organization on earth. I have these documents." The former Deputy Director of the Romanian intelligence service, Ion Mihai Pacepa, has written about Russia's involvement with international terrorism. "Today's international terrorism," he wrote in August 2006, "was conceived at the Lubyanka, the headquarters of the KGB.... I witnessed its birth in my other life, as a Communist general."

In a 1987 book, titled Spetsnaz: The Inside Story of the Soviet Special Forces, a Soviet military intelligence defector writing under the pen name Viktor Suvorov explained the ultimate purpose to which terrorism would be put to use. In Chapter 15 of the book, Suvorov listed various acts of economic sabotage and terrorism to be undertaken in advance of all-out war against the United States. "All these operations," wrote Suvorov, "are known officially in the GRU as the 'preparatory period,' and unofficially as the 'overture.' The overture is a series of large and small operations the purpose of which is, before actual military operations begin, to weaken the enemy's morale, create an atmosphere of general suspicion, fear and uncertainty, and divert the attention of the enemy's armies and police forces to a huge number of different targets, each which may be the object of the next attack." According to Suvorov, the overture is carried out by intelligence agents and by "mercenaries recruited by intermediaries." The strategy they follow is known as "grey terror," described by Suvorov as "a kind of terror which is not conducted in the name of the Soviet Union." Instead, the terror is carried out in the name of "already existing extremist groups not connected in any way" with Russia. According to Suvorov, "The terrorist acts carried out in the course of the 'overture' require very few people, very few weapons and little equipment." The example of 19 men with box-cutters comes to mind, though Suvorov lists "a screw driver, a box of matches or a glass ampoule."

In a July 2005 interview with the Polish Newspaper Rzeczpospolita, FSB/KGB defector Alexander Litvinenko alleged that al Qaeda's second-in-command, Ayman al-Zawahiri, was "an old agent of the FSB." Political writer and former KGB officer, Konstantin Preobrazhenskiy, confirmed Litvinenko's allegation, stating: "[Litvinenko] was responsible for securing the secrecy of al-Zawahiri's arrival in Russia, who was trained by FSB instructors in Dagestan, Northern Caucasus, in 1996-97." Preobrazhenskiy further stated: "At that time, Litvinenko was the Head of the Subdivision for Internationally Wanted Terrorists of the First Department of the Operative-Inquiry Directorate of the FSB Anti-Terrorist Department. He was ordered to undertake the delicate mission of securing al-Zawahiri from unintentional disclosure by the Russian police. Though al-Zawahiri had been brought to Russia by the FSB using a false passport, it was still possible for the police to learn about his arrival and report to Moscow for verification. Such a process could disclose al-Zawahiri as an FSB collaborator."

Litvinenko detailed Russia's role as the originator of modern terrorism in his July 2005 interview with Rzeczpospolita: "I know only one organization that has made terrorism the main tool of solving political problems. It is the Russian special services. The KGB has been engaged in terrorism for many years, and mass terrorism. At the special department of the KGB they trained terrorists from practically every country in the world. These courses lasted, as a rule, for half a year. Specially trained and prepared agents of the KGB organized murders and explosions, including explosions of tankers, the hijacking of passenger airliners, along with hits on diplomatic, state and commercial organizations worldwide." Litvinenko added that the agents of the KGB/FSB were "the bloodiest terrorist in the world." He then listed Carlos Ilyich Ramiros (Carlos the Jackal), Yassir Arafat, Saddam Hussein, and a host of others. According to Litvinenko, "all these figures and movements operated under their own slogans; however, none of them especially hid their 'intimate' ... relationship with the Kremlin and Lubyanka. There is a simple question: whether the Russian special services would train and finance people and groups which are unsupervised by Lubyanka and did not serve the interests of the Kremlin? You understand perfectly, they would not. Each act of terrorism made by these people was carried out as an assignment and under the rigid control of the KGB of the USSR."

Asked if this terrorism continues under the post-Soviet leadership, Litvinenko warned that "the center of global terrorism is not in Iraq, Iran, Afghanistan or the Chechen Republic. The terrorist infection is spread worldwide from Lubyanka Square and the Kremlin cabinet. And until the Russian special services are outlawed, dispersed and condemned, the terrorism will never stop." Roughly 16 months after his public statements about the KGB's connection to Al Qaeda, Litvinenko was poisoned at the bar of a London hotel by Kremlin agents who put radioactive polonium-210 in his tea. He died in November 2006.

In November 1998 I was discussing Moscow's war plans with Russian military defector Col. Stanislav Lunev, who surprised me with an unlikely warning. He said that any future report about Arab terrorists nuking an American city should not be trusted. When I asked why, Lunev replied, "Because it will be my people, Spetsnaz [i.e., Russian special forces commandos]."

For the past five years Robert Buchar has been interviewing intelligence experts, dissidents, defectors and Cold Warriors. What he discovered in the course of those interviews was an altogether different reality than that portrayed in the mainstream media. The sum of what he discovered deserves to be read, studied and discussed. The United States is headed for trouble, and the only way to understand that trouble–in all its complexity–is to turn back the pages of history to learn what really happened in the period 1989 and 1991.

Jeff Nyquist
Eureka, California
4 April 2009

PART 1

THE FALL OF COMMUNISM

The great political upheaval of the late 20th century—the fall of communism in Eastern Europe and the collapse of the Soviet Union—is now generally regarded as the spontaneous product of long-accumulating social and economic pressures, and the political confusion and economic disarray that followed as nothing more than a passing phase in an inevitable march toward a more perfect democracy. One could only wish it was so simple.

It's clear today that developments in Russia didn't go the way the West anticipated. During the final phase of the Cold War, the Soviet Union, under its dogmatic and visibly senile party bosses, was sinking into near-bankruptcy. Yuri Andropov[1], Chairman of the KGB—the only organization with both a full knowledge of the state of the economy and a mastery of strategic decisions—came to the conclusion that there was no cure for the grave illness of the communist system. To preserve the wealth that threatened to slip out of Soviet leaders' hands, he masterminded a nearly unthinkable program—throwing into the fire Moscow's rule over the Eastern European bloc; and, as it turned out, the ruling party of the USSR itself. Though Andropov died in 1984, signs of his influence over the events that followed remain visible through the role of his handpicked successor, Mikhail Gorbachev[2]. The witnesses in this book testify that what appeared to be a spontaneous freedom movement in 1989 was in fact a coup d'état orchestrated from the offices of the Russian KGB[3]. Perhaps for the first time in known history, we have walked through a revolution without realizing who are the real winners and losers.

The consequences are far reaching and people in the West seem to have a short memory. Russia became the perfect KGB state. Eighty percent of government officials are former or active KGB officers, including Prime Minister Vladimir Putin[4] himself.

As we near the final destination of a single world government (the so-called New World Order) it's very important to realize who planned this journey. Do you know what happened in Eastern Europe between 1989-1991? The explanation given to us by the media is an illusion. It ignores circumstances that point to a very different picture of today's reality and how it came about. These circumstances defy coincidence and cry out for explanation:

- All seven Eastern European communist regimes—each of them unflinchingly and often bloodily defended in the past by ruthless and omnipresent security forces—collapsed in perfect synchronism in the short span of seven months.
- Every one of these regimes stepped down smoothly and (except for brief infighting in Romania), peacefully transferred power without a fight to foes they had once despised and persecuted.
- In each country the new leadership agreed not to prosecute their predecessors for decades of criminal oppression.
- The East Bloc parliaments, though still comprised of staunch supporters of the old regime, unanimously rubber-stamped changes that stripped them of legislative power.
- As one after another communist regime fell the Soviet Union, which had for decades taken ruthless military

action to put down any threat to Communist rule, stood by passively.

- Then, in a theatrical farce, the Soviet Union itself collapsed peacefully and its constituent republics broke off with little or no violence.
- All the new governments put under seal the former secret police's dealings with and knowledge of the new leaders and their political allies.
- The new regimes immediately approved so-called privatization laws, turning their countries' industrial wealth and property over to public bidders (as well as to some former legitimate owners) under the terms of "solid financial plans." What is visible today, twenty years later, is a picture far different from what was expected.
- Soon after the turnover, the former dissidents who had been given government positions were replaced by a new layer of "technocrats" and were largely forgotten.
- Some of those most directly involved behind the scenes in negotiations for the turnover of power and the privatization process died of dubious suicides, accidents, unexplained illnesses, or sudden heart attacks.
- Evidence mounted that much of the national wealth had in fact been transferred into the hands of pre-selected buyers who coalesced into power clans with strong ties to the former communists and their security services.
- In a shift already foreseen by political analysts in the early years of Boris Yeltsin's[5] rule, a professional KGB officer, neither politician nor dissident, came to rule Russia.
- Events in Russia have exposed the close cooperation between the FSB, itself a remnant of the Soviet KGB, and its long-infiltrated subcontractor, the Russian Mafia.

The objective of the Soviet regime was to overthrow the United States as the world's leading power. The KGB fathered state sponsored terrorism. Even the PLO was dreamt up by the KGB. In the 1960s, a new element was added to the Soviet/

PLO[6] war: international terrorism. Global terrorism as we know it was conceived at the Lubyanka[7]. As Yuri Andropov once explained to Ion Pacepa, the Muslim world was a Petri dish in which the Russians might "nurture a virulent strain of American hatred grown from the bacterium of Marxist-Leninist thought." General Alexander Sakharovsky[8] (Head of KGB) once said to Pacepa: "In today's world, when nuclear arms have made military force obsolete, terrorism should become our main weapon." Americans and Europeans no longer remember the past and don't realize that history is now repeating itself. More harsh surprises are bound to come upon the America people. However, there is a long history of events that led up to what happened in 1989.

The KGB defector Anatoliy Golitsyn[9], wrote in his book, The Perestroika Deception (p. 205) as follows: "The West has failed to comprehend the deceptive, controlled nature of the new 'democratic' and 'non-Communist' structures which have been introduced in the USSR and Eastern Europe. The West is jubilant that former so-called 'dissidents,' seen as members of the 'persecuted political opposition,' are now becoming presidents, premiers, members of government and of parliament, and ambassadors in these new structures. The communists have succeeded in concealing from the West that this so-called 'political opposition of dissidents' has been created, brought up and guided by the Bloc's Communist Parties and Security Services during the long period of preparation for 'perestroika.'[10] The Bloc's political and security potential has been fully deployed in the interests of the strategy."

Is it possible that the political establishment in the West simply doesn't want to know the truth?

PART 2

PERESTROIKA: WHAT HAPPENED?

RB: *Welcome to our "virtual" panel discussion. I was fortunate enough to interview these very special individuals who would otherwise have never met to discuss the fall of communism in Europe, its roots, and its consequences. Many books have been written on this subject but so far nobody has attempted to connect all the dots in trying to paint the big picture of this event. I believe that our discussion will help to do just that. Let's start with a question that has troubled me for a long time: Why nobody talks about the collapse of communism in Europe? It looks like there is no interest at all in examining what really happened. Why doesn't anybody care?*

Joseph Douglass: Why doesn't anybody talk about the end of communism? Does anybody care about it? I think that a different approach is not so much that they don't care about it but that they are relieved it ever took place. And now that they are relieved about it they can stop worrying about it and forget about it. One of the most interesting aspects in that regard that I found was the reaction of varied conservative political followers to the death, or alleged death, of communism. Many of them were very strong anti-communists. They understood the duplicity, which resides inherently within the communist system, yet they were among the first people who wanted to go out and champion the success of their own strategy in bringing about the demise of communism. I have not seen one of them ever stop to wonder what really triggered its demise and self-destruction. Because what bureaucracy ever self-destructs? It is particularly true in the case of communism, because if there is one thing that communism is noted for, particularly in the Soviet Union, it's centralized planning. They never do anything that seems at odds with the plan. So if they are going to self-destruct then there must be a plan behind it. But none of the former anti-communists in academia and in the government that I have seen have ever asked: "Was there a plan, or wasn't there?" This was very carefully orchestrated and obviously was designed from within. We even had indication that something was coming. For example, one of the most notable spokesman for the Soviet system, professor Georgi Arbatov[1], had written a number of articles which appeared in the Western press, in which he said: "We are going to do terrible things to you. We are going to take away your threat." And these comments came a year before the system really started to self-destruct. And the question in my mind has always been: "Well, why?" Obviously it was planned. What was the plan? Yet it was something that even the most ardent anti-communists don't want to address. Rather, (the attitude was): "communism is dead, let's applaud and take credit." And that seems to be the way it progressed.

RB: *So, how would you describe the end of communism? What happened?*

Angelo Codevilla: In the United States during the 1980s, there was a debate about whether or not the Soviet Union was going to be reformed. Most, especially on the left, the so-called "right thinking" people in this country thought that the Soviet Union was going to reform. Indeed, President Bush staked his presidency on the idea that Gorbachev was a reformer and that he would, and could, change the Soviet Union into something like the West. Others, including myself, and most certainly such wise men as Richard Pipes[2] and Robert Conquest[3], fully expected that the Soviet Union would die some day. We didn't expect it would happen so soon. We fully expected it could die or perhaps that it might live on to cause us a great deal more trouble. We certainly excluded the possibility that it could reform. We believed that it would live and die as Stalin[4] and Lenin[5] set it up but that it could not reform.

Robert Gates: I think that the process of reform under Gorbachev was intended to adapt to a new world and to a new level of competition. However, one problem that arose was the economy. While Gorbachev was prepared to dismantle the Stalinist economic bureaucracy that had been built in the 1930s, he didn't know what to put in its place. And so one of the results was a steady decline of the Soviet economy during the entire time he was in charge to the point when it essentially fell apart. The other mistake he made was that he had little understanding of real sources of Soviet power in the Communist Party. When he took away the fear, he took away the terror and allowed for brotherly dialogue. As a result, all the frustration and anger of nationalities outside and even within Russia exploded. And so in my book I refer to Gorbachev as the author of a law of unattended consequences. He intended to modernize the Soviet Union, to make the Communist Party more responsive to the people, and to get rid of the bureaucracy and an economy that was holding back growth. But because he didn't realize, didn't know, what to replace that economic bureaucracy with, he remained a communist to the very end. And so he couldn't enact the semi-market reforms that have taken place in China and elsewhere and that's why the economy collapsed. So there was a process of internal collapse in the Soviet Union. But the pressure for him to begin that process of reform and change, I think, was from the outside. Not from the inside. But then it began the process of internal disintegration that accumulated at its own pace.

Tennent Bagley: When Perestroika started I was, of course, deeply influenced by my own experience with KGB officers who had defected to the West and became our allies and friends and helpers. One thing they all agreed on was that if fear was lifted from the Soviet people ever, even in a small way, the end of the regime was close. It could not subsist without genuine fear. Fear has been generated by the KGB and its surrogate organizations throughout Soviet society, which has made sure that nobody thinks differently or has wrong contacts, let alone plots against the regime or proposes change. The word dissident was for people who thought otherwise. This was a danger. And my sources, or my friends, all felt that without this fear, without this system being intact, the Soviet regime would be doomed. When Perestroika came they saw it as the end of the Soviet regime. They thought it was inevitable. I was more skeptical. They were right and I was wrong and certainly it didn't take very long, only about five, six, seven years for the regime to fall. I think that Perestroika was an attempt to preserve the Soviet regime and it was ill considered because the Soviet regime could not have been preserved, except through the imposition of fear and terror. These words are not an overstatement for what we are talking about.

Ludvik Zifcak: The system that was in place at that time was over 40 years old and needed a change. Everybody felt that. People in the communist party felt that, people in the military felt that, everyone felt that. Of course nobody was thinking about changes, which would transform the political system, changes meant to replace people at the top of the government. Many people think or believe that in 1989 there was a mass national uprising. Based on what I did, or where I worked, I am convinced that there was no uprising at all. One political system was just replaced by another political system, with help from other elements, of course. It's hard to find out today who wrote the script but it definitely wasn't written in America. America just jumped on the bandwagon at the end. So the script was most likely written in the East.

Oleg Gordievsky: The communist system was not a viable system. You can't direct a whole growing economy from just one group of people. Only a free economy is viable. So the more the Soviet Union got bigger and more sophisticated, the more difficult it was to exist as a viable economic system. Apart from that, Moscow, the Kremlin, spent nearly 50 percent of the national income on the military so the country was drained of resources. That's why in the 70s and 80s it was clear that the communist system, if nothing was done, would collapse. And it collapsed. It didn't collapse like a castle made of cards. The right circumstances were needed. And these circumstances were plentiful. Firstly, there was the low price of oil in the early 80s. Secondly, there was the very impressive military program under President Reagan. Reagan started the SDI program, or Strategic Defense Initiative[6], which was intended to protect against missiles in space. It was an extremely expensive system. So when the Soviet specialists looked at it they said: "We can't compete with the Americans now. We need to do something. Let's try some reforms." Then they started reforms, very weak reforms, to improve the Soviet Union. Not to dissolve it, not to release Eastern Europe, but only to improve the communist system. The Reforms acquired a momentum of their own and eventually led to the collapse of the Eastern European countries and then, three years later, the Soviet Union.

Jeff Nyquist: [The collapse of] the communist system in the Soviet Union and other countries, Warsaw Pact countries, involved a controlled opposition. It was very important under communism that they controlled people who were opposing the regime. They could eliminate some people, they could put some people in prison, but they had to make sure they could lead a kind of opposition themselves. And what happened in those countries was that they realized that they could lead the opposition to power and create false democracies under control of the KGB. Now people can debate to what extent this actually worked. I had defectors, people who defected after the changes, telling me that there was definitely a plan that maybe didn't go exactly the way they expected it to go. But in essence, the origin of the changes that led to the collapse of communism was Moscow. It was planned many, many years in advance and they brought it off. That's the explanation of the changes. It wasn't a spontaneous uprising of the people to sweep the communist regime away. That was never going to happen.

Petr Cibulka: The so-called "Privatization Revolution" in Czechoslovakia was, in reality, the privatization coup d'état of KGB, GRU, and their Czech and Slovak associates. That's all that can be said about the Velvet Revolution.[7]

Ion Pacepa: The KGB played a much bigger—and largely unknown—role in the history of the Kremlin. Behind a facade of Marxism, the KGB quietly took precedence over the original tools of ideology, and became the rulers' main instrument for running the country. Only a handful of people who were working in extremely close proximity to the top Soviet bloc rulers knew that the Communist Party ended up playing no greater role in the Soviet Union than did Lenin's embalmed corpse in the Kremlin mausoleum.

Vladimir Bukovsky: Well, there are many theories as to what happened. Some of them are official. A kind of popular wisdom would tell us that people were fed up and used the opportunity given to them by the policies of Gorbachev to move further than was visualized in the Kremlin. It's all true, except there were some other factors, which normally are not discussed. And if you try discussing them in the West, they look at you with disbelief. Namely, that it was planned in Moscow by the end of 1988 to change the hard line communist regimes in Eastern Europe and to find a replacement for them of a more liberal variety. It never went further then an idea of finding some local Gorbachevs and placing them in power. But it was nevertheless done, as it was a popular revolution—not just pulled off from Moscow. It would itself antagonize the population. At least it looked like local initiative. If not an outright revolution, at least some kind of internal development brought it up. That's on one hand. On the other hand, of course, critical to all of Eastern European and Central European changes was Germany. And it was decided very early in Gorbachev's presidency that the unification of Germany would be the next move provided that unification would happen on their terms rather then on the conditions of the West. Namely, Germany should become demilitarized, socially democratic, out of NATO, and practically in hands of the Soviet Union. That was the original plan. Of course, reality introduced some corrections into this plan. The Initial stages of the implementation of the project were quite successful as far as they concerned replacing and removing hard line leaders in Czechoslovakia and Bulgaria as well as some other countries. It wasn't very difficult to achieve. Moscow traditionally appointed these guys and had all the influences and trusted people in the ruling circles. So it was not very difficult and the scenario was a kind of fake revolution. The whole plan went wrong in the second stage when they wanted to replace these leaders with their own chosen candidates. And that didn't happen anywhere except Romania. In Romania they wanted Iliesku[8] and Iliesku came to power. In other countries they meant for someone else to take power. They didn't endorse the presidency of Vaclav Havel[9], or whoever was in Hungary, non-communist governments and so on. On the other hand, initially the scenario in Poland was quite successful. The Round Table agreement was very good for communists. It would leave them in the hands of some 65 percent of the legislative power and a lot of administrative power. But at the same time, even in Poland, the communists were rapidly losing control. The senate elections were a disaster for communists. They got what they agreed on in the round table agreement–65 percent of legislation—but it didn't look like it would last for long and was not a guarantee to them for total control. So they were complaining that they were losing ground very quickly. What we had there was a runaway operation conducted from Moscow, which brought changes much more radical then what was visualized by the planners. Essentially, they lost control in most of the countries to a large degree. That, of course, backfired again and had ramifications in the Soviet Union itself. The tendencies for separation inspired by a number of examples in Eastern Europe became really unbearable for the center. And pretty soon the Soviet Union would have more or less the same scenario as Eastern Europe. Communists tried to retain power and there were people trying to pull them out. The separation of the Baltic states became inevitable. The attempted coup in 1991, to our knowledge, was not a coup. It was actually the decision of the leadership to introduce the marital law in Poland. But there was a lot of disagreement between them on how to do it. Gorbachev didn't want to be perceived as the one doing it. He wanted it to be done in his absence in order to not spoil his shining image in the West. Of course, without the commander in chief, the army didn't do it. From what we are told, the KGB wasn't as decisive as it should have been. The whole scene actually collapsed in three days, ridiculously quickly. So after that it was only a matter of time. The other Republics definitely wanted independence, and the Soviet Union dissolved in December 1991. That's all the result of their own operation, of their own attempt to modernize the communist system and salvage socialism as much as they could manage. History proved them wrong. Socialism turned out to be impervious to reform. You can cancel it, you can scrap it, but you can't reform it. You cannot restructure it. And the whole system as it was built by Stalin in Europe did not put up with that kind of internal pressure.

Robert Gates: I think Gorbachev evolved over time. I think that when he took power that was exactly where he was; maintaining Soviet power, maintaining the power of the communist party. He had some ideas for modest changes in the economy but the problem is that, as the modest measures he tried to take failed, he would then take further measures and was drawn into a process of accelerating change . . . . I don't think he had a plan or strategy that would move him from where he started as Andropov's and Suslov's[10] protégé to the fairly radical reformer he eventually became. I think that it was an evolutionary process for him that was accelerated by failure.

RB: *So, in contrary to the official version people were told by the Media, can we say that the end of communism was set up?*

Jeff Nyquist: I don't think it was a spontaneous event. I think this much can clearly be said. We got testimony from various countries that the communists themselves, the leadership of these countries, including Gorbachev himself were the authors of these changes. The KGB and the secret police were involved in these changes in Poland, Romania, Czechoslovakia, and Russia, if not in all the countries that changed at a time. So when we look closely at these events, whether it be through the book Andrej Kordiesku wrote about Romania, testimony of the Solidarity[11] that is coming out of Poland, or statements of people I know in the Czech Republic, we see that in each of these countries revolutions were planned in advance, arrangements had been made by the KGB, the communists, and by structures that existed and ruled the country. This was even true in East Germany. They were changing their formation. The communist block was not a success. Neither was the Warsaw Pact or the Soviet Emporium. So they had to change their formation in order to get the things they needed, which were basically technology, money, and freedom to trade more with other countries because they were restricted. Being the enemy of the free world, communist countries suffered a lot of barriers. There were barriers put up against what they wanted to do. It is very difficult to function on many levels when other countries are suspicious of your activity. So it got away from these suspicions and the West was perfectly glad to claim victory in the Cold War. But did the secret structures of the communist system go away? Did they give up their goal? No. Clearly you can see that the activities of former KGB Lieutenant Colonel Vladimir Putin, the President of the Russian Federation, are sinister. And what he does diplomatically, economically and in terms of the internal politics of Russia is also sinister. People are noticing this. But is anybody really going to change the West and say OK the new Cold War is ignited, this guy is dangerous? Maybe these communist structures are re-emerging now and we have a new trend, we have a new problem? I don't think so. I don't think anybody has the courage to go that route. At least not yet.

Vladimir Bukovsky: Well, the changes were very well prepared in advance. There were some contingency plans, preparations of second and third echelons, leaders, and elites. It was done slowly, starting at the end of the 70s, and through the 80s, particularly under Yuri Andropov. The whole plan was worked out then, Gorbachev was not one of its creators. He was not a mastermind. He was chosen as the most likely fellow to implement them. He looked good on television. He was young. He could speak without paper, without reading. He was a smooth operator, but he was not a father of the whole plan. The plan came to him, it was handed to him from the previous Soviet leadership. And of course this plan would visualize all sorts of scenarios and was implemented in the beginning of 90s, particularly from 1990-91. A lot of these things were going on underground with power structures, secret police, and things like that involved. A huge amount of capital was being pumped out of confident safety deposits to somewhere abroad in order to be used later for coming back. Much of it was actually lost in the process because we don't know who was in charge of it, you know. Not all the money remained under control. There was a lot of embezzlement and corruption. But as far as one can judge, the bulk of it apparently still remains at the disposal of this top nomenclature. It was what they called in Russia, and I suppose in Eastern Europe, a soft landing. It wasn't a crash, it was a soft landing. It was well prepared, which allowed the nomenclature to retain its position and to come back a few years later.

RB: *What motivated Soviets to even start this process?*

Vladimir Bukovsky: Well, by the end of the 70s they saw their policies in shambles. The policy of détente[12] was a complete fiasco, a complete collapse. It didn't work. It backfired on them both in terms of human rights and in terms of external problems such as the crises in Poland, and Afghanistan. These things combined to make the policy of détente impossible. They actually found themselves in isolations a result of the crackdown in Poland and the occupation of Afghanistan. So they had to rethink the whole thing. They had to find a better solution, a more convincing, more lasting, more influential solution in order to spread their influence throughout Europe in a peaceful way. At the same time, at the beginning of the 80s they realized they were in a deep economic crisis. The fact was, their economic base was too small for their political ambitions. Their ambitions were global. Maintaining friendly regimes in Angola, Cuba, and Vietnam, not to mention Afghanistan and so on, became an unbearable burden for them. They knew that they also had to do something to adjust their economic production; their economic development. Of course, they never even considered abandoning socialism as a concept. All the adjustments were supposed to be within the system and within the framework of socialism[13]. They hoped to achieve a certain agreement with the West on so-called regional conflicts to prevent from being toppled by its forces and to freeze the situation into some kind of local détente or something like that. They also needed urgently to stop the arms race. That was the other burden on the economy that they couldn't sustain anymore. During the early period when the West was rearming, the Soviets followed suit because they were scared of losing their military advantage in the world. . However, economically they were incapable of doing that, particularly when the idea of "Star Wars", or Strategic Defense Initiative, came along. They suddenly realized that it was not just a matter of money. Technologically, they would not be able to copy it. That was scary for them. If that was reality, the massive army that they had accumulated in Europe just to threaten the world into obedience would have no effect anymore. They would not be capable of delivering enough force to generate fear and détente. That was the main reason behind their strategic thinking. That's why they had to change a lot of things, not only in their foreign policy, but also inside the Soviet Union to modernize it economically and make it more productive.

Jeff Nyquist: I think that Stalin's system was ultimately doomed. It was built on very harsh repression, the elimination of people, and the secret police watching everybody. This created a very tense atmosphere. In the long run it wasn't sustainable. I mean, you see what happened in North Korea. The more isolated the nation, the more rigid the totalitarianism. North Korea became more and more backwards. It can't even feed itself. We know that many, many countless numbers starved to death in North Korea back in 1990s. Russia was faced with the same problem under Stalin, and communist China under Mao.[14] These regimes needed to change in order to open themselves to the West to get money, to open trade, and to get the kind of things they needed to survive. And as long as Russia was ruled by the hard-line type of Stalinism present in the Cold War, they couldn't do that. After Stalin died, one of the things Khrushchev[15] and other leaders wanted to talk about was peaceful coexistence. They wanted things to soften. They wanted the Cold War to soften not because they didn't want to destroy America, but because they needed money, trade, and technology. They needed to keep up and they couldn't do it with their insulated system. They had to be plugged into the world market somehow. And so Khrushchev had his peace coexistence, Brezhnev[16] had détente, and Gorbachev had his Perestroika and Glasnost[17]. Repeatedly, they were returning to the very same theme; they were the good guys, they wanted to have more capitalism, they wanted to have a conversation with the West, they wanted to loosen things up. It wasn't because they were giving up their goals as communists. It was because they needed to have resources and technology to continue to compete on both a military and economic level.

RB: *Let me ask this. How does reality differ from what the public is served up by the media?*

Tennent Bagley: How different is what the public sees when compared to what is actually going on? There is always an aspect of it that isn't known because it is not interesting, except to technicians and specialists like those who are in professional positions. There isn't, in my opinion, an easy way to say what is and what isn't real, what is or isn't known. There is a conspiracy theory on almost everything from the death of President Kennedy to many other things, and I personally think that the truth is hidden almost everywhere. Still, the idea that there is some master plan and some wicked hand pushing this kind of deception and pushing this kind of other reality is something that I personally reject until I see the evidence. Now, in the case of the fall of the communist regimes in Eastern Europe, there surely was a cause .... And in the cases of Czechoslovakia, Hungary, and certainly Poland, things were not as clear-cut as it may seem in the newspapers. There was a different truth in this respect, and that's the truth that was so well hidden that I don't know if it ever will come out fully. In whose interest was the change of the government in Eastern Europe? Sure, it's easy to say that the Soviet regime wanted to keep their Eastern European Empire, but did it or did it not see the handwriting on the wall and see the need to accommodate to changes regardless of whether they wanted to or not? In that respect there is a possibility that they were planning for this inevitable future and using it to preserve their own power, their own money, and to continue the corruption they were already living under with the current communist regime. And to continue, if you like, in the possession of power, from now on it would have to be a secret power and the power of money, not the power of government possession. In general, there is a different truth in most cases. I think everyone knows that from his or her own personal experiences. Things are not always what they appear to be. That's obviously what I am talking about.

Angelo Codevilla: Reality in Russia and Eastern Europe is, of course, vastly different. Beginning with the kind of people, the kinds of expectations that are there. For example, we look at the map and see that the countries surrounding Russia are independent. Well, they are legally independent, but the reality, which very few people in America realize, is that almost no Russians conceive the independence of Ukraine as being legitimate. They simply regard these places as rough runaway provinces that sooner or later will be brought back to the Russian Empire. That is simply one of many, many realities. They also don't realize that the economy that developed in the post-Soviet space is not really free and bears a lot of resemblance to the old Soviet economy. Namely, that like the old Soviet economy, it has very little to do with production to the satisfaction of consumers but rather has everything to do with the appropriation of advantages for those in power for their own wealth, and the perpetuation of their own power. It is not about the production and satisfaction of consumers but rather about the gain of power and the appropriation of privileges.

RB: *Well, did the West win the Cold War or not?*

Jeff Nyquist: You have to ask why the West was silent and went about its business without that much concern for the hundred million that died under communism[18]. The West is involved in consumption, in its own life; its own world. The other world, the world of totalitarian countries, is something we have no deep emotional or intellectual interest or connection to. So the West, in a sense, is its own world as the East is its own world. And, you know, with their nuclear weapons and with our nuclear weapons aimed at each other, it wasn't going to come to war. And in this country, people lived as if the war was not going to come. They just lived for the moment. We didn't build bomb shelters, we didn't prepare, and now we believe it worked out for the best. Communism has collapsed. And we don't want to scrutinize how that collapse happened or who really was behind it. We don't want to look at it too closely because it's just like the good news. It makes us feel good and lets the stock market rise and lets the peace dividend be invested in something we really care about. I think that is where we're coming from in the West.

I don't think anybody won it. I think it's still going on. The United States lost the Vietnam War, lost South-East Asia, basically failed to stop communism in Africa . . . [and] now it's gaining strength in South America. How can you say that the Cold War was won? I don't see any victory here except the one that was proclaimed in Moscow. 'OK, the Russians said you won, we give up.' Did that really happen? Is that really a believable thing? I mean . . . do millions of communists worldwide just say, you know, we are not communists anymore, we believe in capitalism? I don't think they have changed their beliefs. I think they have just told us they changed their beliefs because it's more convenient and it's easier for them to do what they want to do that way. And besides, communism is just a word. Get rid of the word. Let's put it this way, Charles Manson[19] was let out of prison and moved into your neighborhood. He changes his name to Charlie Brown. You can call him anything you want, John Smith; he still will be Charles Manson. It's easy to change the name but it's not easy to change the character of the person or a group of people who carried that name. They changed the name of KGB to FSB. Does that mean that the character of the KGB has been changed? Probably not. There are always changes in people but changes in character are always slow and gradual. And so when you look at changes in Eastern Europe, that's the way we have to look at it. Did the inner character, did the sort of secretive structures that governed these countries change, are they gone, did they disappear? Are those things still there? Their character is to control, and their control continues. And I think if you look at each of the countries in Europe you will find that that control is still there and people will tell you that if you put the camera in front of them and they are brave enough to say it.

Vladimir Bukovsky No, I don't think so. I don't think the West won. I mean, I don't personally feel like a winner. I can't even go back to Russia as a tourist. They don't give me a visa. What happened is a kind of half way victory. It stopped too early. It's almost like the war with Iraq. The first war with Iraq[20]. They stopped three days too early and left Saddam Hussein[21] in power. So more or less the same happened here. Although official communist structures went out, a lot of the nomenklatura remained in power, particularly the KGB and its agents. And through that they would more and more openly control political life, public life, and businesses. There were a lot of operations going on on the part of secret services everywhere in the old Eastern Europe and the Soviet Union in order to infiltrate itself into positions of power, administrative or legislative, into businesses, and even in organized crime. So the control has never been lost entirely. The party and its ideology disappeared. They were just canceled by history. There was no need for them. But a lot of elements of the former system survived, particularly the power of the nomenklatura. Later, within a few years, they felt sufficiently confident to come to the forefront and we finally had the reemergence of the communist power in most of the Eastern European countries and Russia. It actually came in the shape of KGB power, the worst possible scenario. So that's the result of unfinished business. Communism was never conclusively destroyed, and it was never condemned in some kind of court, some kind of Nuremberg Tribunal or something like that. It was just wounded. It lost a lot of positions, but it didn't disappear. And the West is definitely not among the winners.

Edward Jay Epstein: Well, the real question is if the "Cold War" was the right description of the struggle between the United States and the Soviet Union that followed World War II. I don't think it was a war at all. I think it was a series of psychological efforts to throw the other side off balance through the threat of war. But I don't think it was what we call a war. I think it had many, many facets, many fronts, and … who won it? At this point I think the United States ended up winning it.

RB: *Were we duped?*

Angelo Codevilla: I think the Soviet Union and the KGB, for a long period of time preceding WORLD WAR II used their alliances with Germany to create the deceptive image of Soviet intentions, especially in Eastern Europe, that the occupation there was defensive, as opposed to trying to install different regimes. I think they did succeed in that deception. I think that the point of the Soviet deception came from the fact that they were communists. Communists in the Marxist sense. What they were trying to do was bring back a new state. Economic development for the world. Moving from feudalism to capitalism and now moving to socialism. That, let's say, was the deception Lenin was committed to. By the time Stalin took over there was very little effort at anything other than power. There was very little Marxism or socialism in the Soviet Union. And the Soviet Socialist Union of Republics, it wasn't socialist, it wasn't Soviet, it was a union, it was a dictatorship, and there were no Republics. You know, the Soviet deception may have worked up until the 1960s or 70s, but after awhile anyone who visited the Soviet Union, whether it was Eastern European officials or Chinese officials, even North Korean officials realized that there wasn't a socialist utopia there. It was represented by a rather poorly run economy without dedicated people and without any real ideology. So at this point I think I want to talk about the late 1980s. Soviet leadership decided that the cost of maintaining the deception that they were utopian Socialists or Marxists was actually costing them more than trying for another form of power. And I think the original Glasnost was an idea to create a liberal capitalist state with a large state ownership, a place not all that different from Germany or France. Now the question is if that got out of control and they wound up with a revolution that occurred under Yeltsin that they didn't expect. Or did they control it through the entire period? I think that remains to be seen by what emerges under Putin.

RB: *Why did the public never get what really happened, and simply believe that it was a revolution by people?*

Edward Jay Epstein: The successful deception often depends on telling people what they want to hear. Now, when you tell American politicians and American elected officials "You won the Cold War", it's a message they want to hear. Why should they question it? Why should Ronald Reagan question it? Why should George Bush question it? They can now take credit for it. So it wasn't in anyone's interest to question it, and they also believed it, that's what makes the deception. A woman tells a man "I love you, you are handsome, you are brilliant", why should a man question it? And so with Glasnost, and with the issue of Gorbachev moving the Soviet Union from a hard line ideological enemy committed to something called communism to a more flexible, pragmatic society much more like that which existed in Northern Europe it was accepted.

RB: *How much was the fall of communism a surprise for the United States?*

Bill Gertz: In the case of the Soviet Union, the U.S. intelligence community was taken by surprise. And this highlights the flow of our analytical capability. Basically, we have seen numerous intelligence failures over the years. The Iraqi weapons of mass distraction being one, the intelligence failure of September 11 being another, but the collapse of the Soviet Union was not anticipated by our intelligence agencies. To the contrary, the Intelligence assessments at that time in the late 80s and early 90s totally misjudged the severe problems that were plaguing the Soviet Union and ultimately when Gorbachev came to power and tried to tweak the system it ultimately came crashing down despite the wrong analysis of our intelligence information.

Robert Gates: I went to the president in July and asked authority from him to establish very secret, very small working groups to begin the contingency planning for the collapse of the Soviet Union. That was two and half years before it actually happened. And the leader of that group from the National Security Council staff was Condoleezza Rice[22]. So, even two and half years ahead of the collapse, we were already planning for it. And it helped us a lot when the collapse actually happened. The notion that the collapse of the Soviet Union came as a surprise to CIA[23] or the American Government I think is completely wrong and it can be easily documented to show that.

RB: *You didn't buy what Gorbachev was saying?*

Robert Gates: I think that my comments about not taking his comments seriously regarding the new thinking were when he first came to office and began talking about Perestroika and new thinking and so on. The truth is that for the first couple of years he was in power he talked a lot about new thinking but we didn't see anything in consequence on the ground in terms of either the economy or the politics or the amount of money they were pushing into the third world. The truth is that in the mid- eighties, in 1985-86, the Soviets actually increased the amount of money they were sending to places like Central America and Africa and increased the intensity of their campaign in Afghanistan. So, there was a lot of talk about new thinking around that time but not much was happening on the ground. We began to see some of that for the first time in economic measures he started taking in 1987. And I think two events in 1988 that made a big difference in taking him seriously were, first of all, the withdrawal from Afghanistan, which clearly was irreversible at that point and second his speech at the UN in December 1988 when he elaborated specific kinds of units that would be withdrawn from

Warsaw Pact countries in Eastern Europe. We acknowledged in the intelligence community that he in fact did that, that he would significantly impact their ability to wage war against NATO, and that these were very real changes. But I would say that until 1987-88, at least in the arena of politics and their behavior internationally, we didn't see much change.

Edward Jay Epstein: Yes, but not only that. The Soviet Union pulled back from Eastern Europe. It brought down the wall in Berlin. You know, in the strategic thinking, in the Western strategic thinking, Germany was a crucial point of geopolitical balance. So it was assumed that the Soviet Union would never give up its hold on Germany and what became known as Poland, what was once also a part of Germany. It was considered the most strategically important area. But what was forgotten is all those lessons in geopolitics that came out of WW1 when tanks and large armies moved back and forth. Was Germany really strategically important? Why was it strategically important? What was actually strategically important was the control of crucial resources like oil and gas. And food like wheat, corn, and soybeans. Russia really didn't give up control in these areas. It gave up control of areas that were very expensive for them to maintain a political authority over.

RB: *Mr. Gates, you mentioned that in your last meeting with Kryuchkov you felt that Gorbachev was off and that something was coming.*

Robert Gates: By my third meeting with Kryuchkov[24] things were very interesting. The first meeting was in the restaurant in Washington DC, the second meeting was in the safe house, the KGB safe house in Moscow, where we had a lavish dinner, just the two of us and our interpreters, and the third meeting was in his office at Lubyanka. It was quite clear that Kryuchkov, who had embraced the reforms that Gorbachev was undertaking in 1986 and 1987, by 1989 and 1990 had become quite hostile. He felt that the pace of reform was going far too fast and it was a danger to the system. And I told both President Bush[25] and Secretary of State Baker[26] after the third meeting that I think

Gorbachev now has an enemy in his own house. And in fact it was Kryuchkov who would later lead the coup attempt.

Vladimir Bukovsky: The West never understood the Soviet system as such. Well, when I say that I mean mainstream politicians, media, and academics. Of course, the left, left leaning parties and organizations, they did understand it much better, but they perceived them as allies and they would never disclose the true essence of it but they would at least understand compared to the central conservative forces that never understood what the Soviet system was about. It's very difficult to understand for someone who never lived there. To imagine that the whole country could be run according to some kind of a dogma, every nut and bolt of it, and governed by this dogma generated a century ago by some kind of obscure German philosopher. It's so alien to the western psyche. I mean, they don't believe in ideologies and they don't live by any ideologies. They don't understand ideologies. If you talk to politicians, they are all pragmatic. They believe that everything is negotiable. And to explain to them that in the Soviet policy, in Soviet decision-making, nothing is negotiable really, and it's for them to enforce their own approach and their own opinions, they will not believe you. Most of them, even the brightest politicians, have some doubts about it. So they didn't understand. They didn't understand the essence of the system. They never understood why it is inherently aggressive and therefore during the whole period of the Cold War they tried to tie up Soviet aggression with all sorts of bizarre agreements as if a piece of paper could ever stop that monster. For instance, consider the arms control agreement, which had no meaning except giving the advantage to Soviet side, or all kinds of "good intention" agreements, God knows what. That was all nonsense and it just reflected the degree of ignorance in the Western political class regarding the Soviet system. Therefore, if they didn't understand the time of Brezhnev or Khrushchev or Stalin, it was much harder to understand during the Gorbachev period when everything was changing. Everyday there was something happening. It was done quite deliberately to stun and confuse by suddenly admitting the crimes, which they denied for fifty years. And that was itself perceived by the West as a great change. It wasn't any change, it was common knowledge that they committed these crimes except for the fact that they never admitted it. That was a very skilful game with public opinion. And it was, of course, very confusing for Western observers. Within some groups of agents of influence it was very easy to manipulate the West during this time of confusion so they would all believe nonsense, incredible nonsense; to believe that there was a struggle between reformers and conservatives in the Politburo and the leadership. And if something bad happened it would be automatically described as an influence of conservative forces and if something good happened it would always be ascribed to reformers in the Politburo. And that was complete nonsense. The Politburo couldn't operate this way. The Politburo always had unity. All the decisions they had taken were unanimous and they couldn't have any split and never did. When that occurred it would end up in expulsion or execution during Stalin's time when someone deviated . . . . So, that alone was an incredibly skillful disinformation technique. I remember when Gorbachev ordered the massacre of people in Tbilisi in 1989. The world was scared that conservative forces had taken over; 'it's dangerous, what will happen to Gorbachev now?' So he suddenly became the best hope and they supported him even as the Soviet system was collapsing. They supported him with a huge amount of money. Some 45 billion dollars were given to Gorbachev by the West in non-tied loans and credits over seven years of his time in power. They would support him diplomatically. They would oppose any opposition forces in Gorbachev's Soviet Union. They would try to put pressure on some nationalistic forces in Eastern Europe and other Republics in the Soviet Union They would try to restrain them and make them more agreeable with the Soviet center. That was done by the West simply because they believed that Gorbachev was the best option they had. The worst scenario would be a destabilization. They were afraid of destabilization in the Soviet Union probably more than they were afraid of the Third World War. So that was a complete misconception. They never understood what was going on in the Soviet Union. In September of 1991 President Bush came to Ukraine, to Kiev, and made his famous speech. He appealed to Ukrainians not to separate from the Soviet Union. He said that the United States would never recognize the Ukraine and so on and so forth. Of course within a month Ukraine voted in the referendum to separate. That was indeed incredibly stupid but they were loyal to the agreement with Gorbachev. They believed Gorbachev gave them the best option.

Oleg Gordievsky: Gorbachev had one advantage. He was younger than the rest. So eventually the very old Politburo had no choice but to appoint Gorbachev as the General Secretary. The General Secretary had a group of civilian advisers who were more or less progressive, progressive on the communist scale. And the KGB also wanted to have an improvement in the Soviet Union. He won the power struggle and in two years he didn't know what to do. But then in 1987 his civilian advisers suggested some reforms to him to improve the Soviet Union. He started these reforms and slowly they took on a momentum of their own and in the end Gorbachev reluctantly agreed to abolish Paragraph #6 of the Soviet Constitution, which gave the monopoly of power to the communist party. Immediately, Russia was covered with different political parties, groups, movements, and organizations. It was like a stream around 1991 and that stream focused around Boris Yeltsin because Yeltsin hated Gorbachev. It was his vendetta and Gorbachev's vendetta against Yeltsin and vice versa. Yeltsin won the power struggle in the Soviet Union. To get power he technically had to dissolve the Soviet Union. When he dissolved the Soviet Union and took power, he formed the new government in 1991-92, the government that consisted of democratic elements. They started very useful, democratic economic and political reforms. So Gorbachev was not really an outstanding man. But the circumstances, and his civilian advisers in the Central Committee[27] gave him advice, which became useful for the Soviet Union and Eastern Europe.

Jeff Nyquist: You know, Gorbachev was the protégé of Yuri Andropov who was the head of KGB. Gorbachev basically became friends with Andropov when he was the governor of Stavropol. Andropov used to vacation there and he got to know

Gorbachev. He was the agriculture minister and then he became the head of the Soviet Union and the head of the Communist Party of the Soviet Union. The important thing about Gorbachev is that he initiated this Perestroika. He was the liberal. He was the Alexander Dubcek[28] of Russia. He made it all credible. He made the changes believable. He led the way. But all the time these changes were coming from the KGB side. It is Very interesting that he was the KGB's choice to be head of the country. It was interesting what Foreign Minister Andrei Gromyko[29] said when speaking on behalf of making Gorbachev the leader of the Soviet Union. He said that this was smiling Michael Gorbachev. He had teeth of iron or teeth of steel, I forgot the exact wording, but it's like 'this is a tough guy that's going forward.'

RB: *What was the White House thinking?*

Robert Gates: Well, the administration was divided in its assessment of what was going on in the Soviet Union but unified in what we were going to do about it. I think it's fair to say that Secretary of Defense Cheney[30], deputy Secretary of State Eagleburger[31], Condi Rice and I all felt that reforms were going to fail and that Gorbachev was presiding over a process he couldn't control. Until fairly well into the process we also saw that much of what he had done was reversible had he been replaced by somebody else. And so we were more skeptical that his reforms would work. However, we did not at all disagree with the approach that the president and Secretary Baker and Brent Scowcroft advocated which was to get a deal with them. And we had to interact with these folks so we could help manage this process from the West. There was no disagreement on managing the process of collapse. We wanted to manage the relationship in a way that contributed to the continuing change in the Soviet Union and there was no disagreement in the administration on that. I was very pessimistic from the beginning regarding the belief that Gorbachev's economic reforms would work. There was too much information coming to the CIA about what the consequences of his changes were in terms of manufacturing, in terms of research and development, and everything else. And there was a sort of new plan every six months so he could continue to tear up the bureaucracy in terms of trying to find something that would work. And each time he did that the situation got worse. Where he went farther than I anticipated was in his political changes and his willingness at the very end to actually end the monopoly of the communist party on politics in the Soviet Union. And I would acknowledge that I was more pessimistic on that and I did not think that he would go as far as he did. But I think in terms of the administration as whole. During my confirmation hearings in 1991 there was a lot of allegations that the Soviet Union was about to collapse, and there was an acquisition from the democratic side, democratic senators, that the CIA had overestimated the Soviet threat. And I think as we look back and dissect what was going on in the Soviet Union, the level of resources they devoted to the military, and the quality of much of their military in those days, I don't think we exaggerated at all. One of the examples that was brought home to me by one of the arms control people was when the INF treaty was implemented and Soviets had to destroy their SS 20s. They launched virtually almost all of those SS 20s, they withdrew from Eastern Europe, and they didn't have a single launch failure. We did not have that good of a record when we withdrew our medium range missiles.

RB: *But at the end you called it a joyless victory.*

Robert Gates: The reason I called it a joyless victory is that there wasn't any parade like there was on VE or VG day. Again, it was part of Bush's desire not to create attention or take any action that would cause the military or the intelligence services in Russia to react in some way. We were trying to move on to a new relationship with first the Soviet Union and then Russia and it was Bush's view that we had to downplay the magnitude of what just happened. I think we were all in agreement with that strategy and thought that some of those in Congress who had advocated a much more strident desertion of victory were mistaken in terms of our future relationship with the Russians. So I think it was both in terms of the context and the way that the

Cold War ended but also the need to continue trying to develop a new kind of relationship with the Russians, who had just suffered an extraordinary historical humiliation. Bush thought it was very smart, very wise to take a very low-key approach to the end of the Cold War. I think he was right.

RB: *Let's back up a bit. What was the role of the KGB in this process?*

Vladimir Bukovsky: The KGB was an internal part of Gorbachev's Perestroika. For example, all Western parts of the operations they were running came back to the KGB. In 1985 when it was already known in circles that Gorbachev would become the General Secretary, the KGB launched a huge campaign in the West presenting him as a great liberal reformer. God knows why. There was a massive campaign in the Western press orchestrated by the KGB. KGB activity was dramatically increased here in the run up until 1985 and after that when Gorbachev was nominated. They were very instrumental in a massive disinformation campaign trying to present the policy of Perestroika and Glasnost as reforms for democracy and not as an aberration for salvaging the regime. And they succeeded. Most politicians and public policymakers in the West actually believed it. It was very difficult to prove to them this was not the case. So the KGB was quite instrumental, in a sense central, in the promotion of new policies including Gorbachev's policies abroad, and at the same time became quite central in introducing and implementing these policies inside the country. As the crisis increased and progressed, and they tried somehow to switch from a command method of governing to manipulating methods of governing inside of the Soviet Union, hundreds, if not thousands KGB officers were called back from foreign countries, particularly those with experience in manipulating public opinions, and were introduced at all levels of the government and legislative system in the Soviet Union. They became central. They were the people who knew how to manipulate public opinion. They knew how to control through manipulation rather than through intimidation so they suddenly became very visible within the Soviet Union.

RB: *What about Andropov himself. How important was his role in this process?*

Vladimir Bukovsky: What was Andropov's role in the beginning? Andropov was one of the fathers of these changes. I mean, even before he became the General Secretary in 1982 he already started to encourage certain think tanks to work out alternative scenarios by the end of the 70s. This began in a structural sense with foreign policy and later continued in the economic fields. Most of what Gorbachev was trying to implement was worked out theoretically under Andropov in different think tanks patronized by either KGB or Central Committee International Departments or both. The economic things were worked out together with some Western economists of left wing persuasion and socialists. It all happened in Austria in a certain research center created by the KGB specifically to be far away from the Soviet Union so as not to irritate some ideologists in the Politburo. And not only that, Andropov was engaged in training the next generation of elite, creating it. Second echelon, third echelon, it was very tightly echelonized. We still have some politicians coming to the forefront, who were prepared under Andropov. That's still happening. I would imagine a lot of what happened in Eastern Europe was worked out during that time in different research centers. Gorbachev himself admitted that in one meeting when someone blamed him that the reform program Perestroika was badly thought out, he said, "That's not true comrades! When I came to power there were a hundred and two massive research papers formulating what should be done." So he admitted he was not the father of that. It was prepared. And who was presiding over that preparation? Andropov.

Oleg Gordievsky: No, Andropov had nothing do with it. Against all the claims of the West that Andropov was somebody—a reformer, or a progressive—that's total nonsense. He was the most reactionary and most dangerous member of the Politburo. And when he was appointed he was already a very sick man. He was attached to a kidney dialysis machine. He was not the head of the Soviet Union. He admitted to his friends that he didn't know how to reform the Soviet Union. Then he died. As to the fact that he was a Head of KGB, he was one of the most brutal people there. He introduced a mental asylum, putting his political opponents into it. He started concentration camps for political protesters. Andropov is really nothing to speak of. He was a deeply reactionary figure.

Ion Pacepa: In discussing Andropov's legacy, Western historians usually recall his brutal suppression of political dissidents, his role in planning the 1968 invasion of Czechoslovakia, and his pressure on the Polish regime to impose martial law. But the leaders of the Warsaw Pact intelligence community, when I was one of them, looked up to Andropov as the father of the Soviet bloc's new era of political influence designed to save communism from economic failure by making communist dictators popular in the West. "The only thing the West cares about is our leaders," Andropov told me in 1972, when the Kremlin decided to make Ceausescu[32] a success in the West as a dress rehearsal for pulling off the same trick with the ruler in the Kremlin. "The more they come to love him, the better they will like us." It was as simple as that. Andropov came up with the idea to convince the West that communist rulers admired Western democracy and wanted to emulate it. "Let the gullible fools believe you want to perfume your communism with a dab of Western democracy, and they will clothe you in gold," Andropov instructed me. Once on the Kremlin throne, the cynical chairman of the KGB rushed his intelligence machinery into introducing him to the West as a "moderate" communist and a sensitive, warm, Western-oriented man who allegedly enjoyed an occasional drink of Scotch, liked to read English novels, and loved listening to American jazz and the music of Beethoven. I knew Andropov well. He was none of the above.

Tennent Bagley: Andropov? It would be quite clear from information I learned myself after the Cold War ended, and I did have contacts with large number of Eastern intelligence and counter-intelligence officers on purpose, in order to solve some of the problems that were nagging me during my career and still are nagging me after the Cold War and long after retiring from CIA. But in this case I can only say what I heard or what impression I got from several people I talked to in the East: that Andropov was perhaps the key figure in developing the KGB from the mid-sixties till his retirement, his death. As head of their Communist Party in the Soviet Union, he was certainly the key figure in a campaign of terror and diversion. He was the key figure in any long range planning for operations to survive inevitable changes in Eastern Europe. I know of no one who was more influential and manipulative or powerful than Andropov. Certainly not Gorbachev. Gorbachev was more a creature of Andropov then Andropov of Gorbachev.

RB: *Casey was reluctant to involve the CIA in Eastern Europe. Does it mean that CIA actions there were very limited?*

Robert Gates:RB: Again the concern was, even in Reagan's administration, but especially in Bush's administration, not to do anything . . . to interrupt this process. So there was a very real concern that . . . if the Soviets would discover that the CIA was actively supporting Solidarity for example, that they would use that to discredit Solidarity in the eyes of the Poles and to say that it was just a foreign tool. I think that Casey[33] actually was perhaps one of the first to perceive that these changes were important and that it was vital to let the internal dynamics go forward without giving an excuse that would allow them to be interrupted. He was concerned that the CIA actions in Poland might be discovered and then discredit Solidarity. The fact is, beginning in the period of 1984-86 the CIA did in fact began to provide more and more help to Solidarity, mainly in the form of communication equipment, printing presses, and things like that. They were engaging in covert action to try and help move things along if you will. I think we were more comfortable at this point partly because the Western European services were involved in their own activities, and AFL/CIO[34] was involved in supporting Solidarity. The Vatican was also involved in supporting the Poles. So there were enough actors at that point that I think the decision was that it would be okay to proceed.

RB: *Mr. Bukovsky, you got access to transcripts of negotiations in Malta from confidential files in Gorbachev's library. What really happened in Malta? Can you summarize it?*

Vladimir Bukovsky: The Malta[35] summit meeting I remember very well because nothing was reported of what was agreed there. And of course people took it as a sign of some kind of a deal behind the scenes. They believed that Malta was some kind of a replica of Yalta[36]. That was a saying at that time. That it was a second Yalta. In a sense it was, but no agreement was actually signed at the end of the Malta summit. Gorbachev simply told Bush that he was going to change regimes in Eastern Europe completely, that it was already happening and of course Bush could see it was happening, and that he would allow Eastern European countries to go their own way. He would not apply force but he seriously asked the United States and Western allies not to get involved. Not to stir up trouble there because it was a very fragile, very delicate transition period. "We will do it, don't worry, but don't get involved. Don't spoil it." And Bush promised not to get involved. So it was, in a sense, something like Yalta, some kind of division of influence in a sense. However, it was not as clear-cut as it was in Yalta. In Yalta it was actually shaped, or made in the shape of an agreement. But in Malta they didn't sign any agreement. It was all verbal. And indeed everything Bush then did would be completely in support of Gorbachev. He was a very loyal ally until the end.

RB: *So, Bush gave Gorbachev a free hand?*

Vladimir Bukovsky: Yes, because Gorbachev promised democratic changes. He said he will do it. He will give them more independence, they will be democratic, and there will be reforms there. He simply asked that the U.S. wouldn't scare it off. "Don't change the balance." And for Bush, who never understood what was going on in the Soviet Union, [he] thought that was the best deal if the Russians were going to change the system themselves. Why should America be involved? Let them do it. That's how he understood it. He didn't understand the fact that it could be changed in many different ways and with different degree of maintaining control in hands of the nomenklatura. He was not knowledgeable enough to understand what might happen.

Robert Gates: Basically it was a manifestation I think of Bush's experience and his instincts. It was his initiative to push for a meeting as early as possible with Gorbachev. It was his instinct to try and serve as a bridge. It was Bush's idea, for example, to visit Poland in the summer of 1989 as Poland began to move toward significant change. It was his idea to have both Jaruzelski[37] and Lech Walesa[38] to a lunch at the U.S. Embassy. As I recall, it was the first time the two of them were ever in a setting like that together. And it was that kind of effort on Bush's part that I described in the book as him greasing the skids on which the communists were removed from power. And it seemed like he would do the latter with Gorbachev by not forcing the issue or pace and letting these things evolve internally in Eastern Europe before facilitating them by treating the outgoing leadership with some measure of respect, at least superficially. I think he created an environment in which it was easier to slide these people from power and allow reformers to take their place. These were Bush's instincts. And when he felt that things were entering a rough path, it would be his initiative to suggest that it was time to place a phone call to Gorbachev or to one of the European leaders.

I don't think that it was a matter of trying to get in front of a parade that had already left. I think it was a matter of asking how do you manage this process in a way that allows the internal development to proceed while trying to lay the concerns of the communists still in power in all of these countries while denying them any reason to interrupt what was going on. As long as there was no specific event, no crisis, there really was nothing that the hard-liners and the states could rally around. And I think Bush's instincts were to figure out how we would keep the Soviet Union at bay while Eastern Europe began to move toward independence. So it really was the recognition of the magnitude of what was happening in Eastern Europe and trying to figure out a way to ensure that those events would continue without Soviet intervention or without intervention of the military troops of the communist regimes in those states. I think it was more a matter of figuring out how to manage this process and keep the Soviet Union and hard-liners from taking action that would interrupt what was going on. That was really the core of our strategy during that period.

RB: *Well that may be an interesting strategy, looking at it from the outside perspective, but people living in Eastern Europe under Soviet domination may see it very differently. Lets bring some people into this discussion who were actually living through this process and experienced it from inside.*

PART 3

THE CZECH ANGLE

RB: *Mr.Cibulka, you were actively involved in the dissident movement and jailed five times for your anti-communist activities. Did you know what was really going on at the time you were signing the Charter 77 document? After all, many signatories of Charter 77 were former communists.*

Petr Cibulka: No. I had no idea what was going on. When Charter 77[1] was founded it was difficult to find anybody to sign it and nobody asked if those who were signing it were members of the communist party in the past. In addition to that, being among the youngest who signed Charter 77, we didn't know who the others were. I didn't remember those old Bolsheviks from the 1950s to 1960s. I signed Charter 77 in prison in 1978. When I got out three years later in 1981 many years had passed and I didn't know many of the signatories after all. And you are right in saying that everybody who remembered those people, what they did in the 1950s to 1960s, had to have been shocked. The majority of the people who initiated Charter 77, two thirds or three quarters, were former communists. Today, I believe that Charter 77 was initiated by Soviet intelligence, probably by the GRU[2] with help from the KGB. All analyses of KGB, GRU, and the Soviet Army concluded that the Soviet Union couldn't remain a world Super Power in the 21st century if it retained the communist ideology. That's why the intelligence apparatus and the military tried to change the regime in such a way that it would become economically lucrative and they would stay in power. I have information stating that the leading intelligence service outside of the Soviet Union was GRU. Simply said, military intelligence GRU dominated everywhere the Soviet Army set foot.

RB: *So when did you start to suspect that something wasn't right?*

Petr Cibulka: I was released from prison 10 days after the November 17 (1989) demonstration and during the first couple of weeks I believed that the changes were for real. But it took me just a few weeks to realize that the changes were just cosmetic, a changing of the scenery. I realized that power would remain in the hands of the communists and that the communists didn't need to worry about losing anything. From that point I started to critically evaluate the situation, and as I descended deeper into it I realized that everything was just a game for the public, and not just for the local public but mostly for the West.

RB: *How did you come to this revelation?*

Petr Cibulka: The fact that this was not a Revolution but another communist swindle was something that I realized very easily. When I brought up my opinion in the Civic Forum[3] that communists should leave their positions in the government and should be replaced by active opponents of communism such as political prisoners, etc., I was accused of being an extremist. The revolutionary Civic Forum instead fighting communism started to fight me and others who asked for a real de-nazification of communist Czechoslovakia instead of fighting communism itself. This was quite a healthy confrontation and it opened my eyes. When revolutionaries, the official revolutionaries attacked us, political prisoners instead of communists, I realized that everything was different.

RB: *So what actually happened?*

Ludvik Zifcak: Many people think or believe that in 1989 there was a mass uprising of the nation. From what I did, or where I worked, I am convinced that there was no uprising at all. One political system was replaced by another political system with help from other elements.

RB: *Who wrote the script?*

Ludvik Zifcak: It's hard to find out today who wrote the script but it definitely wasn't written in America. America just jumped on the bandwagon at the end. So the script was most probably written in the East. The system that was in place at the time was over 40 years old and needed change. Everybody felt that. People in the communist party felt that. People in military felt that. Everyone felt that. Of course, nobody was thinking about changing the political system. It was meant to replace people at the top of the government.

RB: *So, how did it end?*

Ludvik Zifcak: That depends on whom you ask. It didn't end well for us (communists). For those in the opposition it probably ended the way they wanted. Today, if I were to talk for the division I was working for (StB)[4] then I would have to say that the failure wasn't our fault. The failure was caused by political elements that were holding all decision-making powers in their hands.

RB: *What kind of people rose to power?*

Petr Cibulka: The last two years before the revolution, new people popped up in Charter 77, people we didn't see before. And these people later took the leading positions in the movement. I believe that these people were agents of the KGB, GRU, and secret police who led the so-called anti-communist revolution. And we can say, more or less, that these same people are controlling the situation in this country to this day. Despite the new generation that is coming up now and new cadres that are entering the game of politics, power in the Czech Republic is still in the hands of the group that took power after the 1989 revolution.

When Charter 77 was founded, I saw it as a great opportunity to resist communist oppression, to build resistance against the Soviet occupation, and to inspire the nation to change the status quo. I was waiting many years for this chance to come — Charter 77 and the cultural underground where I was involved as well. After many years in these dissident groups I realized that the majority of the people there only pretended to be dissidents. They were acting in opposition to the regime, but 90 percent of them never really intended to fight communism. Still, all these people took over leading positions after the November 17 revolution. And because of these people, not a single communist criminal faced a court of law to be tried for crimes committed against innocent people.

For example, according to data from the Ministry of Justice, by 1990, 270,000 people in Czechoslovakia were sentenced by communist courts to a total of one million years in prison and were eligible for reparation. Behind each of these 270,000 political prisoners were a few, sometimes more then few, communist criminals responsible for the prosecution. But to this day, none of these criminals were charged and tried in a court of law! So this is what the anti-communist revolution of the KGB and GRU looked like. And I must add that if there is anyone here today who was repeatedly interrogated, accused, tried in courts, and sentenced for political statements, it's me. I was jailed five times during the communist regime and half a year ago I was sentenced again for publishing the name of one StB agent. So this is the state of freedom in the post-communist Czech Republic.

Ludvik Zifcak: Charter 77 became the best-known example of a political group where the most involved members were politicians expelled from the communist party after 1968. And there were other groups as well. Later, around 1975 to be exact, the communist party, through the StB, intelligence, and counter-intelligence, started to build its own so called "dissident groups" and used them to infiltrate groups like Charter 77, Democratic Initiative, etc. So, in other words, by 1988 the majority of the so-called "democratic elements" or anti-communist elements operating in Czechoslovakia were manipulated by the communist secret police.

RB: *To what extent were they aware of being manipulated?*

Ludvik Zifcak: Well, they suspected that they were being manipulated but they didn't have the resources and capability to find out who was manipulating them and how they were doing it. Of course, they knew that StB agents had infiltrated them, but at that time they had no ability to find out who those agents actually were. Once in a while there were some leaks, but even then they were unable to prove that the person they suspected to be an agent actually was an agent. So, these groups knew they were being infiltrated but had no idea who among them was actually working for the intelligence or counter-intelligence services.

Vladimir Hucin: I signed Charter 77 in 1986 after being released from prison. After the 1989 revolution I was nominated by the Confederation of Political Prisoners[5] and KAN[6] to serve in the newly created Intelligence apparatus FBIS[7]. Before that, I was elected by Civic Forum to be the Chairman of the Civic Committee, the body in charge of cleaning up the police apparatus and ridding it of people who participated in past communist crimes. In 1991 I started working at the Federal Department of FBIS in Olomouc and worked my way up to the position of Captain. I specialized in left-wing extremism and terrorism. My idea was that the new BIS should be a "watch dog of democracy." But when I got access to documents from StB archives, I discovered how many people from Charter 77 were involved with StB and how many agents StB had in this group. That was a big disappointment for me.

RB: *Mr. Cibulka, after the revolution you published the names of all StB agents and their collaborators in a list known as "Cibulka's Files"[8], right?*

Petr Cibulka: We published a list of communist StB officers and collaborators in 1992, parts of it actually we published in

1991. The last big record, containing the names of 20,000 StB officers, we published in 1999. But these records are far from being complete. The records were thoroughly sorted out before we got them and they don't include intelligence, military intelligence, and counter-intelligence agents. The names of these people were not made public and probably never will be. So, we published everything we could. However, today I believe that we were deceived. They simply needed to get rid of the competition and released files containing names of people who could stand in the way of privatizing government property and putting it in the hands of former communists and secret police. I believe that the Russians were behind this leak of information to get rid off their competition in the Czech StB.

I believe that the archives were altered months before the November 17 revolution and the most prospective potential leaders, those who run the political scene today, came from this confidential group of science/technology intelligence. Only Moscow knows who they are. They have enough compromising materials on them and can manipulate them.

RB: *Mr.Doskocil, do you want to say something about the destruction of the StB archives?*

Frantisek Doskocil: Documents were systematically destroyed. It wasn't done in one place. Files were transported to incinerators and also all employees of the Communist Party Bureau were instructed to take documents home and burn them. My wife worked in the StB archives and she told me that long before the revolution started, documents were sorted out, packed in containers, and taken away. Some documents from archives were packed and transported to the airport to be taken out of the country, in the Soviet Union. The purging of archives, along with the overall strategy of the communist party, wasn't erratic. Everything was planned and worked out in advance. It was done on purpose. Documents regarding the People's Militia[9] were liquidated first. Today, nobody can ever find out how many former militia members are on the boards of banks and corporations. Our intelligence knew about the deadlines set for the regime to collapse. In May 1989, the Interior Ministry received a document describing the timetable for ending the current regime in Czechoslovakia that was supposedly created by the CIA. The Central Committee of the Communist Party was informed about it in June. The critical dates in the document were August 21, October 28, November 17, and February 28 of 1990. These were the last possible dates for the coup d'état. This means that the Communist Party wasn't surprised at all; they were ready for it. They were ready half a year before Vaclav Havel declared at the Venceslav Square that "The Communists are gone, they gave power to us."

Pavel Zacek: After the revolution in November 1989, the StB continued monitoring the activities of Western intelligence agencies such as the CIA. This intensive pursuit was focused on searching for potential future collaborations with Western intelligence agencies. The big question remains: how does all of this correlate with Aldrich Ames[10]? This pursuit continued even after Vaclav Havel became the President. Evidently this information didn't end up on the president's desk, but was instead passed quickly to the Soviets probably via the Soviet Embassy in Prague or a courier.

Frantisek Doskocil: The StB continued to function for quite a long time, even after it was disbanded. In January 1990 many StB people were still working in the counter-intelligence center and, having access to secret files, were helping others to get rid of their past and infiltrate the new system. That was the main objective of communists in the Interior Ministry and they handled it well. In February 1990, 1500 former StB officers were approved to stay and continue work. On March 27, 1990 Minister Sacher[11] asked for more officers to be call back to work. I was arrested by StB agents in February 21, 1990 and detained in the Ruzyne and Pankrac prisons for seven and a half months. I was never charged or tried. In the end, President Havel pardoned me under the condition that I keep silent for ten years. Without signing that special condition I wouldn't be released.

Pavel Záček: The StB was functioning very effectively all the time. They infiltrated all regional opposition groups. They managed to place their agents in the top leadership positions of regional groups in the Civic Forum and recruited new agents within Czech's Civic Democratic Party[12] and Social Democratic party[13]. There were no documents found about how this operation was run, but documents about these new agents recruited inside the newly formed Social Democratic Party and other organizations, like Obroda[14] for example, exist. General Lorenc[15] managed to destroy tens of thousands of document files within seven days. There are documents proving without any doubt that the StB was helping Marian Calfa[16], the person that Ladislav Adamec[17] put in the post of Premier, and who, in the end, offered the presidency to Vaclav Havel. Adamec's secret meetings with Mejstrik[18] in Klementinum always took place at midnight, and other secret meetings with Vaclav Havel were organized and secured by the StB. It's interesting that the air courier, which intelligence services used between Prague and Moscow, was active until April 1990. Intelligence information was still flowing to Moscow during Vaclav Havel's presidency and ended only after it was leaked to the media that Interior Minister Sacher was negotiating an agreement with the KGB about future collaborations. After this incident, the daily flights of the courier to Moscow stopped.

Frantisek Doskocil: I believe that the StB in Czechoslovakia was under the direct control of the KGB. No agent was signed up without KGB approval. I know this from documents I was able to get just four years ago (in 2002). They (KGB) were checking the background of all employees in foreign trades, in the Interior Ministry, the Ministry of Defense, and all other individuals who traveled abroad.

Pavel Zacek: Unfortunately, files about agents working with the KGB were completely destroyed. The total destruction of these archives was the biggest operation of the StB.

Frantisek Doskocil: I personally believe that Interior Minister Aloiz Lorenc was a puppet following KGB instructions. You will never find any document referring to the KGB. They are always referred to in documents as "our Soviet friends."[19] These links were huge and they continue today. These people knew each other and I believe that, long after the revolution, after Vaclav Havel became the President and disbanded the StB, all efforts were focused on keeping StB people in positions of power or allowing them to infiltrate new political parties and organizations. What amazed me was how easy it was for communist party officials and members to acquire positions in the civic Forum. I believe that the goal of the Civic Forum was to go through the period of change quietly and to make sure nothing that would endanger their future careers could be found in the archives.

Pavel Zacek: In talking about the StB as one of the supporting pillars of the regime, it could be described as a "little sister" of the KGB, copying it in every way. They were aware of the regime crisis and were documenting all the changes. So far, based on the documents found in the archives, it's not possible to prove that the StB was already informed by early 1989 about the upcoming regime change. On the other hand, big changes were already happening at that time at the top level in intelligence services as part of the reorganization process that started in 1988. They fully succeeded in upholding power in the hands of the Communist Party. Regardless of the voices of some radicals like John Bok, whom Czech society only later realized to be correct, the Communist Party wasn't dismantled. Its position was strongly re-instituted in the 1990 elections when communists got many more votes then expected.

John Bok: I believe that [with] Charter 77, even founded with clean minds of Vaclav Havel and Mr. Patocka[20], that the first moment, the impulse, didn't come from their heads. And who was involved in this? Jiri Dienstbier[21], who I think was a high-ranking agent because he was working for the First Division of STB, which is foreign intelligence. He was a correspondent in the UN during the communist regime. When there was the big massacre of the communist party in Indonesia, he was there writing about it. He was angry when I said to him that he was an agent and he wanted me to apologize. I said no, take me to the court and I will prove it, fuck you! And this person became the first Foreign Minister of this country after the fall of communism.

Vladimir Hucin: When I was the Chairman of the Civic Committee I found out that high ranking officials, including well known representatives of dissent like Tomas Hradilek[22], were pushing hard to make sure that there would be no effort to save any documents. These documents were being burned or moved to the Soviet Union at that time. Using a revolver with three bullets, I personally attempted to rob a car belonging to the People's Militia that was transporting archive documents to the military airport. I managed to save these documents. I believe if there were more of us we could have saved a big portion of the StB archives and stopped its liquidation. I was surprised that well known dissident Tomas Hradilek, who later became the Interior Minister of the Czech Republic, was so intensely involved in preventing any actions that would stop this liquidation of StB archives. I began to suspect on November 17. The revolution was not what it seemed. There is more going on behind the scenes and dissidents are part of the political game of assuring immunity to communist criminals. They are helping them survive to keep their positions in the government and economic sector. It was a bitter discovery for me. I got access to archival documents where I saw the names of judges working for StB, and, consequently, how the StB rigged court proceedings. I thought that by uncovering these documents I had achieved something good. But when my superior Jan Princ[23] (Vaclav Havel's protégée) found out about it, I was immediately taken off the case. Then I realized that his job (Jan Princ) was to cover up those who shouldn't be there, those from the old nomenklatura.

RB: *What can be said about the privatization process?*

Petr Cibulka: The privatization[24] was an even bigger fraud then the anti-communist revolution. When the word came out in 1990 that all government property will be privatized, they promised that all citizens of Czechoslovakia, all 15 million of them, will have an opportunity to participate in the process of privatization. At the end of the privatization it became clear that practically all government property was privatized by communists, especially those from the communist elite, such as StB officers and agents. It's unknown how many KGB and GRU agents this includes. But really what we saw was the monopoly privatization of the economy by these communist structures. Communists became capitalists and anti-communists became the proletariat. This is what privatization in the Czech Republic was all about. And when you look at how privatization went on in other communist countries, including the Soviet Union, you find out that it followed the same scenario. Only communists, KGB, GRU, and members of the local secret police privatized. Nobody else. They say that Dusan Triska[25] was the father of privatization, but nobody talks about the fact that he was an elite agent of the StB.

RB: *Didn't plans for privatization come from the Prognostic Institute?*

Ludvik Zifcak: The Prognostic Institute[26] put together the group of people that later, after 1989, ended up in the top government positions. People like Valtr Komarek[27], Milos Zeman[28], Vaclav Klaus[29], and many others were actually gray figures behind the preparation for changes in Czechoslovakia. First of all, they were the ones who, immediately in 1989, were telling the public how everything should be done. And when we look at the genesis of these people, we can see that most of them who later manipulated the public opinion were in fact former members of the communist party.

RB: *What can be said about the "FOND Z"(Folder Z)?*

Petr Cibulka: The so-called "Fond Z"[30] was created shortly after November 17. It actually existed before, but at this time the names of elite opposition people were added to it because the vast majority of them were agents of different intelligence agencies. This "Fond Z" contained the names of the highest representatives within the anti-communist opposition and was initiated by Interior Minister Richard Sachr, who, according to available information, was also a KGB agent. Nobody but him had access to this file.

RB: *But then this file was sealed and disappeared, right?*

Ludvik Zifcak: Yes, this initiative came from Jan Ruml[31]. Jan Ruml was one of very close colleagues of Vaclav Havel. As a Deputy Interior Minister, he ran the Ministry of the Interior after 1989. He ordered not only the sealing of all files about dissidents, but also moved them to an undisclosed location. This action was executed by Mr. Langos[32].

Petr Cibulka: I personally believe that Vaclav Havel is one of those included in the "Fond Z." There are some documents regarding him that we published in the #30 issue of the Uncensored News[33] in 1992. For example, in 1964, Vaclav Havel found an anti-communist flyer in his mailbox and, as a good socialist citizen, took this flyer to the county branch of KSC and they passed it on to StB. StB then contacted Vaclav Havel and visited him at home. During a friendly conversation, an StB officer asked Havel who among his friends could write such a document and he named many of his friends and relatives. So I think that when Vaclav Havel was later chosen to be the leader of the 1989 anti-communist revolution, he was, considering this previous experience as an informant, just the right person that the KGB and GRU could count on 100 percent and never be let down.

RB: *Ok, lets talk for a moment about Vaclav Havel.*

Jaromir Stetina: I believe that Vaclav Havel's biggest mistake was that he didn't use the authority and position he had at the time to outlaw the Communist Party. But after the battle though, every soldier is a general.

John Bok: I like Vaclav Havel. He is a very unusual person, but he is very naïve about many things. He is a person of compromises. He never was a fighter. In his whole life Vaclav was responsible only for himself. He couldn't even imagine being responsible for somebody else. He never helped anyone in his life. And if you don't have this disposition, how are you going to be a leader? The leader must be responsible. Vaclav had the vision. That's fine, that's OK. I am still his defender on that. But he quickly became very friendly with communists like Calfa and Adamec. I didn't want to be friends with them. I wanted them to go to hell. One night, Havel was waiting for Pavel Landovsky[34] in, the Na Zabradli theater. Landovsky came very late and when we were leaving Michael Kocab[35] suddenly showed up saying "Vaclav, I have a very important message for you. Very important information." He was trying to pull Vaclav aside so I couldn't hear them. And Vaclav said "Listen Michael, if John can't hear what you want to tell me, I don't want to hear it. Go on." And Kocab said, "You know, I have just come from the Soviets. They have nothing against you becoming president."

Later that night we were climbing the stairs in Vaclav's house. Being a heavy smoker, he was moving slowly and when we got to the second floor he stopped and said, "You know John, I am afraid that we will wake up and find ourselves in the Ruzyne prison." Even at that time he was taking it all as a dream. This is what I was trying to explain by saying that Vaclav was a person who lived his life like he was inside one of his plays. So it's not so simple when people are angry and blaming him today, saying that he changed over time. He didn't change at all, that's nonsense. He is the same person he always was. People didn't know him at all.

Stanislav Milota: On December 3, 1989 I accompanied Vaclav Havel to a secret meeting with KGB agents. The meeting was organized by Michal Horacek[36] and Michael Kocab. Shortly before leaving for this meeting, Frantisek Janouch[37] came to me and handed me a small tape recorder to record the conversation. We went to what was apparently the safe house, an apartment on Manesova Street. There were five people in the room: Vaclav Havel, myself, two Russian speaking KGB agents, and an old man acting as the translator. The conversation was dragging on and nothing of substance was being said. I didn't pay too much attention to it anyway, being preoccupied with thoughts of the recorder in my pocket. Then, some 30 minutes into the meeting, my recorder started to beep. Trying to save this embarrassing situation, I pretended that it was my pager, excused myself, and quickly ran out of the room. I was so pissed off. I dumped the recorder into the toilet, flushed it, and ran out of the building. I didn't return to the meeting.

RB: *Did it ever come to mind that perhaps Janouch gave you this recorder on purpose? That the KGB needed to talk to Havel face to face alone and this was the only way to get rid of you?*

Stanislav Milota: Now that you mention it, I will have to live with this thought for the rest of my life.

Pavel Zacek: It's not surprising that there was a contact. What was in the play, only Russian archives can tell today. The question is if Vaclav Havel was able, in that situation, to understand what they actually wanted from him. I think that Civic Forum understood that the Soviets would not intervene and that this information was passed to Havel through a personal contact.

RB: *To what degree did Vaclav Havel know he was being manipulated?*

Ludvik Zifcak: Vaclav Havel definitely knew he was being manipulated because he was in contact with counter-intelligence agents very often. Vaclav Havel had his personal file in the 2nd Directorate of StB. It was actually the cover file. Vaclav Havel was pushed in the direction to become one of the leading personalities of the dissident movement. Of course, later it came out that he, perhaps unwillingly or maybe willingly, worked with the StB, which was indirectly pushing him toward the position he was designated to take in the future.

RB: *Mr.Hucin, you were arrested by your own people in 2001! Tell us about it.*

Vladimir Hucin: My investigation led me closer and closer to believing that the Communist Party was connected with groups of extremist leftist and supported their activities. As I kept pushing this evidence to my superiors, my situation in

BIS got worse. One day, Frantisek Bublan[38] (Interior Minister) came to me and handed me a document, signed by him personally, specifically excluding me from further investigation of these terrorist activities. Another funny operation was the buying out of a book about Jan Kavan[39]. He was once the coordinator of intelligence services. This time he was running for political office in Prostejov County and we (BIS) got the order to buy as many copies of the book from bookstores as possible. I was against it and made my opinion very clear to everyone. That was during the time when we were tracking people working for the Iraq Embassy. These employees were supplying money to people in radical left-wing movements, like Ludvik Zifcak for example, to publish anti-American literature. I was not allowed to continue this investigation, which I considered to be important, and I am very troubled by the fact that Jiri Lang[40] is now at the top of the BIS. This man, now in charge of counter-intelligence, was personally responsible for the fact that the bombing attacks in Prerov were never investigated. When I was interrogated by this man in the year 2000, he got very upset when I brought up the name of Colonel Jan Murcenko who, as the leader of the SNB in 1989, actively participated in the liquidation of the anti-communist movement in the past. Today he is one of the executives at the prestigious police academy in Holesov. It seems laughable to me that these people are in charge of the war on terrorism today. Anyway, I was under surveillance since the end of 1999, shortly after the CSSD (Social Democratic Party) got to power. However, open attacks on me came in 2000. I was tailed, my phone was wiretapped as well as the phones of my friends. Then, in March 2001, I was arrested. I spent one year in jail. The trial dragged on for four years till 2006. Most of the time it was closed to the public. In the end I was acquitted of all charges.

RB: *President Vaclav Havel was well known for his generous amnesties but he didn't intervene in your case.*

Vladimir Hucin: Vaclav Havel disappointed me specifically by allowing people who created a lot of damage into the security apparatus and into the justice system. Vaclav Havel surrounded himself with dissidents who were in no way qualified to do their jobs and because of their lack of qualifications they caused a lot of damage. On a personal level, Vaclav Havel didn't intervene in my case regardless of petitions by people who supported me. He practically gave the green light to those criminals to arrest me and start the prosecution against me. He had the opportunity to read my file and see that all the charges against me were trumped up but he did nothing. It was only later that I realized that Havel's and my activities were in two different dimensions. When I was in jail I didn't have the luxury to write "Letters to Olga,"[41] and other things as Vaclav Havel had. I was in the worst prisons of that time, such as Minkovice[42] for example, and I was lucky to stay alive and survive that ordeal. Vaclav Havel was treated very differently in prison. I found that out much later. Vaclav Havel [can be characterized], as the saying goes, "In the land of the blind the one-eyed man is king." But many years passed before we realized this and we paid dearly for it with many painful experiences. It was a brutal awakening.

Ludvik Zifcak: Right, Vaclav Havel was living under completely different conditions than other inmates during his incarceration in Ostrava-Hermanovice Prison. He was allowed to receive gifts and enjoyed preferential treatment. After all, it is well known now that there was a car from one Embassy waiting to pick him up when he was released from this prison to take him directly to the Embassy. So, Vaclav Havel was a one-of-a-kind prisoner.

RB: *Mr.Zifcak, you became famous because of your role in the November 1. 1989 demonstration in Prague, which jump-started the so-called Velvet Revolution. Can you tell us about it?*

Ludvik Zifcak: The purpose of the operation was clear; to create an explosive situation which would later lead to an atmosphere suitable for the replacement of top leaders inside the leadership of the communist party.

RB: *Who's idea was that?*

Ludvik Zifcak: It is hard to say today where the idea came from. It definitely didn't come from the CIA. This operation was organized in the East. That means from the Soviet Union.

RB: *Did everything go according to plan?*

Ludvik Zifcak: Speaking for the people who worked with me, I believe that the operation was executed perfectly according to plan. Unfortunately, the political side of the operation was butchered. It didn't bring the expected results.

RB: *What exactly was your role in all this?*

Ludvik Zifcak: I was the intelligence officer with orders to create and organize a fake dissident group. It was called the Independent Student Organization. This organization became fundamental in organizing the November 17th operation and the students' demonstration in general. This organization was charged with infiltrating other dissident groups and developing contacts with their leaders throughout the whole of Czechoslovakia, groups like Charter 77, Democratic Initiative, Host, and so on. This objective was achieved. This organization's final task was to bring the November 17 demonstration to Narodni Trida.

RB: *Did you really fake the incident of the dead student stabbed by police?*

Ludvik Zifcak: Well, there was a whole story prepared, prepared in advance. The story had to be believable. You can't just send news out that somebody died. You need a foundation. The situation was rigged in such a way that myself along with people working with me on Narodni Trida were surrounded by many personalities from Charter 77 to eyewitness the whole action. The whole story had to be based in "reality." It had to be believable[43].

RB: *So, what physically happened?*

Ludvik Zifcak: There was a confrontation, physical contact with the riot police, and the body of a man on the ground. Other things happened around it that would support the whole fable of the story. The body was then transported to the hospital Na Frantisku.

RB: *And that dead body was you?*

Ludvik Zifcak: Well, yes of course it was me.

RB: *How do you feel about the whole thing today?*

Ludvik Zifcak: I find it quite ironic that I am probably the only living man on Earth who has had his own memorial where thousands of people come each November to honor my "death." I had a false passport, false ID, and a one-way airplane ticket to leave Czechoslovakia after this operation was over. Everything was set, but then, unfortunately, I didn't get the order to leave the country. So till today I have this fake passport and the ticket to Moscow in my possession.

RB: *Well, what went wrong? What do you think should have happened?*

Ludvik Zifcak: After the November 17 demonstration, other steps were supposed to follow; political steps. The . . . executive section of the communist party Politburo was going to meet and some high-ranking officials would step down. The so-called hard-core center of the communist party would take the lead and replace some "fossil" party members. Some security operations were scheduled to help stabilize the situation in Czechoslovakia. What does that actually mean? Something similar to what happened in Poland. The opposition would be arrested within 24 hours and the militia and the army would restore order in the streets. The whole situation could be stabilized in favor of the communist party within 3-4 days. The fact that it didn't happen reflects the fact that the political resolution failed.

RB: *So, from your perspective, the idea of the "people power" uprising is absurd, right?*

Ludvik Zifcak: Of course. There were no conditions for the revolution at the time. People were unhappy and pointed to problems within society, but these problems were not so big. People wanted freedom to travel and a pluralist society. They wanted a political system with more political parties involved, not just the communist party. These problems could be easily fixed. It could all be resolved by the Communist Party Politburo quickly passing new legislation and creating a few new laws. The situation could be settled without changing the political system. The situation wasn't ripe for any revolution. After all, later, in 1990, President Vaclav Havel himself admitted that he didn't want to get rid of the socialist system. That was said just after the revolution. According to the last public opinion poll taken in 1989-90, only 12 percent of the population wanted to change the political system. That means that 88 percent of people wanted to keep the present system. They just wanted some cosmetic adjustments to it.

RB: *As a communist, you admit that all this was cooked up in Moscow?*

Ludvik Zifcak: All this was, of course, cooked up in the Soviet Union. However, it is important to point out who the cooks were. There were what I would call somewhat "healthy forces" in the Soviet Union representing the path of the strong Soviet Union, and on the other side "for-American" forces represented by Gorbachev. They wanted to use Perestroika to install democratic regimes in the former communist countries. As a result, the year 1989 became the crossroad where these two groups collided. The Communist party in Czechoslovakia, but also communists in Germany, Bulgaria, Hungary for example, believed that the Soviet Union would support them. When the system started to collapse and the General Secretary of the Soviet Union Mikhail Gorbachev said, "It's your problem," they felt betrayed.

Jaromir Stetina: After a few years it became clear that the term "the fall of communism" didn't reflect reality. The excitement didn't last for long and I would say that now we are in a state of disillusionment. With help from politicians, the communists are bouncing back. Another form of 'hidden' communism is revealing itself lately. I call it neo-communism. The term that Vaclav Havel uses, post-communism, seems to me like something that already ended. But it didn't end. The revolution wasn't finished.

PART 4

GOLITSYN, SEJNA, ANGLETON

RB: *Well, can we say that the Cold war is over?*

Joseph Douglass: I think that people who think that the danger is gone are just not looking very far. For example, you still have the old communist system. The new system is simply no longer called "communism." You also have China, which is a major threat in many people's minds, and is still communist. And you have a number of communist regimes in various parts of regions where the threat is indeed growing as it is, let's say, in Latin America. But people don't want to look at that. Again, they have other things on their plate to take care of, and they don't want to address this communist threat that still exists, where it's going, and what it intends to do.

RB: *But we had warnings. It shouldn't be such a surprise.*

Joseph Douglass: That's true. I think it was a surprise because nobody was writing about it. Nobody was talking about the possibility. There were maybe one or two exceptions and it was promoted in the Western news media, and media around the world, as an enormous change, as the death of communism. It was almost like a script out of a play. Not that it was unusual. We have had these types of things happen before, though not to such an extent. We had the economic deception in the 1920s in which the idea that communism was changing and was going to allow the intrusion of capitalism was a part of the Soviet plan at that time. And in response, of course, the West came into Russia and helped the economy rebuild itself. It also happened after WORLD WAR II. Perhaps in reaction to the Cold War, Russians introduced what became known as a deception of peaceful coexistence in which they would give the image of wanting to work toward peace. That's causing the enemy, in this case the United States, to stop worrying about the threat. As a result, the Russians can actually bounce ahead of the United States, which they did in many categories during the late 1960s and 1970s. Then we had a similar plan to take over after peaceful coexistence. This came with the new regime under Brezhnev in 1968 and the name of the deception at that time in the Soviet Union was referred to as a period of 'détente.' And of course many people will remember that. Then we had the Perestroika deception, as it has been called, introduced almost as a precursor to the demise of communism under Gorbachev's regime in the 1980s. So, we are positioned to accept the end of communism and nothing applies to what actually happened.

RB: *Why didn't anybody want to see or hear what was coming?*

Bill Gertz: Well, obviously we have had some defectors from the Soviet Union and the KGB. Of course, debate over those defectors continues[1].

RB: *Why didn't anybody listen to the defectors?*

Vladimir Bukovsky: Well, you know, defectors are not the best sources of knowledge because they are deceived, offended people. They listened to them in a limited, technical sense. When a defector from the intelligence service in Russia, formerly the Soviet Union, comes to the West, they are debriefed. At least most of them are. And technical knowledge is used [from them] most of the time; knowledge of structure, chain of command, these kinds of things. What the defectors were never [trusted about], and what we who were not defectors were [dismissed with regard to], is the nature of the regime; the essence, the philosophy of it. It's in their aggressiveness. They perceived it not as knowledge, inner knowledge of the system, but as opinions of some people offended by the system, who defected . . . . That's the reason. They never believed in . . . a strategic vision of it. But technical details were always welcome in the West in the defector game.

RB: *Isn't it all about deception?*

Jeff Nyquist: Well, as one Russian defector said, "New lies for old." That was defector Anatoly Golitsyn. He wrote the book in 1984 called New Lies For Old and in the book he said that the Soviet bloc was going to change. It was going to liberalize. According to him, Russians were going to adapt democratic institutions. They were going to import capitalism. The Warsaw Pact, the alliance, was going to go away. And he said it was all part of a strategy to change the Eastern bloc to make it more effective against the West: against America primarily. In his book, he offered around 140 predictions. Within seven years of writing the book, 93 to 94 percent of those predictions had come true. His model was built on the idea that Russia has a long-range policy. Soviet Russia's long-term policy was, in the words of Sun Tzu[2], "to hold out bait, entice the enemy, feign disorder, and then destroy him." The disorder in Russia, the collapse of communism, has been a controlled collapse. While there were many errors and much of it genuinely collapsed, the communists know that, with the West and the U.S. lowering their guard, they [the communists] could come back. They could re-emerge and get better strategic positions than they had in the 1980s. And it's fascinating, the Golytsin view is fascinating and it should be discussed more. But nobody wants to discuss this, nobody wants to talk about it. Somehow, it's paranoid. But when a person has a rate of accuracy this high, when his model of what the policy-making rationale is in the other country proves so accurate, it deserves your attention. Because that level of accuracy in predicting political events, you can't find it anywhere. And yet nobody wants to touch it. Nobody wants to discuss it.

Edward Jay Epstein: What Golitsyn's eye-opening revelation was, was that there were two KGBs within the KGB. The outer KGB was The First Chief Directorate where the agents came into contact with the West. Now, his claim was that all those agents knew nothing about the actual strategy and what they were sent out to provide was disinformation. Lets say the First Chief Directorate has been given a shopping list to get information about x, y, and z. The Second Chief Directorate was the equivalent of the Counter Intelligence, which never exposed itself to the West and the West didn't even know, I think they knew about it's existence, but they didn't know it's purpose. So Golytsin claimed to be the Second Directorate officer, as by the way Nosenko[3] claimed to be. Now it suddenly became interesting because there was a whole part of the Soviet Intelligence apparatus we didn't know about.

RB: *Did anybody believe what Golitsyn was saying?*

Edward Jay Epstein: Well, initially when Golitsyn defected, he was believed. He was believed by Jim Angleton to begin with. He gave a large number of Soviet penetrations away. And the Soviet penetrations turned out to be accurate so Golitsyn was accepted. But as he kept expanding his story, the pragmatic side of the CIA, the side that was less interested in ideas and producing reports, producing information, began to disbelieve him and believe he was, I guess you would say for lack of a better word, crazy or a myth maniac, and they stopped believing him. Angleton and British intelligence, MI6, especially Steven de Mowbray[4] in British intelligence, they did believe him and they then used his information. So, you know, when Angleton[5] was kicked out of the CIA in 1974-75, then Golitsyn was terminated as a useful agent.

Tennent Bagley: Yes. Angleton did believe him and he had good reason to believe. There was a massive campaign of so-called misinformation, the Soviets called it "active measures," to manipulate and subvert foreign governments and to influence their foreign policies. That was something the Soviets were doing on a very high level in certain countries where they had, as we have since learned, penetrations of intelligence services. We had the penetration in England as well as the penetration of government and political parties in West Germany, and similar manipulations in France and other countries. So there was indeed a general plan to use these assets in the interest of Soviet foreign policy. But to move from here to say that there was some monster plot that was a paranoid conception is again a misrepresentation, it's not true. Golitsyn perhaps believed more strongly in this than others, including myself, but I think it was a misunderstanding. I think that what he was saying was genuinely true as he saw it and we were more or less able to see it from our point of view. Golitsyn was certainly telling the truth as he knew it. And there comes the other story. Because Golitsyn had a lot of information about the penetration of Western governments, when that information was passed to the government it became outraged and unhappy because no government wants to discover this in its midst. It's not in the interest of the government, it's not in the interest of people in power, to find out that they have been fooled and manipulated. Therefore, they will take all pieces of information they can to reject this information. It's, again, the human tendency, but also the bureaucratic tendency. It's politically poisonous because a service which finds, through good counter-intelligence that there is a mole in its midst and gets rid of it by cleaning its own stable becomes the figure of fun, ridicule, and distrust. Our liaison relationships, for example, surely damaged the CIA when it was later discovered that Aldrich Ames, who occupied a key position in the CIA, was a Soviet agent. Certainly nobody before that wanted to find it and, as a result, the investigations that finally led to Ames's discovery dragged on for nine years. That could have been done much faster and would have been done in a different period of the CIA's history. But nonetheless, the things that caused that investigation to drag on were these tendencies of the government not to believe these things Golitsyn was telling us. Angleton did believe it and he did not adapt any wild ideas of a monster plot that was outside of the KGB's capability or that of anyone else. The KGB had the capability needed to do the kind of job Golitsyn was describing. And I think they were purposefully doing it. But later I think Golitsyn, by examining other sources and hearing things, to some degree absorbed things going on around him after his deception. To some degree, I think he isolated himself and sorted things out his own way and developed some theories, which were beyond reason. But certainly they were done with good will. His testimony should be watched, looked at and considered with care because inside, he did care. And he did present it to the world for better or worse and it's there for anybody to see and to be evaluated on its own terms, as I did. I think that Golitsyn was a serious source.

Edward Jay Epstein: I think that Golitsyn is more than a person. I think that people that believe in strategic deception are especially within British Intelligence, people like Arthur Martin[6] and Stephen de Mowbray — people I respect by the way. And people in American Intelligence like Jim Angleton, and people in French Intelligence used Golitsyn by feeding him their own ideas in conversations. And in Golitsyn's book, "New Lies for Old," if you look at the preface and who his editors and advisers on the book were you find it was Stephen de Mowbray and Scott Miler[7]. In other words, I think the book reflects the thinking, and I agree a great deal with this, of the intelligence establishment of the West in the 1970s. So it's not just Golitsyn. He has been talking about publishing a new book, I haven't seen it. That may be pure Golitsyn. But I think the interesting thing about his book "New Lies for Old" is that it's just more than Golitsyn.

Jeff Nyquist: James Angleton became the head of U.S. counter-intelligence [staff] at the CIA in 1954. Angleton was basicaly a fellow who came to believe that the CIA had been penetrated. He had the shocking experience of being very close to Kim Philby[8] before it came out that Kim Philby was a Soviet mole. He trusted Philby. He told Philby things. We don't know what secrets he might have revealed. Philby was in the U.S. from Britain sort of doing a liason thing from British intelligence. It turned out Philby being a mole was a shocking experience for Angleton. When, in 1961, Anatoly Golitsyn defected and told the CIA that it was penetrated by the KGB it created a kind of conflict within the U.S. intelligence bureaucracy. Angleton was hunting for the mole or moles in the CIA and many people felt threatened. Obviously a term like "Witch hunt" comes up. How can anyone feel safe when suspecting their own? It's a nightmare. It's a terrible situation. Angleton found his way into the situation and finally the conflict ended when CIA director William Colby[9] fired him and Angleton and his crew were out. From that point on they characterized Angleton's idea as "sick think." They said it was sick to think that Americans would be traitors and that you would have moles in the CIA. Since discovering multiple moles in the CIA and the FBI, we now know that indeed sick think was correct and U.S. intelligence services were penetrated and almost certainly the moles we found were the tip of the iceberg. What about moles we didn't find? We certainly can't fool ourselves and say we found everyone who was in there.

RB: *Mr.Bagley, you worked with James Angleton for a long time. What can you tell us about him?*

Tennent Bagley: I don't know of anyone whose image was so distorted in the public eye as that of Jim Angleton. In the first place, people called him James Jesus Angleton. Jesus was his middle name and it was never used by him or any of us who knew him well. His mother was Mexican and he had this name which was part of his family background. To call him James Jesus Angleton was to make fun of him already. Jim Angleton was a close friend of mine from the early sixties to his death [in 1987]. I worked with him, each of us in a different brief. I was operational and he was staff. He had no command role over the things that I was doing but he was always there to advise and inform. Often, he took his information from what he was getting from all his sources and, let's say, made his own conclusions and analyses about how things worked. Very often we disagreed. Sometimes we disagreed almost violently, but always with reason and rationality. And to say that he was paranoid and obsessed with pre-conceived master plots dealing with war between the U.S. and the communists is to misjudge the man, to misjudge the situation, and to misjudge the operations in which he and I were involved. He was not conducting a "mole hunt," as people put it. It has been said that the resource, in this case Anatoly Golitsyn, came out of KGB and talked of master plots and great penetrations and so forth and suggested that there was a penetration of the CIA. And from this basis, this general basis, some felt that Angleton chased after this in a mad, insane mole hunt that hurt innocent people. Well, first of all, my experience with Angleton and the whole question of security was that neither he nor CIA security officers ever looked around for moles because they never had any general idea that there was a mole. Never. They only investigated specific allegations or specific indications that there would be a penetration here or there and for these specific reasons. Now, not to go into these specific allegations or these specific indications, not to have done it would have been criminal negligence. And I personally think that what Angleton and what the office of security were doing was their job, and they did it pretty well. There were irresponsible claims where people were spiteful and ill informed. Irresponsible people were trying to pin this label of treason onto some of [their] colleagues, including myself in one case. But I found out the case that was built against me was very thin compared to those against my colleagues. So, the work of James Angleton was serious and responsible. As a human being he was hugely concerned with other people, his friends he was loyal to to a fault. He always helped people in difficulty without others knowing about it. I found out about some of his work by chance, some things he was doing to help some people in trouble. His affection for his colleagues was tremendous. I have many letters from him, which show his concern and his deep feelings. He was a man who was deeply concerned with the danger of penetration and in that respect you could call it paranoia. However, it's not paranoid to be realistic about the possibility of penetration when the KGB, for example, was putting all its efforts throughout the world toward penetrating the American government and particularly the CIA from the counter-espionage point of view to protect itself as well as to get into the American government. Jim was aware of this danger and therefore was a great practitioner of a "need to know" policy. I felt that he was implying a principle that was good. Those who need not know the secrets or operations being conducted should not know about them and he kept these various threads to himself, letting out little bits and pieces to others who may have a need for more, to know more, than he was telling them, things that he knew. This goes back to his experience during the war with breaking German ciphers, the ULTRA operation[10] everyone knows about. This was the most tightly kept secret that one can imagine. In fact, it was unknown until 30 years after WORLD WAR II and even then when it began to leak with the book Enigma by Gustave Bertrand[11] they tried to suppress it because breaking other people's ciphers is the greatest of all secrets besides . . . the penetration of their intelligence services. And in the government, the so-called high-level mole is, along with cipher breaks, the greatest of secrets. Jim was protecting those secrets and many who were deprived of those secrets accused him of paranoia and mole-hunting and other outrageous accusations that have no basis in fact whatsoever. Jim was a decent man, a good man, and a highly professional intelligence officer with long years of experience and a very sharp mind. Now, whether or not at times he became obsessively suspicious I can't judge because I don't know all the things that were in his possession at the time. But I can tell you from personal experience that it was tremendous because we were working closely when I was in charge of our operations at the Polish intelligence service and when I was later in charge of our work against the Soviets and Soviet bloc intelligence services. His work was professional and he was a good man and was totally misrepresented.

RB: *If Angleton lived today he would see that he was not as wrong as everybody was telling him.*

Edward Jay Epstein: Angleton never believed he was wrong. He might believe he was wrong on certain people; people he thought were spies who were not spies, certainly a number of those. That he would understand, because everything he did was in terms of possibility, not probability. So if he speculated that the Soviet Union was involved in a massive deception and they had the means of succeeding in this deception, that they had established feedback within American intelligence community and that they could monitor what was happening, and that they had put agents in place and were spreading disinformation, he was sure of it. While he was right . . . he could always be wrong. I never found Angleton to be an absolutist. He was always willing to listen to other ideas. His ideas were very simple; that the KGB fought the United States as its main enemy. The KGB's job was to penetrate American intelligence by recruiting agents and using those penetrations to advance the strategy of the Soviet Union. I have seen no evidence that he was wrong in any of these three assumptions. We have a wealth of knowledge now proving that the Soviet Union apparatus believed America was the main enemy, he was right there. We have cases like Aldrich Ames and Robert Hanssen[12], actually fourteen of them in all, showing that they succeeded in penetrating the CIA and the FBI[13] and NSA[14] as well as other parts of the American establishment. So, he was right . . . . He never gave the number, but certainly the number is enough now to say there was activity. And the issue of what the Soviet strategy was still remains up in the clouds. Angleton didn't know he was wrong in some of his assumptions as to what the Soviet Union was doing. For example, making a split with China. We now know that the split was real. But of course he was right in saying that the split was temporary because now we see that Russia cooperates with China in every form imaginable; from supplying them with military equipment to coordinating policy. So, he is right in some places and wrong in other places. I remember at one point, Richard Helms[15] was the head of the CIA and he told me, a few years later of course, he said that Angleton kept coming up with very interesting theories, about Chinese-Soviet collaboration when they were supposed to be split. This collaboration was in the area of nuclear weaponry and Vietnam and intelligence agents. And Helms said, you know, I found what Angleton said interesting but when I brought it up to the political leadership they said we don't want to hear anything more. This was in the 1960s. We decided that there was a Soviet-Chinese split and that is what we are acting on, that's what we are exploiting. We don't want to hear any more of this. And Helms said he came back and told Angleton just to shut up on this. In this case it turned out that Helms was probably right and Angleton was probably wrong. But what I am saying is that the way the intelligence is shut down maybe is not always inappropriate and not always wrong but it's always run by a political agenda. Anything that conflicts with the political agenda the CIA doesn't want to hear. It's not what an agent has to provide, it's weather it fits into the political agenda.

Bill Gertz: Counter intelligence in the United States has always been difficult. It goes back to the 1970s when the CIA had very agresssive counter-intelligence, an independent counter-intelligence service within the agency headed by James Angleton. And this created backlash against counter-intelligence because counter-intelligence involves questioning people's loyalities. The positive intelligence people didn't like that. They don't like to be questioned and they don't like to have their sources questioned. Also, in United States, in our culture, we are somewhat averse to secret intelligence activities. That made it difficult to get good aggressive counter-intelligence. Recently, for example, the National Counter Intelligence Executive in the United States saw to develop a new strategy, a new offense-oriented strategy against foreign spies and terrorists, yet bureaucrats within the intelligence system succeded within a matter of months in undermining that new office and this strategy and, as a result, two top officials, Michelle Van Cleave[16] and Ken Degraffin, were automatly forced out of their positions. And counter-intelligence has returned again as a kind of a gate keeper security function. This is something that makes it not very effective.

RB: *Was the Soviet division in the CIA a part of the problem?*

Edward Jay Epstein: What happened was that, as Angleton and his staff began to develop a broader picture of KGB activities, one activity that they believed was prominent was using agents to supply strategic misinformation. Everyone, even the CIA, used agents to provide tactical misinformation to deflect an investigation away from one of the people they were trying to protect or trying to advance the career of one of their agents. Every intelligence service does that. What Golitsyn said, and General Sejna[17] and a few other defectors were saying, was that the KGB had, actually, strategic disinformation. In another way they were trying to paint a wide picture of what the activities and the objectives of the Soviet leadership was and this is what the American Soviet division said: we can't try to get into the minds of Soviet leadership. We can tell you what type of materials they are using such as alloys in missiles, we can tell you where their divisions are, we can tell you how much work they are doing in Siberia on nuclear weapons, but don't ask us about these vast deception plans. So, there was a real separation of interest from the Soviet Division, whose job was to have agents and produce reports, and counter-intelligence, which was trying to get an overall picture.

RB: *You brought up General Jan Sejna who defected from Czechoslovakia just about the time that Golitsyn was shut up, and he was saying pretty much the same things that nobody wanted to listen to.*

Edward Jay Epstein: General Sejna, who I spent some time with, and Golitsyn, and other people, were describing why the purpose of intelligence . . . [was] a means to an end not an end in itself. The CIA didn't know what to make of them. American political leadership wasn't interested in hearing these very complex views of Soviet ambitions. They wanted it to be black and white; to know: "Will the Soviets invade Turkey?" "Will the Soviet Union attack Germany at any point?" "Will they close down Berlin?" "What are they doing in Vietnam?" That was at the top of the shopping list. So when General Sejna came and started talking about the use of drugs, for example, as a means of weakening Western society, that wasn't on the agenda. The CIA is an organization that acts as an acquirer of information that it receives for [the] political leadership. If [the] political leadership doesn‘t want to know about al-Qaeda, it doesn‘t provide the information. If they want to know about the accuracy of missiles, it seeks that. It‘s like a business. It seeks to please its customers. And it has one customer — the President of the United States. It‘s that simple.

Joseph Douglass: General Jan Sejna was a most unusual person. He was the only person that was actually a member of the decision-making hierarchy from a country behind the Iron Curtain who defected to the West, to the United States in particular. He operated at the highest echelons within the communist system from 1954, and especially in 1956, until he left Czechoslovakia and defected to the West in 1968. He knew the top communist leaders not only professionally but also socially. He interacted with every communist leader, I think, around the globe. Most foreign dignitaries who came to the Soviet Union also passed through Prague. He was actually the head of the Secretariat of the Defense Council. And the Defense Council was the highest decision-making body in the communist system. It was above the Politburo in elements of national security, defense, intelligence, counter-intelligence, and foreign policy, as well as the economy for all practical purposes. So, he was at the top of the structure and he ran that Secretariat for a while. He was Chief of Staff to the Minister of Defense. He was a member of the governing bureau to the main political administration, which is the top watchdog over the military system. He was a member of the Administrative Organs Department. He had a whole variety of positions. He was a member of the Presidium, a top governing body, and of the political group that gave instructions to the Presidium. He was clearly at the top. He knew all these people. His mentor, you might say, was Khrushchev. He knew top military and top political people. He socialized with them; he went camping with them for that matter. And this is particularly significant because he had a fabulous memory. He could describe a meeting that maybe took place 20 years earlier. He would identify people who were present and after thinking and translating remarks he could basically tell you what they said. He was a very interesting person with a fabulous memory who never tried to shield the truth that I can see. He only tried to follow the policy he adapted to when he defected, which was never to elevate the importance of information, never talk about what you don't know about, and always be forthright and scrupulously honest in details you provide to questions you are asked. He felt it was the only way he could survive in the Western world because of his importance. And he adapted to this policy. He didn't have to fake information because of his memory. He just knew things, stuck to those things, and, to my knowledge, nobody ever proved him to be wrong or even deceptive. There are memorandums from the heads of some intelligence services complementing him on this.

RB: *What was the most important information he brought?*

Joseph Douglass: In his judgment, the most important information he had when he came to the West was detailed knowledge of the long-range strategic plans for the next 10-15 years and beyond. This was where the Soviet communist system was heading for the next 20, 30, 40 years actually, and the plans behind these goals. He told his handlers that this was the most important information he had but that he would not discuss it until the decision to grant him political asylum had been made. That decision was made several months later and then nobody ever debriefed him on the long-range plan until he and I started discussing it and it struck me as extremely important and I started debriefing him in the late 1970s.

RB: *Are you saying that nobody was interested in what he knew?*

Joseph Douglass: That's true. That surprised me. He didn't say it directly that way. That's what I concluded from what he was saying. So one of the first things I did when I started to work with him was to ask him to identify all the things he had debriefed on during the first year from late February when he defected to whenever his debriefing stopped, which was early in the next administration, less than a year later. He gave me these topics and we talked a little bit about it and then what I did was go back to the intelligence system and obtain copies of all the reports on his debriefings that had been let off and distributed among people with the appropriate access. I went through them and read these things and what struck me and amazed me was that they were precisely what he said to me. They talked about the material precisely as he talked about them with me. And most amazing, they were all focused on trivial things. Things that had no significant strategic importance. Like, one of the things that really disturbed him was that they wanted him to draw out the insignias of all the Czech military officers. It took two weeks, a lot of paper, pencils, and casting for him to draw all the insignias out. He told them, "Why do you want me to do this? You can walk across to the Czech Library in Prague and copy them yourself and get them absolutely right. Why do you want me to do this exercise and waste time?" No answer. Another example of the type of things they focused on for months was getting him to recount all the orders of battle information, like: "How large is a platoon?" "How large is a company?" "How many rifles are in the company?" The tasks focused down to this extraordinary level of detail with no interest in what was happening at the top level. What was happening among thoughts, discussions of the Czech leadership, the Soviet leadership, or the East German leadership? Here was a vast amount of knowledge and they never even explored it. They deliberately stayed away from it. And I would say deliberately, because at one point they also had him start comprising his memoirs. And the British who were also working with the U.S. to certain extent helped him on these debriefings. And when you look at these memoirs, which were cut down and distributed in 1980s by a British publishing company, that's a whole other story. But when you look at the original draft of the memoirs, it's clear that this is somebody who knew an unbelievable amount of information about communist operations around the world. I mean, we would speak for hours about what they were doing in Egypt, Syria, Lebanon; and in Algeria, Australia, and Japan, all around the world. All this type of stuff was included in these memoirs. And not only that. The copy I had of the memoirs was annotated in handwriting with various comments and question marks by the individual who was the deputy for research for Jim Angleton in the CIA. So no one can say that they didn't eventually know how invaluable this guy was. Yet he was never exploited.

RB: *How did you meet him?*

Joseph Douglass: I first encountered him probably in about 1976 after he left the CIA, which is in the time frame of 1975-76 when the new head of the CIA, Stansfield Turner, decided to cut back on a lot of operations and operational people. Jan Sejna was one of the people they got rid of and I asked if I could use him and picked him up and started working with him at that time. What struck me over the following 20 years or so when I was working with him off and on is that we would be discussing many topics of unbelievable strategic importance to the United States and other countries and in every single case he was never debriefed by anybody in U.S. intelligence on the subject. With one exception, and that exception was a group from DIA, a very small group, say 3 or 4 people at most, who started debriefing him in the late 1970s on international terrorism. This is when the Soviet sponsorship of international terrorism was first laid out in detail. Massive detail. These analysts recognized that they couldn't come out with this information as it was, because it would be immediately attacked by the CIA[18], the Central Intelligence Agency. The DIA is the Defense Intelligence Agency[19]. So, what these people did is that, based on the information Sejna provided, they started researching all other intelligence — signal intelligence, human intelligence, collections, clandestine material, and they were able to confirm, and in many respects extend, the information Sejna provided to them across the board in all regards. Sejna was so important because he provided the key to them. He explained how the whole system operated. Knowing this, they were able to ask the right questions in the computer databases files to find information that they never before knew how to fit together. Now, all this information came alive and confirmed everything that Sejna said. They wrote the report on this and the report ended up going into a special NIE[20] process that had been established immediately when Reagan took over to look at the background of international terrorism. Once the report came into this committee that was headed by a top CIA official, what he wanted first was all of the documentation that people from the Defense Intelligence Agency had used. Well, the Defense Intelligence Agency people were smart enough not to give him the documentation, the specific documents, because they knew they would disappear. What they did was give him the list of documents. In the next meeting, the head of this group proceeded to discredit every single CIA source and document in an effort to kill the Defense Intelligence study. Finally, one of the analysts stood up and looked at the representative from the National Security Agency and said, "Are you going to discredit your sources too?" And the NSA guy looked back and he said, "Absolutely not. We stand by every one of those sources." As a result of that, the idea of Soviet involvement in international terrorism finally started to surface. However, there was still a large effort to discredit it by the CIA people who controlled the NIE process and also through the various leakages to the media, which were intended to discount stories saying that the Soviet Union was a focus of international terrorism.

Jeff Nyquist: Jan Sejna wrote a book in 1982 called We Will Bury You. It's an autobiographical book and one [section] is about the communist strategy. Sejna describes how, in 1967, the Warsaw Pact leaders . . . revealed their plans: . . . the fake elimination of the Warsaw Pact was contemplated as part of the strategy . . . . When I read that I perked up and I said, wait a minute, there is another defector saying that they are going to fake a collapse of the Soviet bloc. And so now there are two defectors from two different communist countries saying the same thing. Okay, maybe there is something to this. And I started really looking into this more closely, looking at what other defectors were saying and, in 1987, two years before the changes began in Eastern Europe, I came to the conclusion that this was the policy of the Kremlin and that they were going to follow through on it and sure enough, bang, bang, bang, events happened. And so now, maybe there is another way of understanding this. But I think there is something here. It's frightening to me that nobody in the West wants to acknowledge that there is something to what Golytsin said and that there is maybe a continuing danger from Moscow.

RB: *Can you mention things that Sejna told you would happen that really ended up happening?*

Joseph Douglass: Sejna didn't really read the U.S. papers or magazines to learn what was happening. He knew what did happen in the past and he would tell me things that were planned. Generally, I would identify things that actually did come to pass, or were present that he probably didn't know about. Certainly, his information supported it. One example was, let's say, the targeting of drugs in the inner city. He identified that as well as the rationale behind it and I don't recall if there was an awful lot of new information about it in newspapers that he would know of. He certainly indicated things about international terrorism that were not known before he started to explain it and that, indeed, later on were determined to be entirely right. He identified the existence and supreme importance of the Defense Council which, when he defected, was basically unknown to people in the CIA or Academia with a few exceptions here and there. Still, its power and its role were not understood and he explained that very well. Later on, several years later actually, the Soviets started writing a little bit about it exactly as he said it would be, or said it was. He certainly talked about the development of various areas within military capability such as the use of chemical and biological warfare agents and the Soviets' interest in nuclear operations in the European theater. And as he would identify dates when decisions were made and actions taken, they fit perfectly in what we would later find out was the actual case through other intelligence means. He would also identify various things through special terms, which I would later encounter in documents, clandestine documents that were very highly classified, that indeed confirmed what he said to be the case. In many cases he pointed out things that were taking place, which later on we learned actually took place or found information that supported them. Another example is that, if I looked at times when drug trafficking began, first in China and second out of the Soviet Union, the explosion of cocaine directly correlated almost to the month with when operations began in those areas as was described to me by Sejna. Information on dates I didn't even come across in our own literature on drug use till considerably later was provided by Sejna. There is an excellent account of that which I wrote in the book Red Cocaine.

RB: *Can you talk more about drug trafficking?*

Joseph Douglass: In 1983 I became interested in drug trafficking because my kids were just becoming teenagers. I could see it was potentially a major problem that I knew nothing about. So I started digging into it because I wanted to learn something about it on my own, strictly as a concerned parent. At that time there was quite a bit of focus on drug trafficking as the beginning of the Reagan administration had a number of Congressional hearings. The more I read and the more I looked at the congressional hearings in particular, the more it struck me that there was something wrong here. Because what I was seeing as the picture was developing was a lot of uncoordinated drug trafficking groups that were applying their trade to pushing drugs into the United States for money, but when I looked at where some of the players came from, like Nicaragua, Cuba, and particularly Bulgaria, what struck me was that there was no way that these people who were operating as officials would be involved in drug trafficking if the Soviet Union were not involved. At that time I had developed a very good relationship with General Sejna and I called him on the phone and said, "Jan, let's have lunch tomorrow." So we met at one of our usual hangouts, "Charlie's Place," and 15 minutes into the lunch I started casually asking him if he was aware of any Soviet involvement in drug trafficking. And he stopped chewing and looked up and said, "Of course." And then he proceeded to give me a half hour nonstop lecture on drug trafficking; The countries that were involved, the people that were involved, dates, times, places, and strategies. He gave me the whole works, including his personal involvement. And by the end of this half hour my only impression was that I had hit the motherload of information on the source of all narcotics problems. It would take me a long time to extract the information because there was so much. I spent the next three years getting together with him once a week, sometimes once a month, but usually once a week, sometime more, and talked about various aspects and gradually I tried to develop the whole model, the whole factual description of the origins of drug trafficking: how it came to be, where it led, the countries that were involved, people who were involved, the strategies, and the operations. When I had a tremendous amount of details assembled I thought it would be worth its weight in gold because the United States had an awful drug problem. Most people will remember this. We still do for that matter. It's worse now than it was then but it was still awful bad then. I thought that this would be a good time to send this information to people in the United States government who were fighting this problem because how can you fight the problem if you don't understand it? Because really what you want is to understand what the enemy is, what his strategy is, how it operates. And then you can attack it. And it was clear from everything I read that they didn't understand who was behind it, what the strategy was, or what the motivations or operations were. They had a complete misconception of it. I tried to bring this information to the attention of every single agency I could think of that was involved in the drug problem in the United States. With one possible exception the reaction was one not of disbelief, but of not even wanting to know. The only exception was the Customs Department. I sent a long letter to the Customs Director, I believe it was William van Rab, and he had a couple of customs guys come to talk with me. I met them for breakfast and had Jan Sejna with me so that they had a first-hand source and we talked for about an hour or two hours and then it was clear that things were winding down and it was also clear that they were really not enthusiastic about the information. They basically closed the meeting saying, "Well, thank you very much but there is nothing we can really do. That's a political problem." And that was the end of it. I decided that this stuff was important and the least I should do is write this stuff up so at least the American public could learn where the hard drug problem came from and the strategy behind it if they were interested. I spent about two years writing the book Red Cocaine. Later on, people in the inside had very good things to say about it people as far up as the head of the CIA, people in the FBI. Someone told me it was required reading at one time. Another person indicated quite clearly that everything I put in the book was confirmed. It lays out the entire communist strategy to undermine industrial countries in the West, beginning with the United States, which truly uses drugs more then other countries. The targets initially were youths because paramilitary forces were drawn from youths and it was hypothesized that the use of drugs among them would weaken the military. Youths in colleges were also targeted because this was the place where future leaders of America could be found. Other hard targets were the work force because the Soviets held our work force in high regards and wanted to destroy the high work ethic of the United States. I set up these in the book, the manners in which this whole operation came about in the early 1950s, as well as decisions that were made to make a strategic intelligence operation against the West in 1955. The Soviet operation developed drug schools for traffickers because they didn't want to run the operation by themselves. Rather, what they wanted to do and did was to recruit people from indigenous countries all around the world, citizens there who had clean records, who were not connected to the communist party, and bring them to special training schools, schools for drug traffickers which lasted for about three months, and teach them . . . so that they would come back and become little drug traffickers. If you look at the number of schools, the actual number of students who took these courses, it's a little bit insightful, I would say, to understand that by the mid 80s, assuming just the schools that Jan Sejna had personal knowledge of, that the Soviets would have trained roughly 25,000 drug traffickers. And the number was obviously higher then that. This was all set in motion in the late 50s. It went operational in 1960. And if you look at data on the use of drugs in the United States, what you see is that drug use became very low in the 1930s-1940s and resulted in very few deaths in the late 40s. Then you see a jump in statistics in 1949-1950. The use then plateaus and in 1960 takes off like a rocket. The cause of the jump in 1949-50 was determined by U.S. intelligence and narcotics people at that time to be due to Chinese drag trafficking which was adapted as a strategic operation in 1949 by Mao Tse Tung when he took over the Mainland. Drugs then were directed from China mainly towards Korea, Japan, and the United States. The Japanese also identified China as a main source of this major problem that had suddenly emerged, just as it had in the United States at the time. Chinese drug production remained constant during the 50s and the problem plateaued during the 50s. Then when the Soviet operation came online in 1960 the use of drugs just took off like a rocket. The material Jan Sejna described also looks at the efforts of different groups to improve strategy, and to look harder at different drugs and how to increase drug usage in the United States. This lead to the targeting of inner cities and grade schools. By 1968 drug use was targeted towards professional classes, particularly those in high-pressure job areas. One also sees how the Soviets came to the conclusion in 1961 that the drug of the future was cocaine. They saw tremendous potential in it. So they sent Czechs and Germans to find out how cocaine was manufactured, which they learned because they were already operating in Bolivia, Columbia, and Peru, the key sites for the cocaine industry, as part of their expansion into Latin America. They learned how the process was done, and they brought the information back. The Germans then figured out how to improve the process. By 1964 they had improved the process to the extent that one jungle lab could outproduce almost the whole productivity of Peru, Bolivia, and Columbia. During that same period of time, during 1960-65, they started to develop a dedicated network just to service the cocaine industry, which they believed would continue to grow. The new production techniques were introduced, along with the nucleus of new cocaine operations in Mexico, Columbia, Bolivia, and Peru. In 1967 the operation really began to work. If you look at the use of cocaine you see it take off like a rocket in 1966-67. This clearly correlates with testimony Jan Sejna gave. Between developing the markets in 1960 and servicing the United States, by 1965 they had multiple operations set up in every single Latin American country you can list and in most of the major islands in the Caribbean, particularly those with a tourist industry, such as Martinique. Major trafficking was orchestrated through Mexico, Canada, and into the United States. By 1968, the KGB had concluded that roughly 35 percent of drugs coming into the United States was now coming from organizations they were inside or controlled. They had influenced or controlled something like 32 percent of drug distribution in the United States. And their plan was to expand both of these figures as much as they could. A part of that, I think, was then part of the function of Russian organized crime, which started to really grow significantly, most significantly in the time period of about 1979-80 and it has been known for its interaction with the drug business in the United States. These are massive operations, and most importantly they are ones nobody at the top wanted to acknowledge existed or were even interested in knowing information about back when I was doing this work in the 1980s.

RB: *Did the CIA ever try to infiltrate this business? Somebody said it started during the Vietnam War*[21] *when the KGB started to recruit CIA people for this.*

Joseph Douglass: The CIA has a long history of involvement with criminal operations of all sorts including drug trafficking. Their involvement, I suspect, really became heavy in the mid 50s when they started to move into the Vietnamese problem area. The involvement in Vietnam was clearly major. We were running a secret war in Laos at the time and as the individual I mentioned before stated, 90 percent of funding for that secret war was paid for by money made through the CIA involvement in drug trafficking out of Laos, Burma, and the Thailand area. This was run by the CIA. A blind eye was turned toward it by the head office of the CIA who maintained that it wasn't our policy to interfere in drug trafficking. That may not have been a policy, and so they looked the other away. Other people who looked the other way were chief aids and people who were the main oversight for the intelligence community within the U.S. Senate during that same period of time. So it was swept under the rug and accepted. I think the most damning indictment of this process, for which there is ample evidence to be found, is the problem of the flow of cocaine into Arkansas in the 1980s as part of the effort to fight the war run by the CIA during the Reagan administration and by the NSC people in Nicaragua and elsewhere in Latin America. The focus was really on Arkansas because that's where a number of planes were based or were active in. They were active in both bringing drugs into the United States, especially cocaine, and they were also involved in a massive amount of money laundering that took place and a number of murders that were designed to keep the thing quiet. That has been reported in detail in number of books, very excellent ones, which show the outstanding fact that you always have one person, sometimes two from various federal agencies and state agencies, that got on the trail of this and did their best to bring indictments, to open the thing up, to prosecute people, to shut it down. They were all squashed by higher-level officials within the state or federal apparatus including state police, state attorneys, federal attorneys, the IRS, or Justice Department people. And the trail led up to the Governor's office in Arkansas and to the White House, particularly to the Vice President's office in Washington. I have an interesting article on money laundering in the Wall Street Journal that appeared, I think, in 1988-89 when some of the information started leaking out. This information was available in a Wonderful book by Mara Leveritt, Boys On The Track, and additional material and books written on one of the key traffickers, Barry Seal, by Daniel Hopsicker in the book, Barry And The Boys, as well as a number of general articles written in Arkansas and other places. But they never went anywhere. And they identified officials involved, they identified all sources of judicial cases that were mounted, grand juries that were brought and were then subverted. All the court cases filed were sequestered and put off limits. There was plenty of data, all sorts of facts, that almost every federal and state agency wanted to look at. Nothing ever happened. All was pushed down the memory hole. And this is just a case study in Arkansas at one period of time. One of the most interesting aspects of this was a couple of memos that were dug up from about 1980-81 when the whole thing was started. These were agreements between the head of the CIA and the Attorney General of the United States in which basically it said that CIA personnel who came across these types of activities would not be expected or required to report on these activities to the Department of Justice. In other words, right before everything is taking off, there is an agreement covering the CIA and the Justice Department's backside. Nobody has to report on the information. This is most important because Arkansas is just one state. This type of thing is going on in every state in the Union. Nothing gets out. Occasionally, some people get arrested and thrown in jail, but not because they are drug traffickers. For example, Manuel Noriega[22] was heavily into drugs, heavily into money laundering, but you better believe that that wasn't the big crime he was accused of committing then. And occasionally you get somebody from Latin America like Carol Latter, who I suspect got captured because his mouth got too large, and, when he talked about drug trafficking and it's use against the United States, he used a little too much Marxist lingo, which revealed his origin too much. But the thing that you really find in a number of other books such as the excellent works by Michael Levine[23], a top DEA agent, is that they show how every time a case is developed against some of the top people, all of a sudden agents are taken off the case. The case is closed because we are dealing with CIA operations and they run higher than the DEA or the other people doing the investigation. And after a time, nothing comes out of the investigation. It can't continue because other higher powers are involved. So we have a problem in the United States. We have had one for almost five decades now. It exists and survives because it is politically protected. That's the bottom line.

Jeff Nyquist: In Jan Sejan's book We Will Bury You, he talks about the strategy, about how a Russian strategist came to Prague to talk to them about how the long term strategy worked. And the long term strategy involved knocking out the U.S. economy so American working men would turn against the system and create a pre-revolution condition inside the United States. Also, involving the United States in conflicts like Vietnam would turn much of the world against them. It would also turn the American people against a projection of U.S. power. In addition, the strategy involved using terrorist attacks on the United States to cause disorganization. It's very interesting that the Soviet defector Victor Suvorov, his real name is Vladimir Rezun[24] but he writes under the name Victor Suvorov, wrote book called Spetsnaz. And in that book he talks about Spetsnaz's[25] role in the next world war. And he talks about a period before the beginning of that world war called "Gray Terror." During Gray Terror, terrorism would be unleashed against the United States and other Western states, which would be attributed to people who are not connected to the Soviet Union. They would be terrorists like Al-Qaeda, who are supposed to be independent from Moscow, who would be attacking the U.S. But this would take place before the major operation, to kind of destroy, to finish, the American military. I had a curious conversation in 1998 with Russian defector Stanislav Lunev[26]. We were talking about how Russia could pull off a surprise nuclear attack on the United States. And he said something funny in 1998, which kind of surprised me: "If you ever hear that Arab terrorists have detonated a nuclear weapon in an American city, don't believe it." And I said "Why not?" And he said, "Because it would be Spetsnaz, my people, it would be Russians." And wow, after 9/11 it really got me thinking. And then when you got Litvinenko[27] coming from Russia saying that Al-Qaeda is connected to Russian security services, when you have stories coming from the Wall Street Journal saying that Ayman al-Zawahiri[28] was in Russia and couldn't account for what he was doing there in the 1990s, you put this together and think oh, this is a very bad combination of testimonies. Because if there is anything to this we are confronting an attack from Russia, not from a bunch of crazy Islamists in caves. This is a major power that is making a move against the U.S. And when you talk about somebody playing with nuclear weapons you're talking about somebody bringing the world to the verge of nuclear war. It's very dangerous. And what comes after this? What is the follow up? What happens to America when it's badly damaged?

RB: *Who was really responsible for the fact that Jan Sejna was never debriefed?*

Joseph Douglass: I do not know the answer to that. It was obviously controlled, carefully controlled, by the Soviet Bloc Division within its Operations Directorate and, indeed, by the Eastern European section of that division. That debriefing process is generally controlled by one or two people by having external agencies submit questions that they want to ask or discuss. The problem, of course, with that process as it regards Jan Sejna, and other defectors as well I should point out, is that people were generally interested in tactical level information but rarely, if ever, in strategic information. So they never debriefed them on something of significant influence or interest. Often, tactical interests are fulfilled and followed by people who are interested in technical questions such as a pilot of a plane. When a pilot of a plane defects, that's where you ask him a lot of good technical questions and exploit him for that reason. This is not done in terms of strategic level importance because it's just not a subject fundamentally of interest, nor do they want the enemy's input in that decision-making process.

Tennent Bagley: In the business of collecting intelligence, one is always running up against the possibility of someone trying to give false information for various reasons. Dealing with this kind of thing was a big part of our life in intelligence and counter-intelligence collection in the CIA. I personally became very interested in it because I encountered some of the false defectors and false sources, many double agents working against us. We had many problems working against the Soviets' double agents, and against the KGB. So, deception in the counter-intelligence field is quite different from the field of strategic military deception and we encountered it over and over again. But the most dramatic aspect of it was the false defectors. And, in particular, the defector I can talk about is Yuri Nosenko, a case I was personally involved in. I became interested in why some of these deceptions worked. Why others, in various services, not just in American services but also in some of the other allied services, were so vulnerable to this kind of hoax. And looking at it, I realized that one of the biggest aspects of it is not them deceiving us as much as us deceiving ourselves. I realized that there are other reasons why people are vulnerable. One of the reasons is that you want to believe. And the desire to believe is sometimes much stronger than reason. You have a hundred reasons to realize you are being lied to, but you suppress them. What you keep is what you want hear, what fits your own previous beliefs. I personally think that complicated words for this, like cognitive dissidence and that sort of thing, simply complicate the matter. The fact is that we are deceived because we want to be deceived. And as my wife said, "If we didn't deceive ourselves we'd all shoot ourselves" which is perhaps a cynical view, but nevertheless is not irrelevant to what I am talking about.

PART 5

DECEPTION

RB: *Well, it all comes down to deception. How can we define deception?*

Edward Jay Epstein: To define deception in general? Deception can take place at either a tactical or a strategic level. At a tactical level, it's simply creating doubt in someone's mind. Doubt that you are the enemy or doubt that you mean harm. At a strategic level, which is much more interesting to me, it's painting a picture in someone's mind that actually shapes the way they see the world. And if you can effectively shape the way somebody sees the world, then they can act the way you want them to act. And so it's controlling their behavior, in this case the behavior of states, by creating a false picture of reality. One might also look at it as creating a picture of reality that would bring about the results you want. So, if creating the idea that, let's say you are weak, because it will cause somebody else to disarm, and once they assume you are weak they will take no defensive action against you, then the perfectly viable strategic deception is to project the image of weakness. Or conversely, if you are weak, say like Hitler[1] was in 1932 or 1933, you may want to project an image of strength so countries don't attack you and you can build up your own strength. So you can use different deceptions to shape the reality of everyone around you.

Joseph Douglass: Deception is a hard topic to talk about because it's not how Americans typically think. You know, we all are brought up with the "I cut down the apple tree and I am sorry" point of view which is a kind of truth. When you look at Soviet culture, the Russian culture, and you go back a hundred years, and then forward a hundred years, you find an examination of that culture dominated not by words like friendship, freedom, independence but rather by deception. Two good books to look at in that regard are Hedrick Smith's Russians that came sometime around 1980 and the book that came out about 100 years earlier, A Journey Through Eternal Russia by the Marquis de Custine, which is a sort of counterpart to de Tocqueville's Democracy in America. But in both cases it often describes Russia, in what struck them as a very important difference from the United States, as a culture where the presence of deception is an essential part of the culture necessary to enable people to even survive. So deception is very key. Now, over the twenty years or so that I worked with Jan Sejna, it was very rare that we would ever discuss a topic when at least 20 percent . . . was not focused on deception associated with the topic. Indeed, for the first three or four years that we talked I would be willing to bet that 80 percent of what we discussed was deception. Because deception was so important in the Soviet Union and, of course, because of my own curiosity at not being familiar with it and not really seeing very much of it at all in the United States. Anytime a decision was made in the Soviet Union there was always a political annex to the plan. And this "political annex" was a euphemism for the deception plan. And it would analyze the plan and present one variety of action to be undertaken to protect that plan through deception. They even had sub-annexes within the annex that would explain, by design, actions to be taken to further protect the implementation of the policy, should the true nature of the policy actually get revealed. So they had, you know, multiple layers of deception all planned and set for each and every single decision that ever came out. So it was just a massive topic to the Soviet Union and they were masters of deception. At one time, we spoke at length for a number of days on deceptions implemented under Nikita Khrushchev. And these were fascinating because in protecting the topic you would have deception plans for different countries. And even different groups would get in different countries. And some parts of the plan would be almost internally inconsistent with other parts because they were designed for different groups. That was their function. That was the way they worked. Very complex. Now, at one point I had the opportunity to take a quick read that would allow me to understand the degree to which the United States at its highest level had an understanding of Soviet deception. And what struck me is that we didn't understand then, nor do I suspect we understand now, what the top three layers of deception planning and implementation policy were in the Soviet Union. That was the degree of our understanding. When you were talking about deception in the United States National Security Apparatus, what counted in people's minds were things like disinformation, false information, camouflage, and concealment, none of which are deception in the Soviet system. All are small parts of it but none are deception. Deception is a strategic operation. These might be viewed as tactical components that can be utilized in deception. Another thing about deception is that we had always maintained in the U.S. intelligence community that the Soviets would not reveal state secrets, not for any reason. Yet, as was explained by General Jan Sejna, the release of classified material was used in support of operations of deception. Indeed, there was an entire study developed whose title was basically, roughly translated, "The Use of State Information in support of Deception Operations." And state information is basically secret information in the Soviet Union. The main operations that they undertook, which were eminently successful in the United States, were deception operations. Namely, the whole economic plan under Lenin, peaceful coexistence under Nikita Khrushchev, détente under Brezhnev, and Perestroika under Gorbachev. These are all deception operations. The Soviets live and breathe deception. You cannot understand what they are doing without understanding this. Indeed, you can't even begin to understand communism itself without understanding deception, which is very rarely mentioned in textbooks on communism. The reason why is that communism is 90 percent deception. Communism is mainly a strategic deception designed to entrap and mislead intellectuals. The communist system talks about everything being done for the proletariat. However, unless you look carefully, you don't recognize that the proletariat doesn't exist. A part of communism is therefore directed to bringing about this proletariat, and the only reasonable way they can do that is by destroying the middle class and creating a proletariat that will then rise up against the system. Almost everything about communism is a deception as it's understood from within the system, and at its top levels in a place like the Soviet Union. In working with many defectors, including professors of Marxism-Leninism who have defected, one of the other surprising things that I have learned is that none of them, with one exception, had any real appreciation of how important deception was. Of course, the main individual who did know was Sejna as well as another person who had a hint of it but was not quite as high, nor as important as he was. Other people knew it was there and that it was important but, unless it was a part of their job, they really didn't understand how much of the system was built on deception. Deception is a central part of communism. It's a central part of the Soviet Union. It's a central part of the entire Russian culture. It's not something that can be turned on and off like a switch. It will continue to be like this every day. I wrote extensive articles about Soviet deception, about how they violated the arms control treaties. The new KGB spent a lot of time and energy disseminating information that doesn't exist anymore, that they changed.

Oleg Gordievsky: Deception, specifically foreign policy deception, was very important. It was just a part of the Soviets' massive system of foreign policy propaganda. The KGB was helping to create the most sophisticated deception operations. But it is important to say that the KGB wasn't the main body of deception. Deception was mainly sent to the West through numerous channels of official and unofficial Soviet propaganda—the foreign policy propaganda.

RB: *Who was creating the propaganda?*

Oleg Gordievsky: There was a department on the level of the KGB. They existed under different names. It was a department of disinformation. And in order to create deceptive documents, in order to distribute them in the West, there was a secret department of writers attached to a publishing house. They were usually retired KGB officers who were writing texts containing deception. And deception was always mixed with truth. Sometimes, it was very difficult to find out what was true and what wasn't. But sometimes there were outrageous things. For example, it said that Americans created AIDS in order to kill the black population. That was a deception operation. Then the KGB created a rumor that the body parts of babies from Latin America were sold to rich Americans. There were a number of such big stories. But mostly the propaganda was very simple. For example, Jeane Kirkpatrick[2], the U.S. [ambassador to the United Nations], wrote a secret letter. An apparatchik at some point intercepted the letter. In that letter, one paragraph was inserted which was a lie discrediting the United States. When people read the letter it looked OK. It was written on the State Department's stationary with the signature of Miss Kirkpatrick, but one paragraph in it was a lie.

Jeff Nyquist: It's very interesting when you look at the anti-war movement[3] in the United States during the Vietnam War. It was said by communist leaders both in Vietnam as well as by one defector . . . that . . . the Russian General Staff spent more money supporting the anti-war left in the United States than they did supporting the army of North Vietnam. Money that they spent in the U.S. ended up being very well spent because they turned the American public opinion against the war. They did this by spending huge amounts of money to support the . . . anti-American left-wing pro-communist, pro-socialist subculture. By promoting that subculture, by bringing it forward, by bringing its message forward, they actually shifted the whole country very subtly to the left and got the whole country to doubt the rightness of its own actions. In Vietnam, the United States was trying to prevent a communist country, North Vietnam, from overrunning a country that wanted to be non-communist, the Republic of Vietnam in the south. The act that caused the south to fall was the cutting of supplies by Congress, and that was affected by the anti-war movement. People didn't think South Vietnam was worth defending in the end. It wasn't even worth sending military supplies to. So, in that respect, communist propaganda was shown to be able to effectively cause the fall of countries that were otherwise defendable. This is just one example. Of course, what's happening now is even more sinister.

RB: *It sounds like our politicians never grasped the deceptive qualities of Soviet policies.*

Bill Gertz: This is a major flaw. The deception policies of the Soviet Union, as well as that of other governments that are working against the United States, have been very successful in undermining U.S. policies because our system is based on the Western notion that people, and governments in general, tend to tell the truth when in fact they have very strategic policies to use misleading information, to use deception, to use lies, in order to advance their own interests. And many of our politicians, and especially our diplomats, failed to understand this fundamental feature of America's adversaries. And this cost us serious national security damage as a result.

Ion Pacepa: The whole foreign policy of the Soviet-bloc states, indeed its whole economic and military might, revolved around the larger Soviet objective of destroying America from within through the use of lies. The Soviets saw disinformation as a vital tool in the dialectical advance of world Communism. The KGB's priority number one was to damage American power, judgment, and credibility. As a spy chief and a general in the former Soviet satellite of Romania, I produced the very same vitriol John Kerry[4] repeated to the U.S. Congress almost word for word and planted it in leftist movements throughout Europe. KGB Chairman Yuri Andropov managed the anti-Vietnam War operation.

Angelo Codevilla: There is a strain in American thought, in seeing changes abroad as inevitably leading to democracy, and to the kind of life that we enjoy here in the United States. And, in fact, a number of Americans in the twentieth century have indulged in that line of thought. There were some Americans even earlier that would believe such things. Thomas Jefferson[5], for example, expected that the French Revolution would yield something like the American Revolution had. But Thomas Jefferson quickly realized otherwise and joined the majority of Americans that, at that time and during the 19th century, recognized that America was very, very different from the rest of the world. He saw that most of mankind did not have the habits or ideas, or the religion that would lead to freedom. In fact, they realized that those who made revolutions abroad were not really looking for freedom in the same sense as Americans saw it. Rather, they were looking for power, power over their enemies. This is why most American statesmen had been quite sober regarding these revolutions. In the twentieth century however, they have allowed themselves to believe what they really wanted to believe all along. Therefore, they have deceived themselves. The most difficult thing in the world is to convince people of that which they don't want to believe. The easiest thing in the world is to convince them of what they want to believe. Indeed, no effort is required. People will simply believe what they wish. Now, in the United States you have, since the 1930s, a strain of thought according to which the cooperation between the Soviet Union and the United States and the United States and Russia would result in a kind of peaceful and wonderful condominium of the world. President Roosevelt believed in this, as well as much of the left of the Democratic Party, and in fact even a substantial part of the progressive wing of the Republican Party believe in this. This is a dream, of which it is bad manners not to share in certain circles of the United States. And so, naturally, people tend to interpret what happened not only in Russia but also concerning Russia in that vein. And the reality, of course, be damned. People will simply take what they see and interpret it as they wish.

RB: *How big a deal is this deception?*

Angelo Codevilla: The first lesson to be learned about deception is that it is composed 90 percent or more of self-deception. Again, it is not a matter of trying to convince people of that which they don't want to believe. It is nearly always a matter of helping people to believe most strongly in what they want to believe and to act on what they passionately want to do and to be. This self-deception is enormously important in government. You have sincere people, such as Jimmy Carter[6] or, for that matter, George Bush[7], for whom conscience is, as we used to say, a very good girl. Whose conscience is quite manipulatable, they succeed very well in manipulating them. There is no need to tell these people things that they would otherwise reject. Simply tell them what they want to believe and they will believe you with all their hearts.

Joseph Douglass: I think the fall of communism was a surprise because nobody was writing about it. Nobody was talking about the possibility. There were only maybe one or two exceptions and it was promoted in the Western news media and media around the world as an enormous change, as the death of communism. It was almost like a script out of a play, not that it was unusual. We have had these types of things, not as extensive, but similar things have happened before. We had the economic deception of the 1920s in which the idea was introduced that communism was changing. It was going to allow for the intrusion of capitalism as if it were a part of the Soviet plan at that time. And in response, of course, the West came into Russia and helped the economy to rebuild itself. It also happened after WORLD WAR II. Perhaps in reaction to the end of the Cold War the Russians introduced what became known as the deception of peaceful coexistence in which they would give the image of wanting to work toward peace, causing the enemy, that is the United States, to stop worrying about the threat, so the Russians can actually bounce ahead of the United States — which they did in many categories in the late 1960s and 70s. Then we had another play of the same variety to take over from peaceful coexistence.

They came in with the new regime under Brezhnev in 1968 and the name of that deception at the time in the Soviet Union was referred to as a period of détente. Of course many people will remember that. Then we have the Perestroika deception, as it has been called or introduced, almost as a precursor to the demise of communism under Gorbachev's regime in the 1980s. So we are positioned to accept the end of communism and do nothing but applaud what actually happened. We used to have a number of articles appearing on Soviet deception and disinformation in the 1980s but it all sort of disappeared.

Jeff Nyquist: I ask myself why people know certain things, and why they refuse to accept certain knowledge. Why can't they digest certain facts? That interests me very much. Because it's true that a certain kind of knowledge comes easier to some cultures and to some people than others. There are things that, sociologically, are more difficult to accept for Americans than they are for Russians or Chinese. Every culture is unique and every mindset is different. And to see how those mindsets work, to see how important facts and truths are swept under the rug to preserve our myths, our stories about ourselves, and about other people, that's fascinating to me. That gets my curiosity up. Because as human beings, we think of man as a rational animal. Oh, no, man is an emotional animal. He has reason, but more often than not people are led by their feelings. And what is the IQ of feeling? It doesn't really have a lot of IQ and yet it's present all the way up to the government level. It's up to the level of how people vote and how people manage their lives. Very emotional creatures, human beings. And now our traditions are broken down. The guidelines of rational living, the habits that protected us in the past, they are gone. So now we are adrift in a way and left with just our feelings. And it leaves a kind of opening. Society is moving in a lot of directions that are not right. I am not just talking about morality or the development of our economy. I am talking about national security policy. Hey, what feels better? What's more comfortable feeling than knowing that there is all that stuff out in the mall? It's all waiting for you and all you have to do is to go out and buy it. And then you get a nice job that gives you money. You can achieve that, the lifestyle you dreamed about. It gives you a nice feeling. The idea that you have enemies, that there are weapons of mass destruction, that you have to have a bomb shelter, you have to have food put away — put that out of your mind. That's uncomfortable. That hurts to think about. Any rationalization will do. And I believe that as a society America rationalizes because we want to preserve that good feeling that we can just go out and start shopping, and rent videos, and entertain ourselves. We can entertain ourselves to death.

RB: *Well, Who sees the whole picture?*

Tennent Bagley: I would say that no one sees the whole picture because there is an interesting hiding aspect to this big picture. What I may know on my level is sometimes so complex and so boring, if you like, to others that they don‘t pay attention to it and they don't know these other details. So they take what they want to believe or what they can grasp of these things and make their decisions based on bits and pieces here and there. So I don't think that any decision on the top is fully informed or, let's say, wise. Because it is humanly impossible. I don't, by the way, accuse anybody of anything, I think it's the human condition. I don't believe these are flaws or that they can't be ratified by new organizations in the intelligence community, by putting a new level, which is what they have done since my time. This is not the way to solve the problem or get the whole picture. It may or may not make coordination between agencies a little bit more effective, but it is not going to bring this whole picture, the whole clear well evaluated picture, no matter how one tries. And one does try to bring this picture to the attention, as you say, to the highest authority, which in the case of America means the White House. There are careful analyses, differences of opinions, which are transmitted in these national security estimates of constant debate, but to think that there is any inner automatic truth is to deceive oneself . . . .

PART 6

CIA/KGB

RB: *Somebody mentioned to me that the CIA was interested only in collecting verifiable information.*

Angelo Codevilla: This is a very important issue. Let me tell you about that. During my time on the Intelligence Committee I tried very, very hard to get the intelligence agencies to pay attention to the information they accepted. In other words, I tried to make them conscious of the likelihood of other certainties — that hostile intelligence agencies would try to manipulate their conclusions. And I gave them all sorts of ways in which this could happen. I gave them examples that have happened in the past. Well, one day Bill Casey, then director of Central Intelligence, gathered the top twelve people in the agency for a seminar with me and himself to discuss this subject. After my presentation, Casey asked each person in the room to react to it. Two men said the same thing. They said, "Well, these are very good points that Mr. Codevilla makes and I am sure they are terribly relevant for John and Harry here, but in our group in the CIA we have taken precautions and we are absolutely not liable to any of these difficulties." Now, since they all said the same thing, obviously they all accused each other of being liable to this information but they themselves were surely not. Which of course is the best proof one could have that each and every one was careless about his own sources. Now, what they often do, which helps them to deceive themselves, is to simply verify one or more items in a stream of information coming to them, obviously ignoring the fact that anyone engaged in deception could have at least 80 percent to 90 percent of truly verifiable information. But they would, of course, change or shade a key portion to lead to the conclusion they want to achieve. No, people in the CIA simply don't look at that. They just take the verification of a couple of items as a verification of the entire stream of information. Nothing could be more destructive. The problem with verification certainly goes beyond arms or even intentions. It simply has to do with items of information. If a source has proved that some of these items have been correct, if the items have checked out in one way or other, if they have been corroborated in any way, the CIA will accept just about everything else coming from that source. This is not simply something that has to do with intelligence from the Soviet Union or Russia. This is a general problem. Once a source has given anything which turns out to be factually correct it is simply corroborated whether it is correct or not. The CIA is just terribly, terribly gullible. This is a congenital problem with the CIA. Now, then there is the problem of ideology. Since most people in the CIA are not ideologically motivated and quite alien to religion — very few of them are Christians or Jews in anything but an ethnic sense — they have a very difficult time believing that anybody believes in anything. Those who believe in nothing assume that everybody else believes in nothing. Also, the modern, we should say the modernist's idea of the inscrutability of values is deeply rooted there. Hence, when the CIA talks about terrorism, they simply mean violence by someone we don't like. The famous CIA dictum that one man's terrorist is another man's freedom fighter simply shows their own declaration of moral bankruptcy, their moral and intellectual bankruptcy. In other words, we cannot distinguish between innocent and guilty. We cannot distinguish between good and evil, and indeed, we cannot because we don't know anything about religion, we don't know the difference between the real thing and a fake. And this, of course, is terribly disastrous. It is simply being blind to a huge part of reality, indeed, the most important part of reality.

Tennent Bagley: In the CIA we had categories. The highest category of intelligence was what we received raw from an agent in the field, for example. This intelligence was evaluated with letter and numerical designations. The letter spoke to the reliability of the source, and the number spoke to the believability of the information itself. The highest level of believability was if the information was confirmed from other sources. I thought it was a very bad, or at least self-defeating principle because sometimes we got, as we did when I personally was involved in the case, [information from] the Soviet military intelligence officer from GRU in Vienna, in my time Pyotr Popov[1]. We were getting information that had no confirmation from any other sources. He was the only source we had in the Soviet military at the time. He was a very well placed source, well briefed. He had information, for example, a speech he was giving or a briefing on a new fighter aircraft with details, performance details. Proposed performance details. And this report was so new that it was, I wouldn't say discarded, but not taken seriously at first. Its value later became evident when a U2 began to take pictures and we saw the test stands of new fighter engines, suitable for fighter planes and military aircraft, being developed. A couple years after that, there was a flight test in Moscow, probably on Army Day, or the October Revolution celebration, I don't remember which. A fighter flew over that was absolutely unknown to the West up until that point. Not too long after that, maybe one or two years, a copy of that [plane] was crushed in the mud of West Berlin. The West got their hands on a Sukhoi Su7 fighter, which was the very plane we had known of in its early planning stages seven years before. But in the report it was quoted as "not confirmed by other sources."

Edward Jay Epstein: I think the CIA is interested primarily in information that can be objectively verified because it makes things fairly easy. You can count things. You can count the number of aircraft carriers that the Soviet Union is building. You can compare it with agents' reports and satellite photographs. But when you're talking about Glasnost and deception, or whether or not Soviet leadership is trying to spin off the Soviet Republics and control them without formally controlling them, there is no way of verifying that because, by definition, no successful deception has ever been detected. It's a totality of course. Because if it was detected, it wouldn't be successful. So the problem is, you go back in Soviet history, back to Lenin and Stalin, back to the 1910s and 1920s before they ever got to power, one sees the beginnings of the plan to create fake Soviet Republics that, in a sense, would be independent. These include Georgia, Armenia, the Jewish Republic, and Taneatuva. It's basically the whole map. And in fact, the Communist Party under Lenin wasn't really running the Soviet Union. That was just an informal arrangement. Pretty soon the world saw the Soviet Union not as independent republics but as a block. And it would not be inconceivable for the Soviet leaders to say "We have to recast these republics, like Kazakhstan, otherwise we are going to be in a civil war with every one of them. Let's recreate the idea of independence." And then the question is, could they control them without formally controlling them? And those are issues that are very hard for the U.S. intelligence service to determine.

RB: *Why is U.S. intelligence so vulnerable to penetration?*

Edward Jay Epstein: Well, all intelligence services are vulnerable to penetration. Penetration simply means that you can take the loyalty of one official and, either by bribing him, compromising him, or through some other means, such as putting pressure on his family, get him to change his loyalties. That's part of human nature. It doesn't work 100 percent of the time, maybe 50 percent, but if you try hard enough, you always find an Aldrich Ames or a Robert Hanssen who will change his loyalties for one reason or another. So every organization, especially intelligence organizations, because they are constantly in contact with their adversaries, are vulnerable to penetration.

CIA vulnerability is rounded by the fact that it's arrogance prevents it from believing that it can be penetrated; therefore it makes very little effort to take counter-actions like trying to penetrate its adversaries, actions that would make penetration more difficult. But it's not just the CIA. The CIA is the intelligence organization, but what the Russians would really like to do is penetrate all the positions that input information, all the depositories of crucial information, not just the CIA — the intelligence services — but the government itself. The scientific establishment. It's always aimed in those directions. And America, in the days of the Cold War, aimed in those directions. It wasn't always just the CIA versus the KGB; it was the CIA versus the Soviet establishment and the KGB versus the American and NATO establishments.

RB: *Why didn't the CIA ever accept the idea that the KGB was after political influence?*

Edward Jay Epstein: Well, the CIA was a bureaucracy. It started as a small, dedicated organization mainly dedicated to stopping the Soviet Union. They started on that premise. The biggest division was the Soviet/Russia division. This is were they aimed their energy and, eventually, as the bureaucracy grew and as they hired more and more people who went to more diverse sources, they found that they could only keep track of military or potential military actions, or what the president asked them to keep track of. And the presidents wanted to know very specific things. For example, the progress of the accuracy of Soviet missiles. They wanted to know where Soviet submarines were. They wanted to know about the air defense system. So that's what the CIA focused on. And that's natural. The intelligence service doesn't follow its own ideas. It has consumers. Consumers being the president and the military that they supply with the information they request. The CIA was not set up as an ideological organization, but as an extension of military intelligence. In fact, the OSS[2] was a military intelligence organization. It gathered information about German military capabilities.

RB: *Could we say that this concept was somehow alien for the U.S. government?*

Edward Jay Epstein: Right. Well, here is how I would put it. The CIA, throughout its entire history, was looked at as a pragmatic organization. It was something dedicated to action. The action might even be something like running cover against a labor union in France, but whatever it was, it was action oriented. The KGB was ideologically oriented. It was carrying out the state's purposes. And they were, in a sense, not the same. They were both intelligence organizations, they were both recruiting agents, they were both trying to penetrate each other's organization, but we did not understand the ideological nature of the KGB. And in some sense only with the defection of Anatoliy Golitsyn were eyes opened to the fact that the KGB was involved in much more than simply operational intelligence.

Bill Gertz: The CIA's problem is that it does have a left-leaning culture of kind, a liberal outlook on things. A lot of that remains from the 1950s. During the McCarthy period[3], a lot of liberals and leftists went to work for the CIA and other parts of the government, and they brought that kind of bias with them which resulted in a certain kind of culture that grew up around the CIA. I can remember one CIA official telling me that he worked for the agency for over 20 years and he never met a Republican. I think that kind of tells you what sort of system it was. It was made up of people who came from the left and people who had a leftist Democratic point of view.

Joseph Douglass: U.S. intelligence is a large thing. It has many components to it. It has always had a very strong, let's say pro-socialist, pro-communist component. The actual extent of this has never been revealed till recently when a number of intercepts known as the Venona intercepts[4] started to be released as early as the 1990s. Among other things, they show that within U.S. intelligence, going back to the beginning of WORLD WAR II, there were at least 100 communist that they were aware of, of which some 40 percent were known Soviet agents that were not tracked down and exposed. This provides a very questionable background on certain components of our intelligence services and may help to explain a number of things. For example, it might explain why their estimates of Soviet and Chinese capabilities were very misleading in many regards. It also might explain why, and in an outlandish matter, they almost went out of their way to treat defectors as undesirable people and do everything they could in their power to stop them from talking rather than gaining information from them. This was such a serious problem that it actually led to Congressional hearings in the mid 1970s. It got no publicity to speak of. It also perhaps helps to explain why it is that the CIA did their best to kill the idea that there was a Soviet sponsorship of international terrorism back in the 1970s which continued until the ridiculous nature of their efforts was exposed in 1981 by a number of books and documents that came out and showed how the Soviet Union was indeed the primary sponsor of international terrorism. They were the only sponsor, really. At the same time, like any large organization, you have a number of people that come from almost every [part of the] political spectrum. That's what makes for a diverse organization. But in this case you've got one that Barry Goldwater[5] remarks about in 1964. He couldn't quite understand why the CIA spent all this extra money on influencing opinion in support of socialist causes rather than supporting democratic causes. Again, it didn't get much publicity at the time.

Robert Gates: I knew when I was a Soviet analyst, a new Soviet analyst working on Soviet foreign policy, that I was the only person in the entire unit who actually had a background, an academic background, in Russian and Eastern European history. Soviet history. At that time in the early 70s there were very few people in the CIA who had that kind of background. And so they would bring in Western European analysts or someone like that and that person would become a Soviet analyst. And they would tend to look, they would sort of use a rational actor's approach to the leadership decisions and for somebody who had studied a bit about Marxism-Leninism[7], about Russian and Soviet history, I think I was most prepared to see the role of ideology, not in terms of guiding all decisions, but as the framework in which leadership approached the decision. And, for the most part, that led me to take, I suppose, a tougher approach to the Soviet Union because I didn't see them as just another nation state but one, in fact, driven by ideology, and the messianic desire to expand their sway over as much of the world as they could. We did a lot of analysis on the political side of things. I think we did pretty well in terms of the dynamics in the leadership, pressures on the leadership, the decision-making process, and so on. But we were working essentially with second and third hand information as well as open literature, defector information and those kinds of sources which allowed us to put together the mosaic of the political side of the Soviet Union. So we did a lot of political analysis. It was just not grounded in hard sources, as the information we had on both the military and economy was.

Edward Jay Epstein: Well, you know what intelligence services do, including the CIA, is not public knowledge. You only know in hindsight, you cannot go back to what the problems were in the 60s, the 70s, or maybe the early 80s. But presently the only evidence we have is the case when Russia penetrated the CIA and the FBI in the 90s, with Ames and Hanssen. There has been no apparent improvement in terms of warning or information that's emerged that shows that we are, I hope we are, penetrating other societies. I can't see any evidence that we are doing that. But who knows?

RB: *What about counter-intelligence?*

Angelo Codevilla: United States counter-intelligence has had a very troubled history from the very beginning. Once upon a time the CIA had a small independent counter-intelligence office under James Angleton. That office served the very important purpose of quality control for positive intelligence gathering. That is to say, this office looked at positive intelligence gathering and looked for all the ways in which foreign intelligence services might have got into the operations to change them or corrupt them or use them for their own purposes. Now, this was very much disliked by the intelligence collectors just as any company dislikes quality control. The network was reporting, for example, that Gorbachev was a progressive reformer in the process of transforming the Soviet Union into something compatible with the West. The reality was shown in newspapers and in reports from our State Department political officers, which showed that Gorbachev was in fact a bumbling incompetent who was trying to maintain the communist system but failing miserably. At any rate, we simply did not question the integrity of a system that was yielding results that were so incongruous with reality. After the revolution, the equally unlikely notion spread that Russia was no longer a high priority concern for U.S. intelligence. Therefore, not only did positive intelligence regarding the Soviet Union decline, but counter intelligence also declined. For example, this might include the effort to determine to what extent, if any, the Russians are trying to shape our perceptions. All of that went away. After that, after 2001, the focus of U.S. intelligence shifted to terrorism and counter-terrorism and you basically get a complete absence of significant concern on the part of U.S. intelligence with regards to Russia.

Edward Jay Epstein: I think you have a real shift in the role the CIA is playing in Washington. It‘s now moved into the area which formally was the alleyway of the FBI: domestic security and anti-terrorism and anti-narcotics. The amount of energy the CIA now puts into trying to find out about potential terrorists, especially Muslim terrorists, means that there isn‘t enough room left to operate against Russia or even against other states. I'll give you one example. When the CIA captured Muslim terrorists, al-Qaeda members to be specific, they sent them to other countries for interrogation including Syria and Morocco. But then they have to trust the intelligence apparatuses of those countries to correctly relay information. Now, in the days of the Cold War it would be inconceivable to send someone somewhere else to be interrogated, because they wouldn‘t trust the interrogators outside of their own country. They are outsourcing intelligence, and outsourcing it to countries they don't trust. They're not outsourcing to the British, but to Syria and Egypt, Morocco, Saudi Arabia, or who knows where.

Jeff Nyquist: I think it's so screwed up that they can't fix it right now in the intelligence community. Look at all these reforms that they are doing. I talked to some people about the reforms and I think there are some courageous people making an effort, but it's so bad and the truth is so much worst than anyone wants to admit. And the kind of measures that would have to be taken to straighten it out, the counter-intelligence and security problems in U.S. intelligence, there is a lack of courage to do what has to be done.

Oleg Gordievsky: In the 80s and 90s dramatic events took place between the CIA and the KGB. Several CIA officials, including one important one, Aldrich Ames, agreed to work for the KGB for money. And Aldrich Ames worked for the KGB for nine years before he was caught. Also in the FBI were two to three spies that worked for some time till they were caught. Among them was Robert Hanssen, a very damaging spy. Damaging for the United States. Meanwhile, in the early eighties the CIA and FBI acquired more than 10 excellent agents in the Soviet establishment. Aldrich Ames and Robert Hanssen betrayed them all. In the time between 1985 and 1988 they were all arrested and executed. I, Oleg Gordievsky, was number one on Aldrich Ames' list. I was a British spy, a British agent. I was the only one who survived. And I survived only because the British Service organized for me to escape from the Soviet Union, to escape from execution.

RB: *How damaging were Ames and Hanssen, considering that they were in top positions during all the changes in Europe?*

Bill Gertz: Damage caused by the major cases of spies, Aldrich Ames and Robert Hanssen, are going to continue to plague the U.S. government for years, if not decades to come. These traitors and spies who gave U.S. secrets to Moscow caused enormous damage to the United States intelligence-gathering capabilities; damage that, in my view, will take the CIA and FBI years, if not decades, to correct. What it basically amounts to is the entire infrastructure for intelligence-gathering and FBI law enforcement being hit with a fatal blow. And by that I mean its secrets and the ability to recruit agents, which remains the fundamental activity of intelligence gathering despite electronic wizardy. The bottom line for intelligence is to go abroad and steal secrets. Today, the CIA is trying to rebuild that capability and the FBI is resisting that capability. They have a bureaucratic mindset, a kind of FBI culture, which is averse to intelligence-gathering. They would much rather put handcuffs on criminals than do the very difficult work of gathering intelligence, recruiting agents abroad, and collecting information which is often vital to U.S. national security. The United States is a world superpover with worldwide responsibilities. In order to carry out this responsibility it needs good intelligence. Unfortunately, today we don't have a very good intelligence system.

Jeff Nyquist: Aldrich Ames was a mole for more than a decade and Robert Hanssen was a mole for almost two decades. How did they get away with keeping a secret for that long? Everything that the FBI and CIA knew during that period was known in Moscow. Everything. Do we think that has changed? I don't think so. The kind of confidence that penetrating intelligence services at the top gives Moscow is the feeling that they know everything that we know. And then they can respond to what we know with misinformation to sort of guide, corral or Shepherd us. And I think that's clearly what's happening. They shepherd our perceptions because they know what intelligence we have. They know what intelligence to feed us to encourage our errors and mistakes because they get everything we know fed back to them by the moles. It's a feedback loop. It's a very important concept for penetrating foreign intelligence at the top, and penetrating policy-making institutions. If you've got moles in the policy-planning department of the State Department or the White House, you can hear what the president or the National Security Council or the Secretary of State is thinking. And then you can plan according to those thoughts. You can take what they think and create a whole sociological response. You can sociologically camouflage yourselves while at the same time feeding these people what they want to believe. You can sort of flatter them in that the conclusions they come to are correct.

The ironic conclusions. And then you can guide them down the path of their own destruction. And I think if you look at covert history, if you look at the war between moles and spies, when did we ever have a big mole inside at the top of the KGB? When did we have a big mole at the top of the GRU or the Russian General Staff? In the history of the Cold War we never found such a person. We never found this type of penetration. Instead, all of our spies in Moscow were just being wiped out. They were being arrested and executed or were turned and started feeding us false information. That's the history of the Cold War. We are penetrated. They are not. So, decade after decade, this being the case, we find ourselves in a peculiar position in that we don't really know too much about what's going on inside the Kremlin but they know everything about what we think about them. It's sort of like imagining yourself in a boxing match with an invisible man. He knows where you are. He can hit you and hit you again. You can't even see him. How do you line up a blow when you don't even know where he is or what he's about to do to you? You can't, you are blind. So this is the kind of position that I think the West finds itself in. In modern political conflicts and military conflicts intelligence is the key. You need to know what the other side thinks, what they want to do . . . . That's what you need to know. That's what you must know. And that is what we don't know.

RB: *Would be fair to say that the CIA never recruited a spy who would give inside information from political circles in Moscow?*

Robert Gates: I think it's a fair assessment. I think we had remarkable information on their military research and development and on their war plans. We also had remarkable intelligence on their economy. But in terms of having someone who was privy to the inside thinking of the leadership and what they were talking about, what they were debating, we never really had an agent who could provide us with that kind of information. We would sometimes get it sort of third hand from somebody in the Foreign Ministry or Defense Ministry, but never from the Secretariat or from anyone right around the leadership. Probably the best insight we ever got into the internal dynamics of the leadership was during a period in the late 60s and early 70s when we were able to intercept the telephone conversations of their leaders when they were in their cars, but columnist Jack Anderson[7] blew that source in the early 1970s and it disappeared forever.

Jeff Nyquist: There are cultural reasons why U.S. intelligence is not able to keep up with the intelligence services of other countries. However, one might say that it's not so much that American intelligence is backward as that the enemies are so sophisticated. Russia in the twentieth century developed methods, new scientific methods, of using secret intelligence services to develop new ways of penetrating with sociological sophistication. I mean, remember that there has been a revolution in the social sciences. People may say that sociology is bunk, but there is a lot of wisdom, a lot of knowledge and understanding that can be applied to the manipulation of people. And I believe if you study the successes of KGB and GRU you will find that they have applied very sophisticated methods to advancing their services. In addition, being a totalitarian type of state, Russia has the ability to apply brutal discipline and methods that Western countries cannot employ. And you have an open society in the West. People don't like paranoia. They don't like negativity. They don't like the idea of people being arrested and tortured or questioned about their political views. So in this open society, intelligence services are greatly suspected and constrained. In fact, a lot of civil libertarians don't like the idea of spies and intelligence services because they might turn on the American people. So you have all these inhibitions that we had during Watergate[8] with Congress investigating what the CIA was up to and saying that so much of what the CIA was doing, weak as it was back then, was illegal. And further weakening the CIA and FBI as well at the same time period. You have so many legal restrictions on intelligence agencies saying that they can't coordinate certain things. This is what happened with 9/11. People started looking at this and said, "Wait a minute, this disaster happened because we tied our intelligence services hand and foot with all of these measures because we are so concerned with civil liberties, we are so concern with all these agencies going rogue on us." You know, take an example of basic security, such as securing our secrets or securing our military bases and counter-intelligence. We are not good at it because we don't like Joseph McCarthy[9], who said that there were communists in different parts of the government. Perhaps he was exaggerating, perhaps he was irresponsible, but we have a revulsion against the idea of investigating people. Everything has been done in this country in terms of immigrants coming in and people arriving, but we don't really check people out. And we don't really have any idea how many tens of thousands of spies or terrorists are here living among us. And I suspect that number in some cases could be very high. Higher then anyone realizes.

Joseph Douglass: If you compare 1922, 1924, 1968 and 1978 then you can say that nothing changed. But I think the important thing is to look at operations that really were terrifically effective against the West, not nuclear operations, not conventional wars, but the intelligence operations: narcotics trafficking, organized crime, terrorism, deception, infiltration of the media, and the infiltration of political parties. If you look at these intelligence operations, they were all extremely effective, very successful, and were very good money-makers. The entire operation of KGB's foreign intelligence by the late 60s was being financed on Western money through these operations. The same went for the other countries of Eastern Europe at the time. So they were very powerful. Now, the question is, why would they suddenly discontinue these operations after the dissolution? Number one, they were very good money-makers and number two, nobody from the West was complaining. Indeed, you'd think they didn't exist if you looked at the Western newspapers. And what they knew in the years before all of a sudden no longer applied, because now they were all good friends. But why would these intelligence services in the Soviet Union suddenly cease and desist? They would throw away the entire cost of their operations, leaving them to beg and borrow and steal from the state? No way. Not only that, but when you look at their ability to be politically influential around the world, the main technique of the Soviets for years has not been bribery. It's been blackmail and extortion, that type of thing. These same operations provided them with an unlimited number of names of people in positions of power and influence who were immensely useful in supporting Soviet policy. Because these files were all on the corruption of these people. And I am not talking about five or ten thousand people or something like that. I am talking about numbers in excess of twenty thousand around the globe, all followed by Soviet intelligence, now Russian intelligence. There's no way they would give away this type of asset or state capability. And every day the use of drugs, cocaine and organized crime, and the corruption of public officials and business officials around the world, grows greater than it has been in the past. KGB's archives of files, on people of corruption and influence who can be blackmailed, has grown and grown and grown. This is probably one of their most important assets today. Why would they just throw it away? You have to be naïve to think that this is the case.

Tennent Bagley: The dissident, thinker, and admirable man Vladimir Bukovsky wrote a book, Judgment in Moscow, which was based on the idea of judgment in Nuremberg, a movie that had influenced him enormously in his youth. He felt that the only way the Soviet Union could ever become a functioning democracy was to dismantle the KGB, and put on trial people of the Soviet Communist Party who had driven this country into the strait that it now found itself in. Until then, Russia would be a place where popular morality was destroyed, where any sense of responsibility to society, any civic feelings, were drained out of people, where corruption becomes epidemic, and where the country itself is polluted in every way one can think of. Corruption that began under the Soviet regime became total and, what Bukovsky thought was, that the time had come to be cleansed and recognize the crimes of the Communist Party as a crime against humanity, and as the crime of the century. Unless it was, there was no hope of developing a functioning democracy, which would take a long time anyway, but no chance of developing it without that. Bukovsky's idea was that the KGB's destruction, the absolute destruction of the KGB, was certainly a key piece of this, an opinion that was certainly shared by one man who actually became, very briefly, the chairman of the KGB, Vadim Bakatin[10]. Bakatin genuinely desired to develop a new democratic Russia. And he genuinely desired to dismantle the KGB. In the power situation that existed at his time though, he had no chance to do that. And he didn't last for long. We can even cut it down to weeks, a month. Bakatin was out quickly and those who I talked to from the old KGB said they were happy to see him go because they realized that he would wreck their game. The other person who I think truly desired to destroy the old and build the new was Alexander Yakovlev[11]. He was a key advisor to Gorbachev and a member of the old regime in high places, but nevertheless a man who recognized these crimes. He was appointed in the glory days, the post Soviet days, and was the head of the commission to rehabilitate those who had been unjustly sent to gulags or killed by the Communist regime. He wrote a book, which I would recommend to everyone, called something like "A Century of Violence in Russia," which, in a much shorter way than Solzhenitsyn's Gulag Archipelago, talked about the crimes of the country that had to be purged. Alexander Yakovlev didn't have much more longevity in life or influence then Vadim Bakatin did. He is dead now and it's a pity. There was not a clean-up and the KGB was not dismantled. The KGB is the same today as it was then. It has different names, a couple of different designations that have been changed within the organization, but the same people are in the same buildings doing the same things with the same mindset. And they essentially, incurably, have, in their minds, the same enemy. Despite all the talk of friendship and the mutual fight against terror with the United States, I think that the present regime under Putin is, in fact, friends of America's enemies, and it's relationship with North Korea, Iran, and other regimes of this sort are perfect indications of their lack of change. They did not make the change that Bakatin, Yakovlev, and Bukovsky would have thought was essential.

RB: *The Russians spent a lot of energy on changing the image of the KGB during the time of Perestroika.*

Jeff Nyquist: One of the things they did was announce the purge of the KGB. And that was very interesting. George Tenet[12], the head of the CIA, once characterized the purge of the KGB as window dressing. It was just for show. And so many of the things that had happened in Russia, especially with the reform of the KGB, were simply for external consumption. Nothing really changed within the organization. I mean, you have Vladimir Putin, a Lieutenant Colonel of the KGB, its very representative. He goes on to be deputy Mayor of St.Petersburg. He runs the city. Many other KGB officers went on to run companies or be in charge of government offices. The KGB now, it's been acknowledged and there have been articles in the Wall Street Journal, is running many major institutions in the former Soviet Union. How does this happen? You supposedly get rid of the totalitarian regime and the sword and shield of that regime is the KGB, and yet they are at the top now? What's wrong with this picture? Something is definitely wrong with this picture. If you want to understand how the system actually works, you need to ask who the people are that keep the system going. The Soviet Union was completely dependent on the secret police to maintain order. The secret police stabilized the regime. And they are still doing that. They used to arrest and imprison and kill more people. Now they are experts in fraud. They are able to maintain control throughout, as I said. They are able to control the opposition. [Some of] the people who seem to be pro-American in these Eastern European countries are not pro-American. They have very sinister connections to former secret structures, the KGB in Russia, the StB in Czechoslovakia, or the UB in Poland. These people are suspicious.

RB: *What about the Chekist mentality?*

Jeff Nyquist: The Chekist mentality[13] never left. And the fact is that a Chekist was the President of the Russian Federation. And if you see former communist leaders of outlying Republics still in power, or their close associates, they are the ones controlling regimes in Central Asia and the Caucuses especially. I mean, you can't trust the Orange Revolution in Ukraine, or the revolution in Georgia. I mean, Victor Yushchenko[14] in Ukraine was a KGB officer. So, there you have another KGB officer in charge of a former Soviet Republic. And in Belarus, Lukashenko[15] has always been openly neo-Stalinist. There is nothing new there. So you go country after country and the old Soviet types are automatically still in the control. Then you move on to Eastern Europe and you find out that Klaus in the Czech Republic has a kind of Russian pedigree[16]. The same thing goes for the [former] President of Poland. You look at Romania, Bulgaria and say, "Wait a minute, what is going on with the government?" As I recall, the former prime minister of Hungary was exposed as a former secret police agent and he said, "Well, I was just a patriot. I did what was best for my country." So the secret structures continue and when they are exposed as having connections to these secret structures they say, "well, I am just a liberal patriot and that was the best way I could serve my country at that time." And people in the West, they want to believe that they are nice guys. They don't want to believe that they are following the old agenda. They don't want to believe in a continued Cold War against the West leading . . . [to] . . . subversion, economic warfare, terrorism, and one day perhaps a conflict with the West.

RB: *In other words, we are always on the defense?*

Joseph Douglass: We are on the defense, yes, but worse than that; because we don't recognize that, we don't make any defense. So, are we on the defense? They are on the offense and we haven't recognized it enough to be on the defense.

RB: *When I was still living in Czechoslovakia I witnessed young people from selected families being sent to the Soviet Union for education, many of them to KGB schools. Those people were later, upon their return home, placed in specific positions.*

Oleg Gordievsky: The education of students from Eastern European countries was regarded as a useful thing and had the objective of creating a contingent of people who were loyal to the Soviet Union. This happened over five years in Moscow, Leningrad, Voronezh, Kiev, Minsk, and so on. They recruited several dozens of KGB agents among these students, but the fact was that many of these students were disillusioned with Soviet life. Everybody hated Brezhnev. So many people developed liberal and pro-western tendencies. Of course, there are agents among them, many agents. Sometimes, it is sufficient to have only one agent in the CIA. That's why the danger is not how many students studied in the Soviet Union. The problem is that maybe one of them had penetrated the state machine so dangerously that it will be very bad for the United States. And it happened in Poland when the prime minister turned out to be a KGB agent. That was exactly the case when one student became a very dangerous spy. So, for security services all over European countries that are democratic now, that belong to NATO, that belong to the European Union, their security depends on looking at who may be KGB agents. And they do it very well. This is less true in Bulgaria and Romania particularly, but they do it very well in the Czech Republic, Poland, and the Baltic Republics.

PART 7

TERRORISM

RB: *Now, something always mind-boggling to me was why the CIA played down the Soviets' involvement in terrorism?*

Bill Gertz: Yes, this was a debate within the CIA going back to the 1980s when Yuri Andropov, the KGB Chairman, ordered the assasination of the Pope. And this triggered debate; debate within the CIA between the political appointees and the career intelligence analysts who argued over a benign, leftist view of the world and especily of the Soviet Union. They argued bitterly within the secret councils of the CIA over whether or not the Soviet Union was really behind terrorism. Again, to say [the Soviets] weren't [behind terrorism] was kind of a naïve mindset. It was totally incorrect. They didn't really understand that the Soviet Union was sponsoring international terrorism and that it was doing so as part of a strategy to undermine the United States and other Western governments. This was a kind of classic example of how liberal and leftist bureaucrats within the CIA and the intelligence community caused serious damage to the United States. I would add that a similar thing is happening today in the case of communist China, where you have a certain inteligence mindset at work within our intelligence agencies that says, basically, that the Chinese are not a threat when in fact China today as a communist dictatorship with nuclear arms poses the greatest long term danger to the United States and to the West.

RB: *Were the Soviets' the fathers of modern terrorism?*

Vladimir Bukovsky: Oh definitely. I can show you hundreds of documents proving that[1]. They show how they supplied, trained, created, and governed almost every terrorist organization on Earth. I have these documents. Starting with the Palestinians, the Red Brigades in Italy, Baider-Meinhof in Germany, Action Direct in France, ETA in Spain, IRA in Ireland and so on and so forth. They were all clients of the Soviet Union, not to mention states like Iraq, Libya, and Syria, which were terrorist states by definition who were under Soviet influence and were supplied by the Soviets. So, of course the Soviets are the fathers of modern terrorism.

Robert Gates: No, I don't think that the Soviets were the fathers of modern terrorism. I think that from Bakunin[2] and others, there is a long history of this in Western Europe and a lot of this was presided over by Lenin, the nihilist's in Russia, but it also formed in the Balkans and elsewhere. These were nationalists. Terrorism is always a weapon of the weak against the strong. Russians certainly provided more support to Baider-Meinhof, the Red Army faction, and others than many in the West believed at the time. And they certainly supported terrorism as practiced by many national liberation movements and so on. But most of those groups were not created by the Soviet Union and they didn't take directions from the Soviet Union. The Soviet Union supported something that already existed. And I think that now you are seeing more of these groups and you simply have a different set of states supporting them.

Oleg Gordievsky: The Soviet Union was significantly involved in terrorism, on [a] significant scale. For example, there were numerous training centers organized under the offices of the KGB and the MVD (Ministry of Interior), as well as the offices of the military. This took place since the 60s up into the 90s. They invited friendly organizations like National Liberation Movements[3] and communist parties, which were underground, sometime not even underground, and trained them to be hitmen, counter-intelligence officers, intelligence officers, and saboteurs. Eventually, numerous people, hundreds and hundreds from the PLO, from the Congo, Angola, South Africa, Latin America and Asia, went through these training courses, sometimes for a year or even longer. So, the seed of terrorism was really planted by the Soviet Union. Now terrorism has a momentum of its own because it's spread so much. It is difficult to say that the Soviet Union is to blame, but I must say that a lot of skills that the terrorists have, a lot of the weapons that the terrorists use, have come from the Soviet Union and Russia.

Angelo Codevilla: The Soviet Union was the originator of anti-Western terrorism in a many numbers of ways. Of course, we should not forget that the term "terror" was first used, in a governmental sense, in France during the French Revolution. It was Lenin who instituted terror as a permanent instrument within the policy of the state. The Soviet Union lived by terror; indeed Khrushchev himself, in his denunciation of Stalin, nevertheless excluded the idea that the Soviet Union will abandon terror. Terror has always been an integral part of Soviet policy. As regards of United States, the Soviet Union trained—indeed created—the PLO, and trained terror groups belonging to the French and especially the Italian Communist Parties. It established the Tri-Continental Organization[4] in 1968, which brought together any number of organizations around the world that had been created for the purpose of anti-American terrorism. The symbol of that organization was a globe resting on a pair crossed machine guns. Its conference was held in Havana and it was attended by organizations like [the] Columbian FARC[5], which is still active today and owns about 40 percent of the country right now. As well as PLO, PLFP, and a number of organizations still active today. Now, it is very interesting that immediately after the revolution taking place in the Soviet Empire in 1989-91, there was a hiatus in terrorist activity. Terrorist activity around the world declined. And then in the beginning of 1993, the very same people who had been involved in anti-American terror under the Soviet banner returned to that task; however, under the Islamic banner. These are the very same people to a large extent, though not entirely, but they are nonetheless following the exact same pattern and usually using the same weapons from the same Russian sources.

Tennent Bagley: I knew very little about it. But we knew from some of our sources what was going on. There was no doubt that the KGB and some of the KGB satellite services, the Bulgarians along with the Romanians for example, were training Middle Easterners and other nationalists, Chechens and others, to conduct what we refer to today as terror. It might have been called diversion, sabotage, or something else in those days when the word terrorism was not as common as it has become in our time. Nonetheless, the things we now call terror were being conducted, trained, and coordinated from Moscow. And directed from a section of the KGB specifically devoted toward diversion, which was the Russian word diversia, for sabotage and manipulation. These things were a part of the brief of KGB for a very, very long time before the world became obsessed, and rightly so, with Islamist terror.

Pavel Zacek: I had the opportunity see many documents from the Interior Ministry Archives (Czechoslovakia), documents regarding Carlos the Jackal's group, groups from Arabic countries, and the PLO. For example, I saw documents regarding a meeting of terrorist group representatives that happened in Prague in 1987 under the supervision of the Syrian Intelligence Services and was monitored by the StB.

Ion Pacepa: Contemporary political memory seems to be conveniently afflicted with some kind of Alzheimer's disease. In the early 1970s, the Kremlin established a "Socialist Division of Labor"[6] for persuading the governments of Iraq and Libya to join the terrorist war against the U.S. KGB chairman Yuri Andropov told me that either of the two countries could inflict more damage on the Americans than could the Red Brigades[7], the Baider-Meinhof[8] group, and all other terrorist organizations taken together. The governments of Arab countries, Andropov explained, not only had inexhaustible financial resources (oil), but they also had huge intelligence services that were being run by our "rozvedka advisors" and could extend their tentacles to every corner of the earth. The PLO was dreamt up by the KGB. The National Liberation Army of Bolivia was created by the KGB in 1964; the National Liberation Army of Columbia in 1965, the Democratic Front for the Liberation of Palestine and the Secret Army for the Liberation of Armenia in 1975. In 1964 the first PLO Council, consisting of 422 Palestinian representatives handpicked by the KGB, approved the Palestinian National Charter—a document that had been drafted in Moscow. When I met general Alexander Sakharovsky at his Lubyanka office, he pointed to the red flags pinned onto a world map hanging on his wall. "Look at that," he said. Each flag represented a plane that had been downed. "Airplane hijacking is my own invention," he boasted. The hijacked airplane became an instrument of Soviet foreign policy, and eventually the weapon of choice for September 11, 2001. Sakharovsky's subordinates are now reigning in the Kremlin. Until they fully disclose their involvement in creating anti-American terrorism and condemn Yasser Arafat's terrorism, there is no reason to believe they have changed.

RB: *Is Russia still sponsoring terrorism today?*

Joseph Douglass: It's hard to know because I am not sure what our sources are, and I have heard no direct sources on that. It is clear, however, from books that have been written on al-Qaeda and Osama Bin Laden that there have been contacts. There were clear linkages between this organization and Russian intelligence; that Russian intelligence was effective in providing them with some material supplies and even helping them with financial support. It's also clear that Bin Laden's deputy, who may or may not still be alive, was indeed connected to the Russian KGB or GRU or both. But this doesn't get much publicity because we really stopped looking at them for the most part. Almost overnight it became politically incorrect to drag U.S. intelligence against Russia. Within a year of the Soviet Union's disintegration, the old Russia emerged from its ashes and as it was explained to me by a former key person in the operations directorate of U.S. intelligence, our intelligence collection directed against the Soviet Union was brought to an end. Observation houses were closed, linkages were closed, intercepts were closed. Friends that I knew who were working on strategic threats told me that you had intelligence components that may have numbered several hundred people looking at and analyzing Soviet military developments particularly in the nuclear area that suddenly dropped down to the point that you could hardly find half a dozen people that were still really engaged in following the Soviet strategic nuclear threat. So it was like the key U.S. intelligence units' efforts to understand what was happening in the Soviet Union ceased almost as quickly as the Soviet Union itself dissappeared.

RB: *Could you elaborate on why?*

Joseph Douglass: The only thing that strikes me is that it became politicaly incorrect to continue worrying about the Soviet Union now that communism was dead. So budgets were slashed. The agencies and efforts that were directed that way went out of business because it was no longer popular. Try finding a book written on the Soviet threat published after 1992. It would be a real commodity.

Oleg Gordievsky: I doubt that Russia supports terrorism because Russia wants to look nice in the eyes of the international community. But I think they have some influence in militant organizations in the Middle East because of their old connections in Lebanon, Syria, Iraq, and Palestine. Not everywhere, but in those organizations which are considered Marxist and formerly pro-soviet orientation.

Jeff Nyquist: We had a bombing in London and FSB defector Alexander Litvinenko did this interview with a Polish journalist and said that the ultimate author of the London bombing was standing next to [British Prime Minister] Tony Blair during the G8 summit. He was referring to Vladimir Putin. Litvinenko wrote a book, Blowing Up Russia, about how Russia, Russian special services specifically, are behind terrorism. Chechnya, the Russian Federation [and the war in Chechnya]—it's all part of this huge provocation. And Litvinenko said in a more recent interview that al-Zawahiri, the number two man in al-Qaeda, is an FSB agent trained at a Russian training center in the 1990s. Well, we know that many terrorists in the Arab world, many terrorist organizations such as the PLO for example, were led by Soviet Agents. Yasser Arafat[9], by all accounts, was trained in Russia. He was a communist, a Soviet agent. The same goes for Carlos the Jackal[10], a Venezuelan terrorist trained in Russia. It's very odd that Carlos the Jackal would say that Osama Bin Laden was his successor as one of the top terrorists in the world. If you look at terrorism in Peru or in Columbia, it's communists on one side and governments on the other. So this is a theme, this is something that runs across all countries. The ANC was a terrorist organization in Africa and it was supported by the KGB. It was supported by the South African Communist Party. Terrorism was a main tool used by the Communist Bloc. Different communist countries, such as Czechoslovakia, Poland, and Romania, were all helping the PLO, the Libyans, and the ANC. Meanwhile, the South American terrorists were supported by the Cubans. All of these operations do one thing: spread their criminal networks, their influence, and intimidate people who would oppose their agenda. They care about concessions, gaining [a] negotiation [advantage], and finally getting control. And you see this with the PLO and the struggles in the Middle East. The PLO became this Palestinian Authority. Israel was forced by the United States to give up more and more to the PLO. The PLO was basically an organization allied with Moscow. What is really going on here? How does this relate to the overall strategic situation in the Middle East? I mean, Saddam Hussein himself was receiving support from Russia, from Ukraine, and from other former Soviet countries. Iran is getting support for its nuclear program from Russia and Russia is not going to stop this. Why does Russia want to build up Iran as a nuclear power when Iran calls the United States the Great Satan? Why is this happening? The answer is simple. The Russian government, not the people, but the Russian government, is an enemy of the United States. That's the simple answer.

There was a piece by Andrew Higgins in the Wall Street Journal some years ago about Ayman al-Zawahiri, number two in al-Qaeda, going to Russia and not having a real explanation for what he was doing there. In fact, he had a false explanation. Being caught in a lie, he said, "Well, the KGB/FSB arrested me, they didn't know who I was and they let me go." If al-Qaeda is stalking horse for the Kremlin, or for Moscow/Beijing, then it shows that Russia and China have agreed jointly to a kind of secret alliance in which terrorism is used to knock the legs out from under the United States, to discredit the U.S. government, to damage the U.S. economy, and to cause the fall of the dollar. Then what we are looking at is an attack, by proxy, on the U.S. The stories that emerged from Paul Williams, Yosef Bodanski, and Joe Farah . . . saying that al-Qaeda has nuclear weapons; that al-Qaeda is planning something called the "American Hiroshima"; that al-Qaeda intends to kill four million Americans with a nuclear attack on American soil—if that happens, imagine the repercussions. The dollar will fall, American society will be plunged into chaos and paralyzed by fear, and the Bush's administration will be discredited because it wasn't able to protect the country four years or more after 9/11. The stage would be set for Beijing and Moscow to move into the vacuum left by a collapsing United States. Because if the U.S. economy collapses, the dollar collapses, and there would be massive unemployment in the country. The United States would not be able to project its power overseas. We would have to withdraw from Iraq; our alliance with Europe, which is already in disarray, would further deteriorate. All of a sudden, all these countries that depend on us for their security would have to look elsewhere. And might it be that Russia and China would offer them a new deal, a new partnership? So you are talking about a terrorist attack on the United States with weapons of mass destruction that could completely rearrange the international order and remake it so that Russia and China are on top and the United States is no longer a major power. This, I suspect, is where Beijing and Moscow would like things to go. And if Litvinenko is correct, and if Higgins's report was accurate, if it's true that al-Qaeda has some kind of connection to Moscow, then this nuclear attack on the U.S. is maybe what is coming down the pike.

PART 8

ORGANIZED CRIME

RB: *Another important issue that we haven't talked about yet is the connection between KGB/SVR and organized crime. How did the KGB get involved with organized crime?*

Vladimir Bukovsky: Well, as the regime was entering its final stages of crisis, it decided to use the KGB more actively in internal politics. They were encouraged to infiltrate businesses, administrative structures, and so on, but some parts of the KGB were also involved in creating gangs, or organized crime organizations as well as controlling already existing ones and manipulating them. So they did that. It was a clever move because on one hand, business would be, to some extent, controlled by the KGB and on the other hand, business would be constantly under pressure from the Mafioso structure through extortion, racketeering and things like that. So one would be playing against the other very skillfully. That took place particularly in 1990-1991. That's when part of the KGB deliberately went into operation with organized crime. It wasn't done because of a lack of control. It was a decision. But then, of course, the Soviet Union collapsed and a lot of these things acquired their own life, their own meaning and rationale. For the KGB, it became a question of both survival and enrichment. So the fusion with organized crime on one hand and with the administrative apparatus on the other became almost complete. And today you certainly have this in examples such as a criminal running . . . an oil company, or a former KGB agent controlling aluminum production in the former Soviet Union, in Russia. That's a very interesting arrangement, and one that's unprecedented in history. In the end it's very scary because it's the most powerful thing you can actually imagine. It's almost like the notorious Spectre group in James Bond movies. It is a crime syndicate, which in this case is also governmentally controlled and protected. So yes, it has become one big criminal division. And that, of course, is a very scary proposition.

Oleg Gordievsky: The KGB was, on the lower level, always close to crime. For example, operation officers ran agents who were criminals. They were very close to criminals. After communism fell, many criminals started to appear because it was a private initiative, a private business, and there was a lot of money in it. At first, in the 90s, there was the Mafia, a lot of criminals acquiring money, organizing assassinations, extorting money, and so on. Then they realized, "Why should we let the Mafia have it when we can have it?" Then they started to control different business organizations where the Mafia was strong. Gradually they began replacing the Mafia. So, in a way, today it's less organized crime and more KGB, which is now called the FSB. Around the whole world, especially in countries like Austria, Spain, and Hungary, there are a lot of organizations and activities that look like the Mafia. But practically all of it is run by the KGB/FSB.

RB: *So, is this another way to influence politicians?*

Oleg Gordievsky: First of all, it is a money-making enterprise. Many KGB people became very rich just milking money from enterprises and banks, and by extorting money from businesses. It's really for lining their pockets. But then, when they have too much money, like at the state level, they use it to influence other countries. For example, they offer huge bribes to politicians in Europe and America. Nobody knows if they actually achieve anything, nobody knows, but they think they do. And now the big money in Russia is used to influence the political situation in Western countries. One particular example was, of course, Poland. The Polish public and media found out how Russia was funding and growing different important personalities. Now, after the democratic elections, when healthy political forces have prevailed, maybe Russia's influence will be less than before. But obviously Poland was a great target for KGB influence. By the way, the KGB organized the election of the president in the Republic of Lithuania. It was a great effort on the part of the Lithuanian public to get rid of this person, who was practically a KGB agent.

RB: *How much money are we talking about?*

Oleg Gordievsky: I can tell you one example to illustrate this: the Russian black market is 1.5 times bigger then their official economy. Or rather, the budget, the black budget, is 50 percent bigger than the official budget of Russia.

Angelo Codevilla: Well, you must realize that the KGB was always involved in organized crime. Dzerzhinsky recruited his agents from the criminal world and recruited them to do things that were outside of normal laws and decency. For this reason Lenin, and later Stalin, were always deeply distrustful of the KGB. Now, criminal habits are not easily shed and it is therefore not the slightest bit surprising that the KGB went into organized crime. There should be no doubt that the connections between the KGB and organized crime are systemic and pervasive. So we simply have got to realize that this is the case. We shouldn't marvel at it. This is the way it is.

Bill Gertz: The KGB today has kind of morphed into an international organization that has many ties to Russian organized crime and to some of the established oligarchs in Russia and the former Soviet Union. This has been the result of KGB officials and former KGB officials understanding the nature of power in the system there. When the Soviet Union collapsed, they were able to capitalize on it by getting control of various businesses because they were so integral to the system. They also worked behind the scenes with organized crime in order to advance their financial interests. I would have to say that I think it's possible that the KGB has international connections to organized crime, especially in Europe and the United States. We have seen, through our law enforcement agencies, that there have been some connections, but any good intelligence service is able to cover its tracks. They are able to cover up those connections and create what they call in the intelligence world "plausible denial." By having enough separation between the KGB and direct illegal activities, it's very difficult to make a court ordered case on it.

Edward Jay Epstein: Well, I think it doesn't matter if it's CIA, KGB, French intelligence, British intelligence, or Israel's Mossad[1]. If you have an objective, you need agents of access. These agents don't have to be people who work for you. They can even be unwitting. If you can, use the criminals to give you access and do the job for you. It's better than using your own agents because if they get caught you can blame it on them. So I think every intelligence service uses the people that can best do the job, whether or not they agree with them ideologically. So, for example, Saddam Hussein may not have agreed with Osama Bin Laden, but if he found that Osama Bin Laden could give him some suicide bombers that . . . couldn't be traced back to him, I believe he would have used them, but not because he wanted to advance, or help, or even like Osama Bin Laden. That's what intelligence services do. They use false flags and they recruit the people they need to recruit. Often, the people don't know why they have been recruited or who they have been recruited by. So it wouldn't surprise me if the KGB used the Mafia or even created an equivalent of a Russian sort of gangster capitalism so they could keep control. The point is to retain control, not who you retain control through.

Joseph Douglass: From my perspective, the most interesting aspect of organized crime, particularly Russian organized crime, is how it exploded in the West following the dissolution of the Soviet Union. The image that is projected by our government and by academic studies is that organized crime suddenly exploded, not just in the United States, but everywhere, including Russia itself. Suddenly, we are confronted with the massive problem of Russian organized crime in this country, and this is really all regarded as a product of democratization which would work itself out. This is like saying "Don't bother, it will go away." In a few cases, the researchers and academics would recognize that it didn't exactly start after the dissolution. It really started back when there was a large influx of people from the Soviet Union in the late 1970s to 1980s. They became the criminal element and they exploded in the 1990s. But again, they associate this explosion with the dissolution if the Soviet Union. This, of course, is all a deception. Organized crime was a major strategic operation under the control of the KGB beginning in 1955. It was a major operation designed globally, more or less for its political effect in terms of increasing their ability to influence politics in countries around the world because of the close connection they saw between organized crime and politics in addition to the connection between organized crime and financial operations, which the Soviets were also very heavily engaged and interested in. This was, of course, heavily influenced by the narcotic problem because they had a lot of money and they needed to launder it. As a result, they basically had a cooperative working relationship, with global international finance to help manage the whole money laundering process, which, by the mid 60s, was substantial. Organized crime grew so much that within a mere 10 years the small state of Czechoslovakia organized, or was in control of, 35 different organized crime groups. People say that the Mafia was very hard to penetrate. Well, penetrating the Mafia was, of course, one of the first Soviet objectives so that they would know who was out there and how they operated. Within five years, the Soviets and their Eastern European allies had eighty penetrations into the Italian Mafia. This really gives you an idea of how securely the Italian Mafia was protected against penetration. By 1968, Soviet intelligence services had penetrated something like 80 percent of the organized crime groups around the world. They had agents in over 60 percent of the Latin American banks that covered the total cost of organized crime activities and 40 percent of American and Canadian banks. The banks were very closely connected with organized crime for one simple reason. Organized crime is all about money laundering and increasing the supply of money. They couldn't operate without the active support of the banks which they had because the banks took about 15 to 20 percent off the top for their services in laundering the money and making it all possible. In this respect the Soviet operation was so effective, and had such a problem associated with the money laundering, because there was so much money that in [the] mid 60s they had totally reorganized their money laundering operation. They did this with the active assistance of big international banks. They even identified and ran background checks on people in the various banks who would be handling the money laundering operations.

Jeff Nyquist: You can characterize the Soviet government and the current Russian government in two ways. They are secretive, highly secretive, and they are criminal. I mean, these people are criminals, the people that head these governments. There is enormous corruption in these countries. They don't have the same moral structure as a Western country. Of course, there is corruption in all governments, but in their government you have the kind of corruption that is institutionalized. A long time ago, Khrushchev looked at the drug thing, and Mao suggested [an] opium [war] in the West. Khrushchev said, "We can do it better than anyone. We can penetrate international organized crime, we can take over crime families, we can start our own crime families, and we can export drugs to the West." The significant thing about exporting drugs to the West is not necessarily corrupting the youth or making westerners stupid by taking so many drugs. The significant thing is the dirty money created by drug trafficking. That dirty money is a huge temptation. You have billions of dollars that have to be laundered. Who launders them? U.S. businesses and banks. So when they launder this money, you suddenly have them on the hook. They are engaged in illegal activities with you as their partner. Suddenly you have certain influences over them. You have been in a dirty business with them and they know it's a dirty business. You know, back in the 60s Russia created these schools in Czechoslovakia for training drug traffickers; training them in the business. They were given startup money and sent to Latin America and places like that to begin this process. They put a lot of intelligence assets into looking at whether or not the CIA could detect these sorts of things and whether or not they could be discovered. They found that the CIA was blind to this. In fact, they could even get CIA officers to participate in drug trafficking, turning CIA officers into double agents. Once a CIA officer engages in drug trafficking and you are the KGB officer who got him into it, or you are a drug trafficker yourself, you can turn him over to the authorities and send him to prison. So you can blackmail him. You can say, "If you want to continue to prosper, if you want to be free and not go to prison, you have to be a double agent. You have to work for us." So this has been a very effective intelligence tool for penetrating western intelligence agencies. And, of course, it is another thing that is related to terrorism. If you have this corruption related to drug trafficking spread to the border security of a country, you basically have border control agents that are taking bribes to allow drugs to be smuggled into the country. You could have nuclear weapons or biological or chemical weapons packed in with those drugs. And those border control people are taking that money, so they don't want to uncover these packages because their complicity might be uncovered. So you might have a secure route for bringing weapons of mass destruction into the United States. Huge quantities of drugs, more than 100 billion dollars in drugs, crosses the U.S. border every year. If that quantity is getting into the country, you can certainly get weapons of mass destruction into the country using those same routes and methods.

RB: *I heard something about a guy named Felix Rodriguez.*

Jeff Nyquist: One of the stories I can tell you is this. Terry Reed[2], who was running a CIA front company in Mexico during the 1980s, was working with Felix Rodriguez[3], who was a CIA agent involved in supervising the movement of arms to the Contras in the Nicaraguan conflict. Terry Reed wrote in his book [Compromised: Clinton, Bush and the CIA] that Rodriguez was a double agent working for the KGB. A Mossad officer came to . . . tell him that Rodriguez was a KGB double-agent and that he was moving drugs from Latin America back to the United States through the CIA pipeline that was moving arms. Basically, Terry Reed had to go on the run because of this discovery. This is a really good example of how the KGB turns people through narcotics trafficking. Manuel Noriega, the dictator down in Panama, was supposedly working for U.S. intelligence. He got dirty with drug deals, so they turned him into an agent for Castro. He became a representative for the Medellín Cartel[4]. Of course, the head of the Medellín Cartel had a Cuban advisor. He was a former Cuban intelligence officer. Well, we know almost certainly that he was a Cuban intelligence officer. So, when you look at these drug cartels, when you look at the way they function, you see the way they get people dirty to control them. Once you commit certain criminal acts, you belong to a criminal fraternity. If foreign intelligence services are piggy-backing on criminal activity, they get a great boost from this. This pipeline went all the way back to Arkansas where Bill Clinton[5] was Governor. So how high does this drug trafficking go? How many people have been turned or poisoned or corrupted, and if the KGB is pulling the strings on these criminals, how far into the U.S. government does this penetration go? Does it ultimately compromise U.S. policy? Is this the explanation for why U.S. security officials are not suspicious of Russia? Does it explain how Russia has important agents of influence and moles in U.S. policy-making circles and in intelligence services? Could this be an explanation?

Joseph Douglass: There is not a serious effort to fight organized crime or narcotics trafficking in America. We all know, or should know, that the fight against narcotics trafficking is a fraud, or a farce, depending upon your perspective. In looking at international finance, there are a number of things that Jan Sejna told me that are extremely important in terms of figuring out what is happening. One of the things he said was that,

"Never was there a decision made in Moscow without the presence of international finance." Another thing he indicated to me was that in 1965 the narcotics trafficking operation was so successful that they had to reorganize the entire money laundering operation because there was so much money coming in. This was done by the KGB with the assistance of international finance. Big banks. And indeed, Czechs were giving them the use of their banks and also made up the people in the banks who laundered money. And Czech intelligence later learned that people within different banks had undergone background investigations to determine if they were indeed reliable for that type of operation. The people who ran the background investigation were Mossad agents. That is the Israeli Intelligence Services who were always regarded as having a close connection to the Soviet Intelligence system. The relationship between international finance and the KGB was so close that Jan Sejna also made another very interesting statement. He said, "There was never a week that went by without a meeting in Prague between international finance and Soviet intelligence." The reason Prague was used was that it had a number of highly classified villas where secret conversations could be held since the people from international finance didn't want to go to Moscow. Prague was a much better place to meet, a more congenial atmosphere. But, more importantly, they didn't want anybody to know that they were actually meeting with KGB people. Prague was an ideal place and Jan Sejna knew these things because of his role in one of the departments. When he was Secretary of the Defense Council, he managed a large number of the villas for these types of purposes. As Chief of Staff to the Defense Minister, his access also brought him in contact with other villas run by military intelligence and the Ministry of Defense. So he had the access to know all these things. In terms of size, organized crime today is something that has been blossoming for many years and, of course, it still blossoms. It succeeds and grows because it is politically protected. I think that the size of international organized crime was first estimated in 1994 by the World Bank at about 1.2 trillion dollars a year. In 1996-97 or 98 a study from the UN identified it as 1.6

trillion dollars per year. An Interagency U.S. study on international crime said that the money laundering component alone was estimated at no less then 900 billion and possibly in excess of 2 trillion dollars a year. Over the same period the interest on investments and holdings alone was estimated at one trillion dollars a year as early as 1994. This past year, in 2004, there was a study conducted by the International Studies Institute called Chasing Dirty Money[6], something like that; a very highly regarded study. One only needs to look at it to see the size of the money laundering component. This operation is run out of 21 countries, particularly in the United States, Canada, Europe, Japan, Australia . . . and they determined that today the size of the money laundering component would be roughly 4 trillion dollars a year. That's just for those 21 countries. And that's not even including some of the biggest money laundering havens in the world, places like Lichtenstein, Luxembourg, Israel, Russia, Eastern Europe, China, Singapore, all of the off-shore islands, and all of Latin America. So when you start adding those up, what are you going to end up with? It's hard to imagine since you don't have over 10 trillion dollars a year. Now, what can be drawn from these figures is really very simple. One, there is a massive amount of money out there. It's perfectly adequate to achieve all the corruption at high political levels, the highest, and to influence all the elections you want around the world with absolutely no trouble at all. And not only this, but the amount of money is so large that you really don't care what the precise figures are because it doesn't really matter. It's that large.

PART 9

MEDIA

RB: *We are now living in the so-called communication age. Why doesn't anybody talk or write about this stuff? Where is the media?*

Joseph Douglass: Why doesn't anybody seem to care? I think there are two reasons. Number one, they don't know enough to realize that they should care and number two, the media is not about to tell them or educate them. Because the media is very much under the influence of people who operate on the far left and they are active supporters of changing all United States political systems so they can merge comfortably with communism.

Jeff Nyquist: The media is . . . all about entertainment right now. And . . . when you talk about intelligence battles and strategy and the social psychology of dictatorships or of other countries, these are very technical things. The short attention span of the public cannot really handle these complicated issues. Actual details and nuances, these facts cannot be presented in the correct context when you've got nothing but 30-second sound bites. You get a simplified, reduced version of reality; so reduced and so simplified that the average television viewer, the average radio listener, can't comprehend it. If you really did go into the details you would find that a lot of basic perceptions that people have are wrong. For instance, the idea that the U.S. won the Cold War and Russia is no longer a threat, or that America is a lone superpower, or that China is our trading partner and not a strategic rival. It goes into things like organized crime and drug trafficking, changes that happened in Africa and Latin America in recent years that are very sinister in terms of American security. To explain all these things would go against the fact that the public doesn't even know where some of these countries are. They couldn't locate them on a map. How are you going to begin to discuss details in public and have some kind of public discussion with the kind of low intellectual level that now prevails in a non-literate culture?

Joseph Douglass: Well, the media is not very different from academia really, they are closely related. Their sponsors seem to be allied with powers that have traditionally wanted to hide the crimes of communism going back to the 1920s when it was gaining a foothold in Russia. There was a very interesting book that was written back in the late 1990s by a group of six French scholars who did research. All of them were former communists or close fellow travelers. It's called The Black Book of Communism and it tried to unveil many of the crimes of communism. They did a very good job in terms of the crimes commited by communism against its own people. However, the book was entirely lacking when it came to enumerating the crimes communism committed toward non-communist countries. In one paragraph toward the beginning, the editor of the book raises the question of why we have heard so little about the crimes of communism. We have been awash with all sorts of publicity about the crimes of Nazi Germany; but with respect to communist China, where so many greater crimes were committed, or communist Russia and other communist countries, we have heard practically nothing. Nothing but silence. This is particularly true in respect to the politicians and academics. Well, of course politicians and academics are very sensitive to their sponsors. Large money interests promote research, enable books to get published, and have an interest in who gets reported in the media and what poliiticians get supported and elected. Obviously, these people must ask themselves the reason for this great silence because you have a tremendous silence regarding the crimes of communism going back almost to its founding in 1917. Not only is there a silence, there is also tremendous disinformation and misrepresentation of the system. They talked about how wonderful everything was in the Soviet Union, continuing into the 1980s. Then, all of a sudden they found out it really hadn't been that way. It was all a mirage. People were not able to get in and see how bad these countries were. It's almost like we have been shown a Potemkin Village for 80 years, providing a very comforting illusion to people. The only times there would be a diversion from this main perspective, it would come from a few renegade academics who would ocassionaly publish on the crimes of communism, or when the communists themselves wanted to promote ideas they were changing by publicizing their own crimes and saying how they needed to get rid off that culture and change. The most notable example of this was, of course, Khrushchev's secret speech that was published in 1954 or 56 when they released a lot of information on the crimes of communism against its own people. This was done to basically discredit Stalin, who had recently died, and provide a way for a new era to blow in across the West in terms of what communism was really like. A lot of people accepted this, which is why peaceful coexistence was so effective. However, it was mentioned to me by somebody who was there throughout this process that it was nothing but a large deception.

Angelo Codevilla: The media, the mainstream media in the United States, are a reflection of the mentality that prevails in American Universities. That is entirely conventional, it is entirely unreflective, and tends to reduce the world to certain sound bites, to certain formula. It continues to repeat these formula. And it does so by magnifying them and drilling them into people's heads, coupling them with lively videos. It is a kind of stupefying. It has a kind of stupefying effect. Once upon a time the media consisted of newspapers and magazines that ran lengthy stories full of facts with [which] one could argue. More and more articles became short, images lively and brutal, and repetition nearly insufferable. So generally, they never contributed a great deal to enlightenment; but lately they contributed to simply perpetuating conventional images. Very few people in the media are consciously dishonest. But look at the news. They look for stories and, of course, they run stories that please them. They are wonderfully useful for conveying this information often because they seldom care what they convey.

RB: *Well, how much influence does the KGB have over the Western media?*

Vladimir Bukovsky: It's very difficult to say . . . it's quite complicated. It's done in different ways. There are some people who are simply on the payroll of the KGB. I know that for fact because when I was working in the archives of the Central Committee in this constitutional court case, then the Minister of Mass Media . . . who was in charge of files and secret materials for the court, once showed me a document from a distance. It was three pages, three very tightly typed pages. He said to me, "And this document we will never give you." And I said, "Why? What is it?" "Well, it's a list of Western journalist on the KGB payroll." "Why wouldn't you give it to me?" "Well," he said, "We will use them." So that was one way of doing it. But there were more ways than just getting just some influential journalists on the payroll. They also have a huge network of agents of influence. Kind of "opinion makers." The size of it is not known. I don't know how many. I would notice them on television and in print because I would see them conducting their definite political propaganda . . . that would always be favorable to the Kremlin. They might be in Academia, or in the media. They might be among celebrities or among businessmen. All of them could be coordinated very well from Moscow to push public opinion in the right direction. Were they paid? I have doubts. I mean, some of them might be ideological fellow travelers, and others might be black-mailed. It's difficult to say. Some might have simply been manipulated and deceived. It's known how easily they did that during Stalin's era. Secret police, intelligence, and foreign intelligence were manipulating intellectuals. For example, practically every Beat writer and Beat cultural figure in the West was, in one way or another, influenced by disinformation and manipulation from Soviet intelligence. So, they have accumulated enormous experience in doing that. Sometimes these people were unwitting participants in this game. They didn't do it intentionally. They probably believed in this planted information. So this is a massive scene. You wouldn't be able to type all these names on three pages. It would be quite a big volume if you tried to type them all.

RB: *Useful idiots?*

Vladimir Bukovsky: That was Lenin's phrase concerning some fellow travelers in the West. He used to call them "useful idiots," meaning fellow travelers who were not communist by persuasion; a kind of bourgeois idiots who would play into our hands.

Angelo Codevilla: I don't believe that journalists are on the payroll of foreign intelligence agencies. Things work much more subtly than that. Journalists are invited for privileged tours, they are given privileged interviews, they are treated variety of ways and that is their bribery, if you will. Few journalists . . . actually employed and paid by the KGB didn't have a great deal of influence. Far, far more influential were journalist like Dan Rather who followed the Soviet line because they believed it. That is far more significant than any gross purchase of influence. It doesn't work that way. I wish it did.

RB: *What about these Useful idiots?*

Angelo Codevilla: Look, the best and most successful technique for manipulating media involves giving the media what . . . they want. Finding journalists who have a passion, a tendency to believe in certain causes, and giving them the means to do what they want to do in the first place. It's not a question of inducing them to do something, it's simply a question of helping them to do whatever it is they want to do. That's how you manipulate the media. You choose your people, you make them more effective at doing whatever it is they want to do. It's not a question of buying them or forcing them to do something what they actually passionately want to do. And it just so happens that many of them enjoy being anti-American, and the easiest thing in the world is to give them the means to do what they want. As the U.S. Army used to say, "Be all you can be."

Tennent Bagley: Yes, they had these "friends" in the West who they did use to influence Western policies. This is not a master plot; this is a fact. They had continued these "assets" as we call it professionally. They held onto them, manipulating them and using them ever since. It's very easy also to find new allies in the present atmosphere of anti-Americanism in countries like France, for example. Some of the people who helped the Russians in the Soviet days were not what we would call formally recruited agents or traitors to their country. They were consciously helping the Soviet regime against forces they didn't like and didn't approve of, namely the United States. It's very easy to find anti-Americanism in countries like Germany, where, for example, anti-Americanism was one of the key factors leading to Heinz Felfe's penetration [and the] Soviet penetration of West German intelligence. A primary motivation for him to work for the Soviets was his feelings of resentment against the Americans for bombing his hometown of Leipzig. Today, anti-Americanism is being played on by these same people almost as if they were Soviets, but for their own, different purposes. Now, I don't want to suggest that the KGB has this as a main objective today or that there aren't genuine democrats and patriots among KGB members, but it's also under a different framework now, and the framework is self-preservation and self-enrichment. The connections that the KGB had with the Mafia before the fall of the Soviet Union were immense and long standing. So, it wasn't anything new, it wasn't anything that had to be developed suddenly when the Soviet Union collapsed. No, they simply continued these operations and went private. They were able to go private because of the privatization after the fall of Soviet Union. So, I think that the basic trust of operations continued and they still have plenty of ground today to recruit people in the West who are unhappy with Western policies. This goes not only for American policies, but also for the ways in which

Western European policies are being conducted. So, they had these assets, people inside political parties and sometimes inside governments. Those people were not ever ruled out. Here and there, one or two people were discovered, put in jail, or fired, but in large they survived intact until they died of natural causes, or are dying natural deaths today.

Angelo Codevilla: Harry Hopkins was seduced by the prospect of U.S.-Soviet cooperation at some point. He told Stalin that he saw no distinctions between Soviet and U.S. interests. The KGB considered him to be a Soviet agent. He certainly did not see things this way but it didn't make any difference. And indeed, James Baker[1], Secretary of State for George Bush, told Gorbachev the same thing that Hopkins[2] said to Stalin: "If you want anything, just tell me." Now, this is not being a Soviet agent in the classic sense of someone getting paid, but in practical terms it really doesn't make any difference, does it?

Oleg Gordievsky: The KGB recruits so-called "channels of influence," which means journalists that will spread deception. In some countries, such as Britain, Scandinavia, and the United States, it was very difficult. But in countries like Germany or India particularly, as well as Greece and Latin America, it was easy. Many journalists from these countries helped the KGB to spread disinformation.

Edward Jay Epstein: You know, I don't think you have to have a journalist on the payroll. Journalists are on the payroll of their own organizations. But what they need is news. So if the source provides them with good stories, they don't have to pay them to print the stories. And if you pay them, most journalists are honest — they will not accept money. But I think you can control journalists by controlling their careers. By helping them to advance in their careers. Not in a way that may be witting, [but] probably they are unwitting. I think you control many people in your intelligence apparatus the same way. If you recruit a spy at the State Department, you help him to prove that he is right. You give him good information. You help him to advance. And then maybe, at some point, you get him to give you information. Maybe you never do. I think that career management is a critical part of what the intelligence service does. It doen't just recruit people to work for it, to commit treason and be disloyal to your country. It manages careers, moves them from place to place to try to get at information that needs to leverage the policy it needs. This is true for someone like Armand Hammer[3]. Make him come over to Russia. He might be an opportunist. They need such opportunists to reepresent themselves in the western world in order to sell their cause, to raise money, to act as a laundry. So, in the case of Hammer, they recruited him by making him wealthier, by giving him more credibility, by giving him more power. Agents of influence are just another means of extending the entire false picture of reality. They are the [heart of] . . . the apparatus.

Jeff Nyquist: The Russians were very successful during the Cold War at penetrating the Western press. We heard things about I.F. Stone[4] and [Walter] Duranty[5] and different people in the U.S. who were taking money from the KGB. The insertion of stories, or legends, or false ideas into different newspapers around the world, to get people to think a certain way about Russia, has been a long-standing practice of Moscow. There is no reason to believe that it stopped after the end of the Cold War and, in fact, I am sure there is plenty of evidence from defectors to show that they are still recruiting reporters and that they are still slipping money to people to do certain things. It's just that now people don't see it. It doesn't have a stigma [any longer] . . . talking to a [KGB] agent. You are not talking to a KGB guy anymore. You are talking to Russian representatives of a democratic country; a country that's moving toward democracy. There is no more Cold War and they are not our enemy. So what's the big deal in taking money from these people now? This makes it easier for them to achieve their goals because now people's consciences don't bother them when they do things for Russia. Talking about perceptions management, the Russians are just brilliant at it.

RB: *Well, again, how different is what the public sees from what is actually going on? Can anybody see the big picture?*

Joseph Douglass: There is another point . . . while touching on this subject, and that's the difficulty involved in really learning what happened in various communist countries in the past. People talk about archives in Russia. As all of the books were opened, go to find what you want to find. That's not the case. The only things you can really get a hold of are things that you accidentally find, or things you are allowed find because it suits their purpose. But you can't find information dealing with subjects of strategic importance; and even if you did, you probably wouldn't find them to be of much use because they are written in codes that only people who were a part of the operation know. This is especially important because the manner in which these operations were conducted . . . was so tightly restricted that there really weren't too many people who knew what was actually happening. This is especially true today, since fewer of the original participants are still alive. So back-tracking and finding out what actually happened is extremely difficult. For example, as large an operation as narcotics trafficking actually was . . . so highly classified and so carefully controlled that very few people who were working on the operation actually knew what they were doing. So it's very, very difficult to delve into the past, particularly into anything that still has a significant relevance today. Ironically, this probably includes 80 percent of the past. Historians cannot really tell very much because they just don't know very much. What they do know, or think they know, is itself designed as a cover to protect the real people behind the power.

PART 10

RUSSIA TODAY

RB: *Is there still a danger in Russia's power, or can we all sleep well?*

Vladimir Bukovsky: Today's Russia is dangerous because of . . . its system. They are not likely to present a serious military challenge to the West as they did during the Cold War. Their military is in bad shape, and it will only get worse and worse. As a counter-balance to the West, a military counter-balance . . . in a military strategic sense, they are not going to emerge for probably 20 or 25 years. I don't know. It's difficult to say. But the remaining structure, which is more and more entrenched in Russia and elsewhere through their tentacles, is also still quite threatening. It is some kind of alliance emerging between KGB and organized crime, which is rising up under these businessmen. This can very easily infiltrate a whole country . . . . We are offering freedom of business so that is the instrument that they are using in Eastern Europe and more and more here. These huge businesses, these conglomerates, are emerging in conjunction with Western partners that used to be ideological partners as well in the 70s. So this is currently the biggest threat: the spread of organized crime, corruption, and to a degree, some of the control that comes with that. That is the biggest threat to stability. There are also some other potential threats emerging from Russia. For example, Ecological disasters pose a threat. We still have something like 30 potential Chernobyls in Russia, and who knows what will happen? There is the threat of spreading nuclear technology and selling nuclear material to third parties, including states and terrorist groups. We don't know. This does happen occasionally. Radioactive material leaks from Russia. Occasionally it is intercepted, but more often it is not. So we don't know whom they sell it to or what they do with it. There is also the danger of Russia manipulating so-called international terrorism. It's not a new thing. People keep forgetting it. In the 70s it was already in place and it was controlled very tightly from Moscow. In every country in the West, particularly in Europe, we had some terrorist organizations that were quite impressive and skillful. They were supplied, trained, and harbored by Moscow. Some of them were operating through Czechoslovakia, and others were operating through Bulgaria. It doesn't matter. Either way, it was by proxy. The real master was in Moscow. It also spread to the Third World with all those liberation armies and liberation fronts that were all supplied, trained, equipped, and financed by Moscow. With the war in Afghanistan, it spread to the Muslim world very actively to such an extent that I am pretty sure today's Islam, or Islamic extremist terrorist organizations at least, have contact with their former masters and suppliers in Moscow. I don't think it's done for ideological reasons today as it used to be. The concept of Brezhnev's time was promoting world revolution. Today they don't. They don't believe in world revolution, but it's still a very useful instrument for global policy. I mean, they stir up trouble and then they become indispensable in the eyes of the United States as partners in the fight against terrorism. They create the problem and then join the United States in trying to solve it. It's the kind of unique technique that they practice in almost every part of the world today. So that's another danger.

RB: *What is the situation inside Russia?*

Vladimir Bukovsky: As far as we know, they have internal control over these things. How tight the control actually is is difficult to say. It looks like the top generals of the KGB are actually in power and they alone make decisions about the country right now. I mean, it's definitely them who promoted Vladimir Putin and made him the President. He is their man in the Kremlin. Their power is much greater than it ever was in the Soviet system.

RB: *So, who is running the government now and setting foreign policy?*

Gordievsky: Basically, Mr. Putin is in charge of foreign policy but he has many competent advisers. In particular, the bosses of the Ministry of Defense and the military, as well as some important grey figures in the presidential office whom we don't know exactly.

Vladimir Bukovsky: I would imagine that governing is done by the top senior officers of the KGB, mostly generals I suppose. There are some rumors about an organization named SYSTEMA, which is run by former and active KGB generals, GRU generals, and some members of the military. It possibly looks like an arrangement for governing because Putin and his entourage definitely are not governing. That's for sure.

RB: *How much of the old structure is gone and how much is still there?*

Vladimir Bukovsky: Well, the power of the Communist Party and its official ideology is entirely gone. Their ideological control completely disappeared. The party as all-powerful, all controlling, no longer exists. There is some kind of communist party, which is oppositional, but as I said, the power of the nomenklatura didn't go anywhere. And particularly in the last five years the KGB retained all the structures, all the power, and all the ability to control things. It actually increased them. Today they are probably more powerful than they were at any other time in Soviet history.

RB: *How is that possible?*

Vladimir Bukovsky: Well, after Stalin's death, the ruling Central Committee of the Politburo realized the danger of the secret police running around uncontrolled. Under Stalin it was controlled, because it was controlled by Stalin personally. That force was capable of killing a lot of people in positions of power in the Central Committee and in the Politburo. None of them wanted to repeat that. They wanted a guarantee that leaders will not . . . be shot, tortured, and so on. So the decision was made to get the KGB under the tight control of the Central Committee, and that's what was done. Everything since Stalin's death, although more likely after Beria's execution[1], became more and more under the control of the Central Committee. I have seen documents showing that the KGB couldn't do anything without the approval of the Central Committee. They had to submit a request even to search somebody's apartment. Without that approval they couldn't do it. So that was one of the major changes in the post Stalin period. And, of course, once the Communist Party disappeared as the controlling hand over the KGB, the KGB became completely uncontrollable. It became a power of its own. Very quickly they began to utilize more and more power for personal wealth and for increasing their overall influence in the country. Vladimir Putin, their nominee, became the President. We are talking about 80 percent of the top positions in the country. They are all occupied by former KGB or active KGB officers.

RB: *What can be said about Vladimir Putin?*

Vladimir Bukovsky: There is nothing significant about Putin. He is a most unnoticeable person. He is a non-entity. I know some people who used to be in school with him at the University. They all say that no one ever noticed him. He was kind of a gray figure. He was very insecure, very pitifully minded, and very vengeful, which is more or less the typical psychologically for underlings and small people. He is tiny. I don't know how high he is, 1m 56 cm, something like this. This type of person is known by psychologists as being susceptible to a complex. People of small size usually have a complex and hunger for power. They are insecure. He is one of them. As far as his KGB career, it's very exaggerated now. He was never in intelligence, or in foreign intelligence. He was posted in East Germany supervising his East German comrades, not recruiting foreign spies, but acting as a secret policeman against his own comrades. He reported them coming in late, being drunk, or having affairs. He was just an informant. He never had any experience in a foreign, non-communist country. He was never posted anywhere like that. To say that he was is just an exaggeration, image-building. His spin-doctors invented all that. It has become part of a mythology in Russian that he was in intelligence, and in the West as well. He wasn't. He was a secret policeman. He was posted in Dresden and he stayed there running the Society of Soviet-German Friendship. That's it. He was supervising the GDR.

RB: *Is it true that his grandfather was Lenin's cook?*

Vladimir Bukovsky: Well, that's what they say. I don't know. Apparently, he was a cook in Gorky. Gorky is a place outside of Moscow where Lenin usually was . . . . Now it's called Leninsky Gorky. Apparently he was a cook there. I don't know if that is true or not. I didn't try to verify it. He [Putin] is a third generation KGB man. That's for sure.

RB: *So how did Putin get into the game?*

Oleg Gordievsky: In the 80s, Putin was a small-time KGB security officer in Dresden, in Eastern Germany. He didn't know anything about Western life. As was said, he was not an intelligence officer. After leaving Dresden, he went to Leningrad and the KGB put him undercover in the University. There, in corridors of the University, he met his old teacher professor, Professor Sobchak, who was a democrat. Professor Sobchak said, "Oh, Vladimir, you work for KGB, you speak languages, join my staff. It's much better than working for KGB. And Putin was clever enough to understand that, yes indeed, it's better to be on a political trajectory. Still, he remained loyal to the KGB. He started to work for Sobchak and [eventually] . . . Putin got into an important department in Moscow. Because Putin was clever, very bureaucratic, very well organized, and a good administrator, he started to move up the ladder. First, he was head of the

KGB, then Deputy Prime Minister, Then Prime Minister, and then, I don't know why, but Yeltsin appointed him to be President. So Putin is an absolutely accidental person appointed by President Yeltsin to be the new President. And now we have the big picture. We have a country run by a KGB officer, and everybody in the government including the Vice President, who is a KGB Colonel . . . . The KGB is everywhere. The important point is that the KGB is not only in the government and important departments; it also has a network of agents that act as secret informers. They sit everywhere, in the presidential office, in the Duma, in the ministries, and in the army. So the KGB is controlling Russia from above and from below. It is the perfect KGB state. The Communist party is not in power, it is a small organization in the opposition now. Democratic parties have been made very, very insignificant by Putin's manipulations and by the KGB. Television channels were taken by Putin from independent owners, so the country is now entirely controlled and ruled by the KGB.

RB: *So, is he now the most powerful man in Russia?*

Oleg Gordievsky: Mr. Putin is now, without a doubt, the most powerful man in Russia. After so many years in power he has consolidated his power and put all his buddies in the important departments and positions. The KGB controls all sectors of Russia's society, particularly its economy, finances, the Ministry of Foreign Affairs, and the Army. So it is, as I said before, a perfect KGB State. It will remain that way now, and probably forever, because there is no other political force to compete with them.

Jeff Nyquist: According to testimony from former STASI[2] people, Putin was in Germany[3] to set up a network that was going replace the communist network that they were preparing to collapse when they let Eastern Germany go. That means that in 1984 they were planning to let the Berlin wall go down. In describing himself Putin says he is a "Soviet person." His instincts and his thoughts are Soviet. When he was on Larry King[4], I remember this was very interesting, Larry King asked him why he was wearing a cross. Larry King was trying to get him to say he was a Christian, which is the impression somebody gives when wearing a cross. Putin couldn't bring himself to say that he was a Christian and when he was asked if he believed in Christ he gave the answer, "I believe in the power of man." It's a very Soviet answer. So Putin is not a democrat, he is not a person that the West should trust. In fact, considering the way he behaves, and his relationship with the Russian military and security services, he is a person who is almost certainly a totalitarian type. He is moving Russia back to a totalitarian order step by step, very slowly. You probably read the news report saying that at his inauguration they toasted Stalin. This was shocking to some people. Putin has been at these anniversaries of the Cheka, of the KGB. They celebrate them every December. Here is an organization that was founded by Felix Dzerzhinsky at the beginning of the Russian revolution. This organization killed tens of millions of Russians and oppressed the country, and it is celebrated by Vladimir Putin? His nickname was "little Andropov." Andropov was the ultimate Soviet bad guy, the head of the most powerful criminal organization in Russia, the sword and shield of the Communist Party of the Soviet Union. How can such people truly be democrats? How can they really change what they are inside? So Putin is the problem. President Bush, you may remember, said he looked at Putin's soul, or something of that manner, and saw a man he could trust, a man he could do business with. Putin is a spy. He is only lying and manipulating people. You see this when you watch interviews with Putin. He has a kind of smug demeanor when he is interviewed by Western Journalists. Gorbachev had that same smug demeanor when he was interviewed by Western journalists. It is like they are thinking, "I know what you don't know! I know something about the future. I know what is really going on." There was an interesting statement that Putin made when he went to Cuba. They asked him what his ideology was, if he was socialist or not. And he said, "Call me a pot but heat me not." Just a very strange thing for the President of Russia to say. Call me a pot but heat me not? Puzzle that one out. What do you make of that? But speaking an Aesopian language is an old communist way of communicating with people who will understand what you are saying—people from your secret organization. The rest of the world would be mystified. What do you mean by that? What are you saying? We are left to put our hopes into Gorbachev or our hopes into Putin and to say, "Oh, they are really good guys" or "they are democrats." They kind of form a blank screen onto which we can project our hopes. But what are they really? They are Soviets. They are the KGB. They are sinister. They are a part of this giant gangster milieu. That's what they come out of. That's what brought them up. That's who promoted them.

RB: *Well, where does Russia stand now?*

Angelo Codevilla: Russia, as it is, is a much diminished version of what the Soviet Union was. Vladimir Putin would really like to play the role that the previous General Secretary of the party would have played, that the previous chief of KGB played, but he cannot. He doesn't have a disciplined party at his back. He doesn't have a base of people who are responsive to that party out of fear and habit. He doesn't have the kind of armed forces that the Soviet Union had. He may have the same dreams that his predecessors had, but he does not have the means to live them out in reality. Still, the new Russia bears very, very strong similarities to the old Soviet Union; people count for nothing, leaders count for everything, and the economy is not an economy of production. It is a very sad place. The sadness is different from that of the Soviet Union, but it's still not a place where people get ahead through honesty. It is not a place where people would like to raise their children. Indead, it is a place where fewer children are born than ever before. This is a sure sign that there is very little hope here.

RB: *So is there still danger from Russia towards the United States and the Western World?*

Edward Jay Epstein: I think there is actually more danger from Russia and its exceeding influence over the world than there was at the height of the so-called Cold War. The danger of a military confrontation no longer exists. Nuclear exchange?

Russia still has ten to twenty thousand nuclear warheads, and we could always have a nuclear exchange. That didn't diminish. The probability diminished, but the possibility didn't. Russia now controls a larger proportion of the oil and natural gas needed by Europe, the United States, and by the entire industrial world than they did at the height of the Cold War. In addtion, it actually has more influence over Western Europe than it ever had before.

RB: *In other words, Russia can't be trusted, right?*

Edward Jay Epstein: Well, I think in the game of geopolitics no country can be trusted. It's assumed that all they can be trusted to do is follow their national interest.

Oleg Gordievsky: The prospective plan of Putin's Russian government is to become the boss of Europe. That's why there is so much pressure on countries that don't want to dance to the Russian pipe. These are the Baltic Republics, Poland, Ukraine, and the Czech Republic. Russia will pursue them and try to undermine them as much as possible in the future. The Soviet Union wants the "Finlandization" of Europe. They wanted to make West European countries like Finland, very dependent on the Soviet Union. Now, Russia understands that that's impossible and that they are too weak to do it. But they can still achieve some political advantages over Western Europe. Using money, deals, exchanges, talks, and friendship it achieved great success on the German front. Now Germany is a best friend of Russia in Europe. And this is dangerous because Germany, after all, is the biggest country in Europe. It's the most important country.

RB: *What is the KGB influence in Europe now?*

Oleg Gordievsky: After the collapse of communism, the influence of the KGB in Germany was temporarily undermined because the huge STASI, the Russian spy ally, was destroyed. But since the late 90s Russia sent so many spies to Germany that now it is full of Russian agents. The KGB is also very influential in countries like Finland, Hungary, the Yugoslavian Republics, Bulgaria, Austria, and is also fairly influential in

Italy and France. It's all through organized crime and the KGB. In the Czech Republic, the Russian influence is maybe 10 percent. In Poland, 15 percent. In Austria, 5 percent, which is a lot for a democratic country, but it's still not dramatic. For example, here in Great Britain the Russian influence is very, very low. The KGB station is kept low, only 20 officers, compared with the 400 officers in the United States. There are more KGB officers in the Czech Republic than in Britain. In Britain I'd say 20, in the Czech Republic 30 plus 20 GRU. Together, that makes 50 officers.

RB: *Why is Russia still so anti-American?*

Jeff Nyquist: That's a very good question and people need to ask it more often. Russia has a hand in working with Germany and France, with this whole business of stopping movement of our troops through Turkey during the assault on Iraq. The Russians had a hand in that. The Russians are drawing our Europeans allies away from us. Here is the thing about this. Russia, not the Russian people, but the Russian state, sees the United States as its primary enemy. Russia is a centralized state. The Russian government, the Kremlin, is really in charge of the entire show over there and they see themselves as the strategic rival of the U.S. They don't want the U.S. to be the dominant power in the world. They would rather be a dominant power themselves or share power with China than have the U.S. in its present position. They are doing whatever they can to stop that. They are doing whatever they can to weaken the United States on every level: diplomatically, economically, and militarily. This is clear when you see Russia offering a sort of special relationship with Hugo Chavez in Venezuela. Hugo Chavez hates the United States. When you see Russia forming military ties with China and making a friendship treaty with them, keep in mind that the Chinese see the U.S. as their major strategic rival as well. The Russians are selling them submarines, missiles, and fighter aircraft. Why are the Russians doing this? You know, twenty years ago the received wisdom was that Russia and China were rivals, that they were right next to each other in Asia and they were going to butt heads. Now they are working together like they were allies all along. It is a strategic reality that Russia and China are different kinds of countries. They are different from Western countries and they see the U.S. as a barrier to their greatness. They are going to oppose the U.S. every chance they get, but they are going to be careful about it. They don't want the U.S. to realize what's going on and react to their moves. They do it slowly over a long period of time and they use a lot of clandestine methods.

Ion Pacepa: In the 1970s, when I last met Andropov, his elongated, ascetic fingers always felt cold and moist when he shook my hand. "We are replacing all those so-called professional diplomats, who do nothing but sit around drinking and gossiping with deep-cover KGB officers," he began. His habit of plunging directly into the subject of a meeting without introductory remarks was legendary among intelligence chiefs. In his soft voice, Andropov laid out the historically Russian roots of his new technique, for he was a Russian to the marrow of his bones. Some two hours later, the KGB chairman concluded our meeting as abruptly as he had started it. "Our gosbezopasnost" had kept Russia alive for the past five hundred years, "our gosbezopasnost" had made her the strongest military power on earth, and "our gosbezopasnost" would steer her helm for the next five hundred years, he concluded, looking me straight in the face. Andropov was also a dependable prophet. Today, his gosbezopasnost is still running Russia.

PART 11

CONSEQUENCES

RB: *Mr.Bukovsky, I never asked you, how did you get access to all of these confidential documents in Moscow?*

Vladimir Bukovsky: Well, I got access to some of these files in 1992 when the Communist Party of the Soviet Union, being banned by Yeltsin the previous year after the coup, actually protested and disputed that ban in the Constitutional Court of Russia. They argued that this ban was unconstitutional. And the court took the case. That frightened Yeltsin's entourage enormously because they knew they had a very good chance of losing this case. And if they lost it they would have to return all the property to the party. The property of the Communist Party amounted to probably half of the country. So that really scared them. Yeltsin's adviser called me. I knew him from previous years, and asked me to come and help them with the court case. I agreed only under one condition: that they open the archives because without the archives we would have no case and I wouldn't have a motivation to get involved. So he agreed and I came to Moscow in June 1992 and had open access to secret archives during that time. Of course I was not allowed to copy anything, but I took precautions, a notebook computer with a hand scanner. I guessed that they wouldn't know what it was and I was right. I was scanning thousands of pages with this device for half a year. That was the initial bunch of documents that I got out. Based on these documents, I published the book "Judgment in Moscow." Then, years later, a son of my friend in Moscow who I used to know as a kid was showing more and more interest in history; specifically, this kind of research. He read Judgment in Moscow, and remembered it almost by heart. He was growing. He became a student and without really realizing that there are copies of lots of documents, secret documents of the Politburo in the possession of the Gorbachev Foundation in Moscow[1], he found them through the Internet by chance. Someone published a work based on the archives of the Gorbachev Foundation and we could see that they were actually Politburo documents. What apparently happened in the turmoil of 1991 when the Soviet Union ceased to exist and Gorbachev was ousted from power, was that he actually took the trouble of making copies of almost all the files and secret documents concerning his period of power, from 1985 to 1991. So I instructed this young fellow to go to the Gorbachev Foundation, ostensibly pretending that he was writing a paper for his University course and asking permission to work in the archive. Permission was granted, although it was very limited. He was only allowed to look at some parts of the archives. However, being a bright young man with a good knowledge of computers, he actually broke the administration's password and copied the entire computer. So that's about 2 GB of material that he was sending to me for almost a year in small portions. 5 MB in ZIP form would come to my email every day, and I collected all it. Finally, when he copied the rest of it he came here to England. The most remarkable thing is that, two weeks after he finished copying the presidential administration files, the Putin administration learned that Gorbachev had made these documents accessible and explicitly ordered him to block all public access to these documents because they were originals and were still secret in the archives of the Politburo. So suddenly, right after he finished copying all these documents, access was closed completely. He was very lucky. Anyway, we suddenly had 700,000 pages. We had transcripts of all the talks Gorbachev had with local leaders, foreign leaders, and public figures. We had all the reports by his aids, memos, the ministry of Politburo meetings, and so on and so forth. This was a huge amount of material. That's how I've come to know a lot of things now that I didn't know at the time I was writing Judgment in Moscow. I guessed most of them correctly but I didn't have documentary evidence at the time. Digging into these files is an endless process. Even finding a particular document in that collection takes us hours. Because of different file formats we can't find a way of searching through them quickly. Someday we hope to convert them into a single format, but that would take several months of work.

RB: *What was in your book, Judgment in Moscow, that pissed the Russians off so much? The book was never actually published in English.*

Vladimir Bukovsky: It's difficult to say. They were annoyed by the fact that, being a sworn enemy of the Soviet system throughout my entire life, since the age of 15 to 16, I had suddenly gained access to their most secret documents. That fact itself was really annoying to them, but they couldn't do anything because it was Yeltsin's order. He wanted to win the case in court. So the KGB couldn't do anything about it. They were very annoyed. I have seen lots of documents which they would prefer me never to have seen, including some agents that they were running, as well as friendly connections to some politicians in the West that you might describe as, if not agents, secret collaborators. This includes quite prominent politicians and business figures here. And I, of course, published as much as I could. So that in itself was very annoying for the KGB. Publishing the book in English was blocked by the left here. They threatened my publisher, a small, family publishing house, respectable. They are proud of publishing Lord Byron[2]. They were the ones who translated the book and published it in their catalog. But then the lawyers came and threatened the publisher with endless libel cases if the book was ever published. They said it quite openly: "You may win in the end, but you will be bankrupt by then." The publisher was scared so they suddenly suspended the publication. They stopped it.

RB: *Shouldn't the public be concerned about all this?*

Angelo Codevilla: The American people are, in a way, rightly unconcerned with what happens in the world. This is a very big country, it's a lovely country that takes up most of our attention. It is very difficult for anyone, even one who goes abroad a great deal, who studies what happens elsewhere. Living here in the midst of all this peace and prosperity, common sense, gentility, and civility makes it hard to realize that people in other places think and act very differently. They would rather not see the world in a different way . . . . It is very difficult for people to realize that others are different from themselves. Americans, being part of a large country, have difficulty doing that. And indeed, Russians can hardly imagine what Americans are really like. And when they do come and see us they don't believe it. This is a purely human fact, and a very important one.

RB: *How dangerous is this for us?*

Angelo Codevilla: It is a very great danger for people to not understand reality. And very often, reality comes knocking the hard way.

RB: *Can we say that there is a "Strategic Blindness?"*

Angelo Codevilla: The American foreign policy establishment is very blind for a variety of reasons. The establishment is primarily homogeneous in its progressive outlook on the world. This is a chief source of blindness because the establishment really does want us to believe that the world has meaning that corresponds to its own prescriptions; that Iran wants to be like America . . . and that the Israelis are willing and able to learn from the Americans. In that sense it is blind. It is also blind in that it is absorbed in its own functional difficulties. One of the truest things I ever heard when I got to Washington was that all talk (when I got inside the U.S. intelligence establishment) was not made up of various arguments concerning the Soviet Union—they were not about the Soviet Union at all! They were about the people next door. The people down the hall. The great controversies were among various agencies, various power centers within the agencies. Certain personalities and views about the Soviet Union were made to fit into these struggles, to serve these struggles. So there is another reason for strategic blindness . . . . A certain type of miotic concentration on our own internal difficulties. Then, of course, the other reason for strategic blindness is the continuing decline in the quality of personnel in the American foreign policy establishment. Fewer people have a real acquaintance with the outside world, and they are simply of lower quality. We have a tendency to choose people for high places who are not abrasive thinkers but people who get along; people who say pleasant things. Bush's National Security Council is full of pleasers rather than thinkers, and pleasers are not strategists. One of the most profound enduring truths about politics is that the system . . . [lives] according to the pattern of their founding. They are what they are and really cannot be anything else. This was true of the Greek city states, of Rome, or any other regime that ever existed. These regimes will live and die as they are. They cannot change. Attempts to change the regime are akin to trying to rip a tree from its roots and expecting it to grow again. Sometimes you just get a tree stump that doesn't resemble its origins; but most of the time the tree will die. So we really have to be aware that regimes and people . . . change very slowly, and regimes really never change at all. They live and die as they are but reform . . . they cannot.

Jeff Nyquist: You know, Americans are very idealistic. They believe in some sort of automatic victory of democracy. So when people say that democracy is succeeding in Eastern Europe, or Russia, or wherever, we immediately want to believe it because we believe that these countries are inevitably headed toward democracy and capitalism because democracy and capitalism is the only real way to live. After all, look at the way we live. This is the product of democracy and capitalism. Doesn't everybody want to live like people in America? Well, of course it doesn't quite work that way. The leaders in these countries don't necessarily want democracy because that might mean that they wouldn't be able to hold onto their positions. So they like to continue the system that keeps them in charge as a ruling group. Part of our mythology is that we believe democracy was triumphant in Eastern Europe, in places like the Ukraine. It's only a matter of time before we find out that this most recent democratic revolution in Ukraine was again a disappointment; that nothing has changed. The old structures remain. And as soon as we discover that, they have another democratic revolution; we'll say, "OK, this time it is the real one." How many democratic revolutions do we have to see in Ukraine . . . or wherever, before we realize that it's just for show? It's just something to keep us going, to keep us believing in the myth that democracy will always triumph. The reality is that for most of human history governments have been dictatorships. Most of our history is about the rule of small oligarchies, or of single monarchs. Democracy, the flourishing of democracy, is a recent development. And there is reason to believe that it may not last very long, even in the West. It's a very delicate thing and it needs to be protected. It needs to be looked at not as something that is inevitably triumphant, but something that takes a day-to-day struggle to maintain. It is not to be taken for granted.

RB: *Well, can we say that the power behind the regime in Russia survived and is probably stronger then ever?*

Tennent Bagley: The major power, the essence behind that regime, is intact. It survived, it prospered, and it has taken other forms. I don't believe there is any particular KGB element that is masterminding the world of pseudo-democracies, not for a minute. But there is no doubt that KGB elements are continuing their work. For example, if you want take it strictly down to my level of espionage against the Soviet regime, when the Soviet regime collapsed it made no difference whatsoever as one can see through their handling of spies or moles within American intelligence. Namely Aldrich Ames, who was not discovered until three years after the fall of the Soviet Union, and he was still actively collaborating with them and was actively exploited by them. Then you have Robert Hanssen in the FBI. It made no difference. They were continuing the fight against the old enemy and it may continue to this day.

RB: *What do you see happening in the future?*

Tennent Bagley: I wouldn't dream. My experience with the past is troubling. I wouldn't dare to look at a crystal ball. The Russians today are aiding our enemies in the Middle East, maintaining relationships with them, perhaps playing two ends of the thing in Iran and its assets in Iraq, in Syria, and in other countries. I would say that they have long range goals, [they] have no interest whatsoever in . . . the survival of the United States, much less its prosperity. So, what may happen in the future is anybody's guess, but I predict more troubles with all of these countries as well as perhaps the development of the atomic bomb by Iran. If so, this will be a whole new ball game with new possibilities which I think could be the end of everything. I have no idea. It could be that bad.

Edward Jay Epstein: Countries still want to win in the arena of power and influence. It's not something you can abdicate or give up. If America takes no action in the strategic arena, they are still taking action by letting other countries take action. So yes, we should be concerned with strategic intelligence. We should be concerned about the information we are receiving from other countries. We should be concerned whether or not that information is meant to drive us in certain directions, to deceive us about reality, or whether it's simply accidental information that we are gathering and confirms a view of reality. But one needs to carry a sophisticated apparatus to examine this information, its sources, its credibility, and to see what it adds to other information. Then we need to try and penetrate the source of the information through quality control. Because if it turns out that, lets say, everything that journalists from Russia and Eastern Europe are telling us is confirmed by our penetrations into their intelligence service, one can just relay that there is no plan against us. On the other hand, if there is a contradiction, we should be concerned.

Joseph Douglass: I guess the main thing I would tend to go back on, or back to, is one question, "is communism dead?" It's easy to recognize why this is a very serious question because most people believe that it is dead. You rarely hear about the death of communism that took place . . . with the dissolution of the Soviet Union. However, when you look at communism today, you can easily see it as a threat that's worse than it has been in the past. Because it's still massive, it's still effective, it's still growing and we recognize its existence less than ever. To really look at some new places where it is growing we only have to look to ourselves, and not just Cuba, but Central America where it is still in possession, as well as places like Venezuela, Bolivia, and Argentina where it is growing significantly. Then of course there is China, which we are busy fueling so that it can become a superpower, a power that doesn't worry about losing one or two hundred million of its own citizens in a war. As a matter of fact, they are probably looking forward to it because it would reduce a number of the problems they have. So, because we try to act as if it is dead, as if it doesn't exist, it can well be considered a threat more serious than it was in the past.

Angelo Codevilla: I don't believe there is any more danger from communism per see, no. I think that the ideas of Marx and Lenin are quite dead and that no serious person espouses them in their original form. However, the essence of Marxism-Leninism survives in very, very different ways. For example, I recently had a conversation with the Ayatollah of Iran. He interpreted the Koran in ways that really were quite indistinguishable from those of Vladimir Lenin. I pointed this out to him and he was a bit shocked. Nevertheless I showed him exactly how that was so and he said he didn't realize it and was quite dismayed by it because he was a sincere Muslim. He was not one of these Islamists, he was a sincere Muslim. Nevertheless, he didn't realize how far these ideas had crept into his own religion. Basically, what is happening is that Islam has been re-defined as anti-Americanism. And that has happened according to a logic that would be very, very familiar to Boris Ponomarev or any of the leaders of the International Department of the Communist Party of the Soviet Union. They may be dead, their system will most certainly not be revived, but some of the driving ideas of the system have survived them.

Bill Gertz: I would say that I think the problem of communism is certainly growing in the Western hemisphere. One of the problems in the global war on terrorism has been the lack of attention focused on communist advancement in Latin America and South America. I think this is an important danger that needs to be addressed. A lot of people would like to say that communism is dead, but if you ask people in China or Cuba or North Korea whether or not communism is dead they will tell you for certain that it is not. I think Communism as an idea is on the decline. However, communism as a practice and as a culture is still very much alive. One of the main missteps since the early 90s has been the failure of the free world to demand a de-communization process similar to the de-nazification process that took place after WORLD WAR II. There wasn't a clear statement of the fact that communism is not just a false ideology, but an evil ideology and that it has to be recognized as such by its current and past practitioners.

Ludvik Zifcak: The communist movement is not weakening, definitely not. I believe that the communist movement is gaining strength now. And not just in the former socialist countries but, most of all, in the West: In France, Belgium, and even in the United States. I believe it's getting stronger because it got rid of people who joined the communist party just for some personal, materialistic reasons. Now the people in the communist movement are not looking for a personal advantage but because they truly believe in it. That's why the power of communism today is much stronger than, for example, it was in 1989.

RB: *So, the idea of global socialism is still around?*

Oleg Gordievsky: The Soviet Union wanted and tried to force the idea of global socialism upon the world. But, in the end, it was Soviet socialism. It was the Soviet version of socialism, and it collapsed. Now some people, particularly in America, believe that the idea of global socialism is dead. But it is not. If you look at its development in Europe and Latin America, you see that there is now more socialism than ever before. Because of public opinion, or rather, the media, political parties, political movements, parliaments, and institutions are all becoming more and more socialist. The European Parliament is a socialist organization. The Spanish government is a socialist organization. Even the so-called "bourgeois" French government is practically a socialist organization. For many years in Germany, socialists were getting 55 percent of the vote. It is getting stronger and stronger. You can see it in the press, in academia, and in the Universities. There is no sign, even in the United States, that socialism is decreasing. On the contrary, there is even more of it. Unfortunately, the social democratic, Western European idea of socialism is growing. I am very sad about it because it's not what I want. We, Soviet dissidents, wanted a liberal and free society in both Europe and America. Now Europe is moving toward socialism again.

Vladimir Bukovsky: If you look at the overall trends in the world, yes. You have these progressive, persistent attempts at integrating the world more and more, solely in the European Union. If you look at regional arrangements in other part of the world, you see the same tendency. This is not a natural tendency. This is a tendency pedaled by the political elite. For example, when you look at the situation here in Europe, in Britain, Germany, France, and Italy, keep in mind that the Eastern European countries are being dragged into integrating with them. Most of the population is very distrustful of the European Union and this integration process, but the elite favors it. They use their position of influence and power to carry this process through, even in the face of the silent resistance of their population. So, in reality, it's a shift toward the left, not the extreme left. With the end of communism, that model disappeared. It's not our future anymore. We are not going to see an Orwellian[3] future. We are most likely going to see a world of the sort described by Huxley[4]. That's where we are shifting now.

RB: *How did the idea of the EU come about?*

Vladimir Bukovsky: The idea, to a degree, existed for some time. It was the dream of Sumeria[5], Rome[6], and Napoleon[7]. It was also the dream of Hitler, not to mention many politicians after World War II who wanted to consolidate in the face of Stalin's threat. This idea was kicked around for centuries. It never succeeded. In our time, starting from the Treaty of Rome in the post war period, the basic idea was not a political integration. It was the idea of creating an economic integration. Open market. Have the trade barriers removed and simplify the custom regulations, which would both be good for the European economy. More open trade and more easy movement of capital, goods, and labor across the borders would help stimulate economic growth. So initially, the project had nothing to do with political integration. They never sought the political advantages of open trade. And that continued till the early 80s. By 1985 the process of economic liberalization in Europe was finished. It did create an open common market here. There was no need to go any further than that. But at that time the left wing parties in the West, and the people in Moscow, as well as the leadership in Moscow, became increasingly worried that the socialist concept was going to be damaged by this development, that it might actually be in crisis. They might lose all of the achievements of socialism, meaning themselves. Their own power would be sacrificed. That was intolerable for them. So the first to alert Gorbachev to that eventuality were Italian communists. They came to Moscow and explained that the only way out of this crisis of socialism was to try to impose it on all the countries in Europe at once, because if you lose it in one country it doesn't work. Others simply become more successful through competition in the world market. So they had to impose it at once. And the way to do it was to hitch-hike [onto] the European project. They took the common market project and turned it upside down. Instead of simply a common market agreement, they decided to make it into a state. They wanted to make it into a federal state, a united state. That would allow socialist forces, leftist forces, to get entrenched permanently in these structures. What that means is that, no matter the outcome of elections in different countries, that power will be perpetuated in the superstructure of this European super state. That was their basic concept. Through this arrangement, it would be very easy to introduce more and more socialist innovations and changes into every country, even if the population there is widely against it. So that was really the concept that they proceeded with. They very quickly agreed, in particular the leftist parties, on a bigger role to be played by French President Mitterrand[8], Spanish prime minister Felipe Gonzales[9], and Willy Brandt[10] of Germany as well as other social democrats in Germany and so on and so forth. Of course, British Labor also played a part, although they were not initially in on it too much. They became attracted to it later. But now they are a part of it. So anyway, that was worked out between them throughout the 80s. By 1991-92, the crisis in the East happened, catching the Western leftists off guard. They were counting on the Soviet Union being a partner. They were already very well into it. Gorbachev's angle was slightly different from that of the European left. Not entirely, but slightly. He perceived both the West and Moscow as converging. It was an idea that was popular with many politicians long ago after the war that one day the big divide between East and West would disappear as a result of convergence. The Soviet model would mellow, would become soft, more tolerant. In other words, it would be, "socialism with a human face," while meanwhile, the West would become socially democratic. Then there would be a convergence which would be a great achievement because there would be no threat of war in Europe and all problems would be solved. It would be almost like a paradise. So that was a concept, a theoretical concept in the 50s. In the middle of the 80s this concept became dominant. The Western left perceived it as a convergence. So this is why the European structure was built so similarly to the Soviet structure. They were supposed to fit each other at one point. Gorbachev was officially calling this project The Common European Home. It was perceived and supported as a convergence by the left. So they were doing it gently. The advantage for Gorbachev, among others, was having access to the unlimited industrial potential of the West, which was a dream in Lenin's time. Apart from that, it would help to sandwich Central European Countries between the European Union and the Soviet Union in such a way that they would be completely controlled. If they wanted to run away to the West they would be embraced in the European Union. To save themselves from the European Union they would have to be embraced by the Soviet Union. That was a very neat arrangement discussed at length between Gorbachev and Mitterrand. They both understood how important it was in terms of controlling Europe. The European Union resembles the Soviet Union more and more structurally and even philosophically. It's a very mild version of the Soviet system, but the similarities are undeniable. Also, the Soviet Union is not a part of the project anymore, at least it was not under Yeltsin. The European project continued only on the basis of remaining parts. Still, it spread to the East, including Eastern European countries, and because of this kind of utopian thinking they never stopped. They have to continually expand. It's like the Soviet Union. If these totalitarian ideological structures stop expanding they start collapsing. So that's why the European Union will continue to expand. Their next agenda, if you saw what Prodi said before he retired, will be the Middle East, North Africa, and so on and so forth. It's going to grow like the Soviet Union and, of course, collapse one day. I believe it will have the same faith as the Soviet Union. It will overextend itself, crack, and collapse. Eastern Europe, in this sense, will be in the worst position. Their economy is still fragile and their democratic institutions are still not terribly stable. Once this call comes, they will be the worst affected parties. The West is always entrenched in traditions and a rather high standard of living. It's very experienced when it comes to profound crises as a result of collapsing structures. It will survive. What will happen to the rest of Europe is anybody's guess. It will be a terrible shock to them. That will be a shock that is very difficult to absorb. Meanwhile, since the Russians are now trying to revive their former expansion in terms of economic influence through controlling businesses and so on and so forth, they will become a much easier target for Russia. So that is a future danger which we can visualize. Russia itself by that time may be in deep crisis as well. They survive today because of the very high price of oil and gas. That might go down, and then they will be in a deep crisis as well. That may not be so dangerous for their neighbors, but one can imagine another scenario where the European Union collapses and Russia benefits from it. That's more or less what we can talk about when we discuss the future.

Robert Gates: I think that nothing is permanent in history. I think that for a long time to come the notion of socialism has really been discredited. I think what you have now is a variation to a degree, which is the welfare state. It's not the state taking over. In some ways you have to return, to the examples of France and Russia, to something similar to seventeenth century mercantalism[11] and the debate on whether or not free trade or national champions are best paths to follow. But I think in terms of direct state ownership as the means of production. I think people see that as a losing idea. I think that even the Chinese see it the same way. It certainly failed them. It cost them tens of billions of dollars a year in subsidies in remaining state industries that are owned by the state. I think they would like to get out of it as soon as possible, but they can't figure out what to do with the 100 million people who work for them. So I don't think that socialism will be a valuable cause, at least for some considerable period of time.

Jeff Nyquist: There is a funny thing about Marxist strategy. Marxists always claim that you can't really build communism until capitalism is destroyed around the world because the capitalist mentality . . . pollutes the communist countries. You can't make a new socialist man unless the world market collapses and you have a true experiment where they try to operate the world economy without money. And, of course, anybody who really understands economics knows that you are talking about the death of 4/5's of humankind by starvation if you attempt to smash the world market. You get rid of the international division of labor. You interrupt world trade. But this is the kind of thinking that animates Marxist-Leninists. And Marxist-Leninists are in charge of China, and autocratically in charge of Russia. They have the upper hand in the world, and if this is what they are thinking, we are talking about a calamity of major proportions. We are not just talking about a calamity in the United States with weapons of mass destruction. What we are talking about will devastate people of the Third World, people in Europe, and people in Asia. So any destruction that would happen in the United States would not be on a scale any greater than what would happen in other countries. People don't realize the extent to which the United States has been the center of a kind of order that allows for prosperity, economic growth, and technological growth worldwide. You would never have the population explosion that we have today, I believe, without a world order mediated by American power. American power created this stable market, this intensification of the division of labor. All of these things have led to tremendous development and tremendous population growth in the Third World. It certainly elevated global poverty, but you have this period of sixty years now since the end of World War II marked by tremendous stability in Europe, in Asia, and tremendous growth. It can't last forever. And . . . if America is displaced, this whole order is broken, and there is no guarantee for what would come after. Can we maintain the kind of stability and pattern that would allow for growth and allow for the feeding of 6 billion people worldwide? So it's very important to know when people are tampering with [or] breaking the American global system; The global economy. They are putting at risk the lives of billions of people across the world. To understand that, to understand how the world economy functions, that is absolutely key. But it is also important to know that the totalitarian mind, whether it's Nazi[12] or communist or whatever ideology you want to call it, doesn't care. It's already a kind of inhuman way of thinking. And it dehumanizes others as well as it dehumanizes itself. Whether it is al-Qaeda, Stalin, Mao, or the successors of Stalin and Mao, that mentality continues. It was the mentality of Genghis Khan[13] who conquered in degrees of longitude and latitude and swept away whole cities and civilizations. History repeats itself. This is what we are facing.

RB: *What about Zbigniew Brzezinski and his vision of Global Management?*

Angelo Codevilla: This is a very important point to make, you see. Another part of what we may call "diplomation professionale" of the U.S. foreign policy establishment is the belief that human differences can be transcended; that politics itself can be transcended and we can move from politics, which are the adjustment of differences, enduring human differences, to a kind of apolitical management of the world. Roosevelt[14] always believed in that, and even Zbigniew Brzezinski[15], who is, after all, a Pole, and therefore distrustful of Russians down to his roots, nevertheless believed that somehow under American, not Russian ostracism, under American ostracism, it would be automatically possible to transcend all of this and to move from politics and conflict to a kind of apolitical management. In other words, turning the world into a great EU. This is quite a divorce from reality, but recall in 1999 the most popular book in America was Francis Fukuyama's[16] The End of History. Now there is absolutely no basis to believe in that, except for the passion of so-called right thinking Americans. How else could one believe that history really has ended, that there will be no more controversy, no more major differences, and that everything can be administered rationally. Now, to my mind, it is sheer madness. But a lot of people really want to believe that.

RB: *Who makes strategic decisions in the United States and how?*

Jeff Nyquist: Politicians and policy-makers probably make the strategic decisions. My perception is that they make strategic decisions concerning the country predicated on maintaining the status quo, on keeping the economy growing — "it's the economy, stupid" — and trying to deal with threats like al-Qaeda in a way that doesn't distract the system. The problem is that threats may be greater. It may not just be al-Qaeda, there may be very serious threats from a re-emerging Russia, or the Soviet Union and China, extending to Latin America and Africa, Asia, and even taking over Europe. If this threat is serious in the long run, that would require changing the economic system. And we are not psychologically able to do that. It would take . . . a nuclear bomb falling on an American city for America to change its way of life or to think about the way we are living now and revise it. To meet that challenge, to meet the kind of challenges that are out there appearing on the horizon, it would have to take that much.

Joseph Douglass: It's probably based on political agendas. The one thing that we can generally say is that it's certainly not based on intelligence. Intelligence is designed mainly to support decisions, not to aid in the decision making process. It's very difficult to know where the key decision-makers are. Obviously, the White House is the center. Certainly, various lower level departments act in accordance with national policy, which is set by the White House. But there is also a significant powerful influence from outside the government that has been regarded for two hundred years as having tremendous influence on the decision making process. Who and what, as well as from where and how this decision-making process is implemented is not entirely clear.

RB: *Can we say that, regardless of the intelligence input, decisions come from somewhere else?*

Joseph Douglass: Yes. You know that intelligence, the CIA let's say, is an agency that serves only one person and one organization, the person being the president and the organization being the National Security Council. It has no international intelligence capability. It is really just meant to support the White House and, presumably, the White House's decision-making process. The problem is that too many presidents have not been interested in intelligence, or know what to do with it once they have it, or how to believe it. Too many of them look at intelligence mainly just to answer questions; does it support our policy or is it in opposition to our policy? And if it makes our policy look silly, how do we best bury it or send it away? So, intelligence is not highly regarded in the White House except perhaps to know what alligators may be working in the shadows ready to pounce on them from behind. However, it's not really a challenge to the political decision-making process.

RB: *Did Europe gain anything by the end of the Cold War?*

Angelo Codevilla: Europe gained one very great thing from the end of the Cold War. And that was that it lost the legitimate fear that it would be overrun from the East and that Russian soldiers and commissars would do to it, as they had done at the end of World War II. That is a very real and legitimate fear, which, since they have lost, has been eased. However, they have allowed themselves to continue down the path that they have embarked on many years before. I am speaking of the path to depoliticization, to becoming subject to an administrative state. Europe is no longer free in the sense that people no longer make decisions about their own lives. The decisions are made by a vast administrative bureaucracy. Europe is a place that has lost its soul and its freedom. It is a sad place in many ways, and a place which is slowly, or perhaps not so slowly, being taken over by Muslim immigrants who, pure as they are, and as rich in spirit and courage as they are, still frighten the Europeans. So Europe is by no means in good shape, but I don't think that comes from the fall of the Berlin Wall and the end of the Cold War. Those events simply left the current problems alone and made others more evident.

Edward Jay Epstein: What happened is, of course, that there was a division between Eastern Europe and Western Europe. Few countries failed to fit in neatly, like Yugoslavia. Still, there was a division and there was hegemony of Russia over Eastern Europe, but it had no influence over Western Europe. It had no influence outside of its so-called sphere of influence. Then the Soviet Union pulled back from Eastern Europe. It brought down the wall in Berlin. You know, in strategic thinking, in Western strategic thinking, Germany was a crucial point of geopolitical balance. So it was assumed that the Soviet Union would never give up its hold on Germany and what became know as Poland, which was once also part of Germany. It was considered the most strategically important [part]. But what was forgotten is all those lessons of geopolitics that came out of World War II, when tanks and large armies moved back and forth. Was Germany really strategically important? Why was it strategically important? What was strategically important was control over crucial resources like oil and gas, as well as food like wheat, corn, and soybeans. Russia didn't give up control of those areas. It gave up control in areas that were very expensive to maintain political authority over. Now, because countries in Western Europe, including Germany, are dependent on the supply of natural gas and oil from the former Soviet Union, it has an influence that exceeds what it had before. It has more influence but less power. A difference between influence and power is that power can compel someone to do something while with influence you can simply lead them in the direction you want without forcing them.

Vladimir Bukovsky: I came across some documents regarding the Trilateral Commission[17] in connection with the European Union, which were kind of stunning for me. In January 1989, the delegation of the Trilateral Commission came to see Gorbachev. We have a transcript of their conversation. Included in the conversation were David Rockefeller[18], Giscard d'Estaing[19], Henry Kissinger[20], and Yasuhiro Nakasone[21], the former Japanese Prime Minister. Ostensibly, they came to prepare the report for the Tri-lateral Commission on the development of things in the Soviet Union and they had questions for Gorbachev. They also came to encourage him to start integration into international financial systems such as GAT, WolfeBank, IMF, and things like that. They also asked him what he would think about making Russian rubles convertible. In the middle of all this conversation Giscard d'Estaing suddenly took the floor and said: "It may be 10 years or maybe 15 years, but Europe is going to be a single state. And we have to prepare for that. And we would pretty much like you to be a participant in it. What would you think, what would you say, if in due time one or more of the other Eastern European countries, or Warsaw Bloc countries would actually like to join the European Union? Would you have any objections to that?" That was a discussion in 1989. At that time, evidently there was a master agreement, the agreement which was moving the European project into political and financial integration. It wasn't even drafted at that time, Let alone voted on in a referendum. But these people already knew that in 15 years Europe was going to be a single state. Now, what is even more puzzling was the reaction of Kissinger. I mean, now we are told that European integration is a kind of counter-balance to the United States. It's almost anti-American. Kissinger didn't perceive it that way. He actually said: "Oh yes, we would like it to happen and we would like to help our allies go along with it, but we think that you should be a part of it and that the United States should be part of it." So his only concern was that the United States might be left out of this arrangement completely, and must be tied to it somehow. That's all Kissinger said. So all the talk about being a counter-balance to America, the anti-American project, is complete nonsense. They used anti-Americanism very often. Francois Mitterrand in particular used it when trying to consolidate forces in Europe for his projects. Very often he would do that, particularly in talking to the Soviets, knowing their anti-Americanism and so on. But I think that it was a tactical thing. In reality, they were talking about this kind of monolithic idea of uniting the whole world under one government and things like that. That's why Kissinger was not against it in general. He would perceive it as a move in the right direction.

RB: *What about Eastern European government and politics now?*

Vladimir Bukovsky: Well, as far as I can judge, Eastern Europe is a total mess right now. This is precisely for the same reasons that there is a total mess in Russia: because the old regime was not conclusively finished. It was never dismantled. It was never uprooted. Its remains are still very powerful. So periodically we have a return of communism to power, which is ridiculous. Poland and Ukraine are probably the most anti-communist countries right now. However, they themselves let communists govern, which is ridiculous. It still happens because the structures of the old nomenklatura are still very powerful. There are infiltrations of business that are quite successful, so they suddenly require other additional leverage in the society. Therefore, you cannot write them off. They will be a factor in the politics of Eastern Europe for a very long time. They will be influential behind the scenes, sometimes occasionally coming to the forefront. That is a fact of life. It is very difficult to deal with this issue. It would contribute to the instability of Eastern Europe. Plus, their hasty integration into the European Union is going to add to their problems. Even in the initial stages, you may know that they may not comply with the criteria of the European Union before joining it, or after joining it. They have to include something like 80,000 pages of European rules and regulations into their legislation. Eighty thousand pages! It's unbelievable. And a lot of policies common in Europe right now would be very damaging for Eastern Europe. For example, the agriculture policy would wipe out Eastern European agriculture, and that is quite a big danger. Imagine the situation for, let's say, Poland, where about 30 percent of the population still lives in rural and agricultural areas. So the upheaval was created on one hand by European integration, and on the other hand by influence from Russia and its Mafia-type businesses that were going to be a burden for Eastern Europe for a very, very long time. It would be a burden at least for a generation, I imagine. It would be very difficult to cure any of these countries from this illness.

Jaromir Stetina: Russia is still a danger, mostly because, in addition to its strategic weapons, it is starting to use the pipeline valves as a weapon. This means that Europe and the United States are facing the same problem. I believe that Russia has the best diplomats in the world and I know for sure that Russian diplomats understand two things well: the power of money as well as smashing a fist hard on the table. I think that we have to start with the question of how far Russia spreads. Russia is not sure where its own borders are. Negotiating with Russia will only be possible when this dilemma is solved. At this time, Russia is an unpredictable, imperial element that we should be scared of. But we should not just be scared of Russia, we should also worry about Russia. That's the only way we can help them. And in the meantime, membership in NATO and the EU is our only guarantee against the hand of Imperial Russia grabbing us again. Communists know how to hide, lie, and wait. There is the prospect of some kind of mix between Communism and Fascism[22] rising up. It's already happening, this strange symbiosis.

Jeff Nyquist: There is a point about the changes in Eastern Europe that should be made, and that is—that both conservatives and liberals have their own reasons for accepting change in Eastern Europe and the collapse of communism at face value. The conservatives love to take credit, especially giving credit to Reagan for winning the Cold War. And they, of course, are eager to turn this victory into profit; the peace dividend. They love the idea of not having to invest in this Cold War. We can take that money and put it back into private resources. We can get tax relief and lower taxes. The liberals have their own reasons too. Decreasing defense spending means there is more money available for social spending. The defense spending decreased since the end of the Cold War, while social spending had a proportional increase. So both groups have something at stake in their political agenda for accepting the collapse of communism, and they are not looking at it too closely or critically and saying, "Hey, wait a minute, maybe this is something we have to be careful about."

RB: *Is Western democracy in danger?*

Oleg Gordievsky: Western democracy is not in big danger now. But in 20 years it could be in danger because Russia will improve its nuclear weapons, it will improve its air force, and it will create smart weapons like Americans have. As a result, Russia will be a threat to Western Civilization.

Joseph Douglass: In my judgment, the non-military aspects of the threat, which were the most important, still receive no attention and still, from all evident appearances, continue in one form or another. In other words, we have more of a change in strategy and tactics on the Russian side and not necessarily any change in goals. But this itself gets no attention, and, in many respects it may be a stronger threat to us because of this.

Angelo Codevilla: The political establishment in the United States, like the political establishment in any large country, is concerned, certainly over-concerned, with its own internal difficulties. It tends to see what happens in the rest of the world through the lens of its internal difficulties. It isn't so much that it prefers to see that which is not there. Of course, everyone wants to see the world the way they wish to see it. And of course, they are preoccupied with internal matters and seeing things through that light [as well]. It isn't that they have a positive appetite for self-deception. But nevertheless this is the way self-deception works.

Edward Jay Epstein: The KGB has been replaced by the Federal Intelligence Bureau of Russia (FSB); and the CIA, which oddly enough has left its original purpose, is now involved in fighting terrorism and international crime like narcotics and things like that. I think that, in a sense, the KGB or its successor is better positioned now because it has no countervailing force. And if it has any strategy, it can carry it out without concern that it will be penetrated.

RB: *Does that mean that we will always be on the defense, never able to be offensive?*

Bill Gertz: Unless there are fundamental changes at the top of the U.S. government, no. In other words, if the president and some of his closest advisers make it a top priority to fix this problem, to be able to go after foreign spies and to do it in an aggressive way, not simply identify foreign spies but be able identify them, to understand what they are and then conduct double-agent operations to go and turn some of these spies into agents or double agents, that might fix the problem.

RB: *And if this doesn't happen, then what?*

Bill Gertz: Well, I think that unless they fix U.S. counter-intelligence, we are going to see more and more extremely damaging spy cases. This might include the theft of technology by the Russians, the theft of technology by the Chinese, and more importantly, influence over our operations. They may be able to recruit agents of influence within the government who can not only obtain secret information for these foreign governments but who can actually conduct influential operations to undermine and subvert U.S. policies.

RB: *In other words, the United States will deteriorate on a political and economic level?*

Bill Gertz: Yes, the United States is facing a major strategic assault on its system. Yet, because of denial and the deceptive activities of countries like Russia and China, it is ill-prepared to counter these activities. It will take tremendous leadership. It will take leadership that is willing to divide our national interest from our diplomatic interest. This has always been a big problem for State Department diplomats who would like to play down foreign intelligence activities in order to play up diplomatic relations and the ability to conclude agreements with some of America's main enemies. It is about a political mindset and it's going to require that the United States come to grips with the fact that its bureaucratic system of government is severely broken, severely damaged, and is ultimately working against the national interest of the United States. Clinton's administration, for instance, caused grave damage to U.S. national security[23]. They had a naïve view of national security, which stands from the fact that many of his senior advisers ascribed to a view that I call "anti-anti-communism." In other words, they were not necessarily communists, although they probably held some Marxist-Leninist views. More importantly though, they were opposed to anti-communists and conservatives. This was at the core of their problems. For example, in the case of communist China, the Clinton administration wanted to treat China as a normal nation when in fact China today is a nuclear-armed communist dictatorship. And this was a fundamental flaw, which led to flawed policies. When it came to the Russian government, Clinton's administration didn't have a good understanding of it. And it wasn't just limited to the Clinton administration. It was again based on the opinions of left-liberal advisors within the Clinton administration who had a naïve view of America's enemies. For example, I think it was the late United Nations Ambassador Jean Kirkpatrick who described them as the "blame America first" crowd. That means that when it came to bad governments, like the Russians, they had a bias against the United States and saw the United States as the source of the world's problems when in fact the Russians and others, who did not wish the United States well, were behind those problems. Bill Clinton also did a lot of damage to our intelligence agencies. One of the key problems there was the left-liberal notion of political correctness, which has no place in national security. As it relates to the CIA, Clinton's administration imposed seriously flawed restrictions on intelligence gathering that made it almost impossible for our spies overseas to collect information. And this came home to hurt us on September 11. Even then we had information within the system that some of the September 11 hijackers were in the country. The restrictions placed on our law enforcement and intelligence services were so great that we were unable to stop that attack. Unfortunately, I still see this as a continuing problem. You may still vote people into office who might have conservative or moderate ideas, but the fundamental view of the bureaucrats and the careerists in government is fundamentally flawed in the sense that their initial outlook is that America is a problem and other countries are generally better than the United States.

Angelo Codevilla: This administration [the Bush administration] has had a greater-than-usual propensity for self-deception. Condoleezza Rice, who fancies herself an expert on Russia, is one of those who, in the language of the Foreign Service which I was a member, has "gone native." In that regard, she really does see the Russians as she would like to see them. She has made enormous concessions to them, especially with regard to U.S. missile defense. These are concessions, by the way, that she has kept secret from the American people. This, of course, is the very, very worst offense that any diplomat can make. To make a deal on behalf of a country while keeping the country in the dark about what deal has been made is really the number one sin for any diplomat. No professional diplomat would ever do that, but she is not a professional diplomat.

RB: *Would it be fair to say that we may see some "socialization" of American society coming our way?*

Bill Gertz: I think what we will see is that America will become so weakened that it will be unable to act in such a way to fulfill these global responsibilities. That is, to be able to help in promoting the concept of democracy and freedom around the world.

RB: *Didn't we learn anything from the past?*

Bill Gertz: I think that the lessons of the Cold War are still to be put into practice. As I said, one of the most important lessons to me was the fact that there wasn't a de-communization process with the collapse of the Soviet Union in 1991. And I think that this was a fatal flaw for reform within Russia. The fact is that communism should have been outlawed. There should have been an education process for Russian leaders and former Russian leaders to go through to make sure they clearly understood the evil of communism.

RB: *Do you see Russia becoming a superpower again?*

Bill Gertz: I think that's clearly the objective of the Russians — to become a superpower once again and to regain the territory that it lost when the Soviet Union collapsed. I don't see them doing that. I have seen some efforts within the former Soviet Union to try and realign. Belarus comes to mind. But I don't see an example that suggests Russia will ever be able to retain control over Ukraine. If you understand the Ukrainian mindset, it is that the Ukrainians have one enemy and that is the Russians. Of course, the Ukraine takes up a large land area in that part of the world. But I think that Russian policies, Russian military buildup, and Russian intelligence activities are directed at trying to regain the lost Empire of the Soviet Union.

Oleg Gordievsky: The objective is clear now. It's to make Russia a global counter-weight to the United States again. To compete for influence in the world with the United States, which is, of course, very much against the wishes of democratic and liberal elements in Russia, and in the West as well. Because everybody is saying: "Join the United States, join Europe, don't be in alliance with China and Iran. They are the wrong friends for you." No, they don't want to hear it. They want a strong Russia, which will be a smaller super power, but still a super power, because they have several thousand intercontinental ballistic nuclear missiles. That's nearly as many as the United States has. So in a hypothetical case of nuclear war with the United States, Russia and the United States would destroy each other completely. That's their most important asset. "We have Nuclear Weapons the same as you Americans. You can't do anything against us." This is dangerous for the Western world. But so far the Western world prefers not to speak about it. They don't want to boost Russian pride and Russian confidence about their nuclear weapons. The West is pretending that they forgot about Russia's nuclear weapons. But they do exist. Do you know how many nuclear missiles are in the United Kingdom? I think less than a hundred. Only one British nuclear submarine is on duty all the time. That's nothing. With five to seven thousand nuclear missiles, Russia can dominate the world. Russia has missiles in silos underground, in submarines, and some can be launched by the air force.

RB: *So, is the threat of nuclear war still alive?*

Oleg Gordievsky: Yes. The threat of nuclear war is very much alive. Because Russia is very proud, I mean their military, the chauvinistic Russia under Putin is very proud of it. The nuclear weapons are like a favored baby for them, and they keep creating new, modern nuclear weapons.

RB: *What do you think Russia will look like 20 years from now?*

Oleg Gordievsky: It's very difficult to make a prediction about the future. I think Russia will be about the same as it is now. It will be very corrupt and still in the hands of the KGB. Because of oil money other cities apart from Moscow, cities like St.Petersburg, Rostov, Nizny Novgorod, and some others will also have a chance to prosper. So, more prosperity will arrive in Russia. It's inevitable because most of the money goes into pockets—whose exactly, we don't know. Every year Russia receives billions and billions in oil money. Where is that money? Nobody knows. Ask anybody in Russia, "Where is the money?" But that money goes to Russia, and while a lot of it goes back to private accounts in different countries, some money will remain in Russia and Russia will become richer and more prosperous as a result. Globally, Russia will improve its position because it will be stronger, but it will also suffer humiliating defeats. This may happen in Moldavia, Ukraine, Georgia or perhaps in some other areas. Also, the northern Caucasus will remain an open wound for Russia even 20 years from now, I am sure. It may become an even bigger wound because the Chechens were punished and tormented so badly. They say, "OK, you don't want to give us freedom? Now we will make the whole region of Caucasus a bonfire." And that's what is happening now. Now is just the beginning. In 20 years there may be a war and Russia will spend all its effort on the war in the Northern Caucasus.

RB: *How concerned is the U.S. government with Russians spying on the United States?*

Edward Jay Epstein: I think there is much less concern than existed in 1990, or 1980, or 1970 about other states running intelligence operations against America. And I think there will be less in the next few years because the enemy is no longer conceived of as a state. It's conceived of as, I hate to say it, a religion. As Islam. Islamic fundamentalism is now seen as the enemy. Narcotic gangs are also seen as the enemy. Russia . . . has interests all over the world. It is interested in controlling the price of energy, gas and oil. It has interests in assuring itself a supply of natural resources, and of controlling it's own former Soviet Republics. It has ways of controlling them. It is interested in influencing China. So, in some way, Russia has a strategy. I don't think that America has a strategy to counter-balance that strategy.

RB: *Why is that?*

Edward Jay Epstein: Well, I think that what is happening is, especially after 9/11, that a division of interest regarding the focus of resources in the government has gone from geopolitics, the geopolitics of Henry Kissinger, Richard Nixon, Ronald Reagan, Jack Kennedy[24], if you like and Lindon Johnson[25], or even Jimmy Carter, where there was a strategic view of what America should be doing in the world, to much more defensive attitude of how we can prevent, say, the shipment of bombs through ports by small groups of bandits, groups that are unconnected and have no hierarchy and no state backing. My own view is that state sponsored terrorism, or, if you like, state sponsored covert actions, still remain the main threat, and the job of intelligence services should be penetrating states, not going after groups of, or gangs of potential terrorists.

Oleg Gordievsky: And then there is China. Russia wants to make China its ally and China doesn't object. They carried out joint exercises and the hint was given to prepare China to get Taiwan, which really is equal to hostility against the United States. So China is a very good partner for Russia and Russia is trying to woo China. For example, I can tell you that China is now desperately spying against both the United States and Russia, while Russia deliberately pretends it doesn't see that China is spying against them. No arrests are made, and no efforts at stopping them at all take place because China is an important strategic partner for them.

RB: *Is it somewhat similar to America looking away from Russian spies in the United States?*

Oleg Gordievsky: The United States knows very well that there are roughly 400 Russian spies in the country and they don't do anything about it. They don't do anything because, like China for Russia, Russia is an important junior partner for the United States. And why? The United States doesn't want to irritate Russia because of nuclear weapons and because Russia is participating, at least verbally, in the war against terror. Russia may be useful in the solution of the Iranian problem as well.

Vladimir Bukovsky: I don't understand why Americans need so many Russians as American partners. But one thing they do, which I can see quite clearly, is that they manipulate public opinion here into believing that the war in Chechnya is part of a general struggle against Islamic terrorism. This is total nonsense. The majority of the people in Chechnya are not Islamic extremists at all. They are like other Muslim nations from the former Soviet Union. Like Tatars, Baskies, and Sunnis, they are very moderate Muslims, there are no extremists there. Nevertheless, that's kind of a useful technique for the Russians to recruit citizens' support in their bloody war in the Caucuses.

Jeff Nyquist: The intelligence services of the West have bumbled their way through the decades including the Cold War and everything else. You look at the biography of Peter Wright[26] at M15, for example. He was the Deputy Director of MI5, a big British mole hunter. This guy writes a biography in which he says that he thinks his boss at MI5 was a Soviet agent. And he says that the Russians were ahead of us during the entire game. In the U.S. we find out that Aldrich Ames and Robert Hanssen were moles, these top guys in the CIA and FBI. The fact that we were penetrated by these foreign intelligence services is something that our intelligence agencies denied for decades. Now that they can't deny it anymore, they don't know what to do and, of course, now they prefer to say that the Russians are spying on us but that they are not really our enemies, so what's the big deal? It is an inteligence fiasco. Also, I should make a comment about intelligence analysts. You know, intelligence analysts today that know their jobs may depend on giving the "correct" analysis. They Give the analysis politicians or higher level buerocrats may want to hear. Maybe if they actually looked at the facts honestly and with intellectual integrity they would eventually come to a conclusion that would conclude their careers. They don't want to do that. They don't want to end their careers. So maybe instead they are going to persuade themselves that the opinions held by politicians and the general public are correct after all and then they can shift the context or use the evidence that sort of denies that there is a threat.

Bill Gertz: I think that even in the United States today there are debates over whether or not the United States should promote democracy and political reform in the case of communist China. This is one of the more urgent debates facing the country, because China is a prime example of a communist system that has given up Marxist-Leninist economic policy but has not abandoned its Marxist-Leninist political system. This poses a threat not just for China, but for the entire world. As the contradictions between the economy and the political system become more sharply marked, this could lead China's rulers to miscalculate. To take some type of military action that could possibly trigger a major confrontation in the world.

Jeff Nyquist: What's happening now is that you have all kinds of regimes that are actually led by communists, such as the South African regime. The ANC[27] is basically a communist front. It's led by people who are communists. South Africa, even though it has a certain degree of freedom, is in the Communist Bloc now, or is at least in a group of countries that used to be called communist. So South Africa is a strategic country near a strategic waterway with a lot of strategic minerals, and it is no longer part of the Western Bloc of countries. You have Venezuela, an important oil producing country, the most significant oil producer in the Western Hemisphere, and it's led by a man who is described in the Western press as a left-center populist. I know from interviewing people that have worked with him that he is a communist who hates the United States and wants to attack it in any way that he can. But is the American public aware of how dangerous he is and what his agenda actually is? No. So you have many governments in the world who you can call stealth communist governments, or stealth enemies of the United States. People say that China is never going to act against the West because of our trade relationship with them. China isn't really about trade. They are using it to achieve their current goals, but in the end it is a country that wants to be a great power. Of course, I am not talking about the average Chinese citizen. I am talking about the leadership of the country because it is, after all, a dictatorship. And that dictatorship, the leaders of that dictatorship, hate the United States. They want to see the United States destroyed. And they will combine forces with anyone who has a similar feeling. And they will promote anti-American propaganda through whatever venue they can while smiling to us and waving saying, "What a wonderful trading partner America is." China's economic policy has been to export to the United States and penetrate U.S. business, Canadian Business, and Mexico, in a way that makes the United States seem very vulnerable economically, militarily—and in the eyes of terrorists. But people want to have that economic relationship with China, because the business of America is business. And doing business with China is doing business with the country that has the most people. And what can you say about that when your country is all about capitalism? Their country, however, is not all about capitalism. Their leadership is communist. They are using capitalism to get to an advantageous position later on. That's when you see Russia and China signing military treaties, having joint military exercises, while what's going on should be obvious and should be discussed. However, most people really don't want to talk about it or dwell on it very long. You might see a flurry in the press about China being a threat and then it just fades away. There is no sustainable public interest in this reality.

Bill Gertz: If we look at the combination of China, Russia, and Islamic extremism, there are not too many countries left to fight it, or with a will to face it. The immediate problem of international terrorism is, to me, a very serious one, but I think it is a problem that can be solved in a matter of years. Wherever there is a strategic long-term problem of communist ideas, the leftover communist ideas possess a greater challenge. I see this in the United States where left-liberal Marxist ideas are finding their way into our education system to such an extent that, for example, when new intelligence analysts come out and work for the intelligence community and they are asked about Bolivarism, the new left ideology of Hugo Chavez[28] in Venezuela, they identify this movement simply as a social justice movement. They fail to recognize it as a Marxist-Leninist ideology or the pro-Cuban communist ideology that it is.

Jeff Nyquist: It's very interesting how so much of the world has turned against America, how the constant drumbeat of certain anti-American propaganda has emerged. You hear it in Latin America, in Europe, and if you actually examine the anti-American propaganda that's here now, it's structurally identical to the Soviet era anti-Americanism, the anti-American propaganda that you would see in the 60s and 70s. It has such a similarity that one has to suspect that the ultimate origin of this anti-American way of thinking is the former communist structures of the Soviet Union. And, of course, when you see people like Hugo Chavez or Castro[29] basically saying these things today, you know that this is consistent with the communist view of the world. Even people on the right, like Europeans who are supposedly independent thinkers, are mimicking these exact phrases or ideas about the United States and American imperialism.

Edward Jay Epstein: I think . . . Hegel[30] said "The Owl of maneuver flies at dusk," meaning that we don't know things in history until they have already passed. It's very difficult to predict what is going to happen in terms of the end of the Cold War. When people look at it, lets say 50 years from now, they may find that Russia established itself as a legitimate power with the greatest, or the second greatest I should say, nuclear arsenal — the accurate weapons capable of deterring everyone including the United States and China. They may find that Russia gained control over the world's resources; that it built up an organization based on opportunism and wealth that was far superior to the one built up on ideology and Marxism, and that it retained power and achieved the purposes that Stalin had been aiming at in the 1920s. You know, Stalin wasn't Hitler. He didn't want world domination. He wanted the protection of the Soviet State; he wanted a huge sphere of influence over Iran and most of Asia. I mean, the big ideas might speak to it, but it wasn't that he wanted to be a world dictator. He wanted control over natural resources; he wanted the recognition of the Soviet State. I think it will take history to judge whether the transformation of the Soviet Union into an extended Russia was part of a plan or whether it was reflected in the victory of the West. I don't think we can make that determination now. I think we have to wait until it's too late.

RB: *Should people care about all this?*

Jeff Nyquist: Well, people are busy with their private lives. People should care. It's the future of our country. It's the future of all the western countries. It's the future of freedom. Are the countries that were threatened by the Soviet Union during the Cold War being threatened again? I think they are. Maybe not in the same way that we saw before, but there is a threat there. And if we don't face up to that threat, if we don't realize the interconnection between Moscow, Beijing, al-Qaeda and other terrorist organizations, the emergence of communism in Latin America, and the neutralization of Europe — you know Europe is moving away from America. America can be isolated and separated from its Cold War allies. You don't have the same structures in the West to oppose the reemerging of Russia, or of China, that you had before. In that case, maybe the tables will be turned. The new situation, the new Cold War, could take place with the United States as an underdog unable to cope. That might be a situation that is coming, and it's coming sooner than anybody realizes it.

Angelo Codevilla: And so, of course, reality catches the American people by surprise. This has happened quite a few times in the 20th century. The more idealistic as it were, the more people have been indulged in their own ideas of the world rather than in dealing with it as it is. The more harsh surprises have come upon the American people.

Jeff Nyquist: There is another point I want to make. There are two ways to think about power. One thought is what Chairman

Mao said, "Power comes from the barrel of the gun"; the other one is the idea that money is power. In the West, it's commonly understood that money is power. Money-power. We always talk about it. It can buy elections; it can make things happen. Money is power. It's very interesting. What happens if you have all the money and I have all the guns? I stick you up. Then I have all the money and all the guns. People who believe in guns, people who believe in violence, have a more fundamental kind of power than people who believe in money. You can use money to buy guns, but in the end the fundamental belief in violence, in using weapons, which is the fundamental basis of regimes in Russia and China, is of a different order, a different kind of thinking. This is not the type of thinking that animates Western elites. Western elites see economics as having primacy. Elites in Russia and China see weapons, violence, and military power as having primacy. Whoever has the most nuclear weapons wins. Whoever has the biggest army wins. And this is what we have to be careful of. If we assume that our idea of power is the truth and we predicate everything on money, we are going to be hurt in the long run because it's not really about money. "Man does not live by bread alone" as [Christ] once said. That's a point that has to be made in order to understand the difference in psychology between East and West. Let's look at the things Russians are brilliant at. For example, the Russians say, "OK, things are falling apart. Our military is in disarray. We can't afford the security on our nuclear warheads. Our early warning system has degraded so we are very jumpy on the nuclear button. You know what? If you don't want an accidental nuclear launch against America, you'd better give us billions of dollars so we can fix these problems." That's a very subtle, very brilliant kind of nuclear blackmail used in order to get the United States to give Russia billions. There was a facility in Russia that the United States was to pay hundreds of millions of dollars to build so it could be used to take apart Russian nuclear warheads and to dispose of weapons-grade material such as uranium and plutonium. As I understand it, the U.S. ended up paying a billion dollars for this facility. There was a cost overrun. A highly placed U.S.

intelligence analyst told me that people in the intelligence community suspected that the Russians were not taking apart the warheads in this facility but that they were instead making new ones. So we basically paid for a new nuclear weapons production facility without even knowing it. And the Russians are very good at saying, "No we can't have you come to the facility," or "You can only come under these circumstances; you can only see this." It was, in fact, in the New York Times a few years ago that we have yet to calculate any accurate amount for all of Russia's nuclear warheads. We don't know how many of them there are, and we don't know where they are. In the United States, of course, we've gone down to some 6000 nuclear warheads [as of 2005]. President Bush unilaterally said that since Russia is not our enemy anymore, we will go down to 2000 or 1700 nuclear warheads [close to the actual 2009 number]. Some nuclear experts are saying that going below 2000 warheads is exposing the United States to the danger of a successful first strike in which all of our nuclear missiles and weapons are destroyed or unable to launch. So we wouldn't be able to hit back at all. That really counts for a country like Russia that has the advanced missile power to launch such a strike. This is not a strike to destroy American cities, but a clean strike to destroy American weapons. And then, once America is stripped of its nuclear power, stick them up. "We will bomb your American cities if you don't surrender; if you don't agree to these terms." It's the old nuclear blackmail scenario. So, the nuclear balance really does matter, but our politicians don't think it does. Now with all eyes focused on al-Qaeda as the enemy, a greater emphasis is put on taking American missiles and nuclear weapons off alert. This has been suggested by some U.S. senators. "Let's take U.S. missiles out of politics, let's not have to aim them at Russia. After all, our enemy is al-Qaeda, our enemy is not Russia." But I'll bet that the Russians won't take their missiles off alert. They never gave us proof that they are not aimed at us. After all, it takes just a few seconds to aim them.

Bill Gertz: Well, I think that the West, the United States and the Western World, is clearly the last best hope for our civilization.

That said, we are beset with serious moral problems. The decline of the family; the decline in the understanding of moral values; the basic understanding of right and wrong. And I think that this is a serious problem, and one that the West and the United States needs to address. Often, people criticize the United States for being so engaged in the world trying to promote democracy and freedom. Even some voices of isolation in the United States say that we should fix our own house, and fix our own problems before we go out. I think that the opportunity is too great. The United States is the world's only superpower. It does have a moral vision for promoting freedom and democracy, and it shouldn't be sidetracked by its internal problems so that it can take steps to fulfill what I feel is an important global mission.

Jeff Nyquist: I want to talk about the issue of left-right conversion and all these conspiracy theories that are emerging now. It is very interesting. You listen to the far right. They talk about this New World Order and the conspiracy of these elites that are against freedom and against the people. You hear this from the far right. This is very interesting. When you study the structure of this right-wing propaganda, and right-wing conspiracy theories, you find it has a spooky resemblance to the propaganda of the Communist Party in the Soviet Union during the Cold War. Who is the enemy? The rich people and the capitalist West, that's the ultimate enemy. This is the same enemy the communists talked about. So, it's a convergence wherein the right and left are saying something closer and closer to the same thing. I mean, the extreme right and the extreme left. So if you had a very radical event — a nuclear attack on the U.S., for example — a radicalizing event and an economic collapse where the center disappears and people start to move to extremes, would the ideology that emerges on the right or left be pro-capitalist, pro-democratic or anti-capitalist and paranoid? Is that what we would end up with? And would totalitarian forces or ideas then be in a position to take over the United States? That's something that worries me. Also, if you look at different racist groups, whether they are black or white, or Hispanic, they have a thing about conspiracy too. It's a Jewish conspiracy; it's a conspiracy of the man; it's a conspiracy of those people who wish to hurt the white race. Whatever it is, whatever group it is, their paranoid beliefs fuel a similar totalitarian mentality of divide and conquer. This possibility might make violence in Yugoslavia, the break up of Yugoslavia, look like child's play in comparison to what could happen in this country. If somebody wants real civil disorder, civil war, revolution in this country, it could be argued that we are not as stable as we think. If we took a major economic hit, this country, the U.S.A., would fall apart. I hope it's not the case. I hope that there is enough residue of patriotism left. But when I look at all these different groups, these different hate groups, and I look at how loud they are and how many followers they have, I begin to wonder. You know, I had the thought when I was teaching at school, I saw a kind of narcissistic psychology that was emerging in the students, that was promoted by the media and our consumer culture. And I looked at that and I thought, what would happen if these people weren't rich? What if these people didn't have all the money they needed to spend in a store, if they lived lives that were not comfortable? Would they be strong, would they be patriotic, or would they look at races to blame? Would they succumb to these ideologies, this hatred? And I wonder if ideologies of hatred naturally appeal to narcissistic personalities. If we know that the majority of Americans are narcissistic, would we then just completely succumb to an ideology of hate? I hope not. That's the other fear in this situation. So the prospect of destabilization in the United States, and the possibilities what may follow from that, are horrifying. Vilfredo Pareto[31], the Italian sociologist, had an interesting theory that there were basically two political types in the world: The lions and the foxes. And when a civilization is young the lions prevail, but when the civilization grows old the foxes prevail. The lion confronts, and the fox negotiates. The foxes, in the end, outnumber the lions. When they predominate, they make everything about talking and negotiating and making treaties. But what happens in the end is that a civilization led by foxes becomes soft and gets swept away by barbarians who are more lion-like. This is maybe what we are seeing play out in our time. There is also another interesting analysis of civilization given by Jacob Burckhardt[32], the Swiss cultural historian. He said that civilization is made up of three things: culture, the church, and the state. These are the three basic components of civilization. If the state became predominant you have a type of oriental despotism that crushes the culture and makes it into an instrument of the state. If the church became predominant you have a sort of theocracy where the church uses the state for the religious oppression of people who don't believe, and ultimately religion crushes the culture and tries to turn it into a kind of extension of the church. But what happens, Burckhardt asks, if culture becomes predominant over the church and the state? He said all three of these elements have an important function. The state protects society, religion spiritualizes and humanizes the society, and culture, well, it makes life comfortable. Culture gives us art, it gives us wealth, it gives us scientific advancements. But if culture triumphs, culture then tries to make the state into an extension of the culture. We see this with political correctness. We see it with the way politics in America works. Culture is taking over everywhere and imposing its values and prerogatives. Culture is all about fashion. It is anti-authoritarian. Notice how authority in America has declined. The Church has lost authority in the United States, and more and more Churches are like businesses run to appeal to worshippers the same as somebody who is selling soap. If everything becomes about business and everything becomes about making money, then the defensive function of the state starts to lose its coherency. The spiritualizing function becomes just another example of commercialization. Maybe this is how our civilization is developing. The triumph of culture over state and church ultimately becomes a catastrophe.

RB: *Can America survive?*

Jeff Nyquist: Oh yes, I think America can survive. History is complicated. Best-laid plans do not always come out the way you planned it. And you talk about if the world economy, if the American economy, suffered a major blow, nobody can automatically predict the sociological, social impact on the whole world. We don't know what kind of chaos would be unleashed and if anyone could really guide the chaos. If Russia, for example, thinks it can guide and control the chaos, they may be sadly mistaken. And if you are talking about unleashing weapons of mass destruction, once you start unleashing weapons of mass destruction there may be no way to control the sequence of events. It can go out of control in any number of ways. Disastrously. And this is a big concern. How responsible could a country be when it [is] . . . engaged in supporting Iran in getting nuclear weapons, or terrorists having nuclear weapons, or even using terrorists as a stalking horse?—to launch a kind of secret attack on the United States? If these things are going on, even if they think they have a reasonable chance to gain the world, there are many things to think about. [So] it's a harebrained scheme. You know, the plan can sound very rational and very doable but when you go to do it it's very difficult to make it come out the way you want.

RB: *Are we better off now than we were 20 years ago?*

Robert Gates: I think the struggle against tyranny is never-ending. There is something in the human DNA that makes some people want to rule over others and control their lives. And we will deal with that as long as any of us are alive. I think we are definitely better off. I think if you look at conditions at Eastern Europe today, the lives of Eastern Europeans are significantly better than they were when they were under communists. I think the lives of most Russians are better than they were under communists. There is no terror in Russia today. There are no gulags in Russia today. Is there a clamping down on freedoms? Absolutely. Is Putin determined to restore the Great Russian power views and approaches? Absolutely. Does he want to control Russian's natural resources? Absolutely. You have a more authoritarian government in Russia than we would like, but it's a very different kind of government than existed under the Soviets. And what's more important is that there is always an opportunity for change in the current environment. A different leader with a different set of priorities could always be in the position to change things. I think that there is significantly greater freedom in Russia and, in many areas, it is better off. And the world is better off because we don't face, on a day-to-day basis, the potential for cataclysmic nuclear conflict or major war in Europe such as what existed under the Soviet Union. So I think we are much better off. But we are facing the kind of world that, in many ways, existed before WORLD WAR II. And that is a number of great power states that are contending for authority, economic power, and military power. We are dealing with despotism in various places. There are societies in the middle of change and the threat of terrorism and radical fundamentalism. But even terrorism isn't a new problem. Terrorism is something that has been with us for a long time. Most people don't remember just how effective terrorists were in the last quarter of 19th century. They assassinated a Russian Czar, two American presidents, and various figures in Europe including Francis Ferdinand. I think we have returned, in many ways, to the kind of multi-polar world that existed prior to World War I and World War II. It's a more complicated world, no doubt about that. But I think at the end of the day it's still a safer world.

PART 12

WHO FRAMED ROGER RABBIT?

A few years ago I had an informal meeting with a former high-ranking official of the CIA. During our conversation I asked him the following question: "You knew that the dissident movement, specifically in Czechoslovakia, was organized and controlled from Moscow by the KGB, but you financed dissidents with help from George Soros anyway. How was that possible? What was that all about?" Smiling at me he replied: "Would you give up such an opportunity?"

The issue here is a very complex one. Do you remember the movie Who Framed Roger Rabbit? We sort of know who the bad guys are but we can't prove it. On the other side, the good guys seem to be so nuts that we have a hard time believing them either. As Pete Bagley mentioned previously in the discussion, nobody can see the whole picture. The strategy of the game was laid down, but with so many players involved and so many variables that many unintended consequences came along. Many questions will never be answered. That's what deception is all about. The important data and information is destroyed. History, as we are allowed to see it, can be altered. We all would like to find a convenient truth because an inconvenient truth is, well, inconvenient. This book may be labeled as another piece of conspiracy-oriented nonsense, but we can't pass up the opportunity to search for the bits and pieces of information that are available before it all evaporates with the passing of time. We must try to connect the dots and, with an open mind, come to our own personal conclusion. There are many things the media will never tell us. The valuable information is scattered over many books written by experts. You may not like or accept what you learn, but so be it. The future may not be as pretty as we would wish. Regardless of all the efforts to suppress facts, nobody can say today that the fall of communism in 1989 came as a surprise. Many defectors came to the West warning us about Moscow's deception strategy. But the West didn't listen. Or, we just didn't want to hear about it.

It was Anatoliy Golitsyn, a KGB Major working in a KGB think tank, who defected in 1961 and brought information nobody wanted to hear: since 1959 the KGB was developing a long-term deception strategy to manipulate public opinion on a global scale, fooling the West and economically crippling and diplomatically isolating the United States. In his book New Lies for Old published in 1984, he made 148 falsifiable predictions of what would happen. According to him, during the process the communist bloc would be dismantled. He said that the dissolution of communism would be impressive, that the Berlin Wall would fall, that the European Parliament would become completely socialist, and that cosmetic changes in the KGB would be publicized to support the myth of democratic changes. By the year 1993, 139 of these predictions had been fulfilled and only 9 turned out to be wrong. There is no question today that Perestroika opened the door for the KGB to become the central power in Russia. As Gorbachev once said, "Hug Europe to death." The KGB did everything they could to minimize the damage and discredit Golitsyn, even approving a plan for his assassination. But politicians and the CIA didn't want to hear any of that at the time anyway. Other information he brought about KGB penetrations also turned out to be true and led to further embarrassment for Western governments. But just when Golitsyn started to fade away from the spotlight, two other defectors from Czechoslovakia emerged in 1968: Ladislav Bittman[1] and General Jan Sejna.

Bittman, the officer of Czechoslovakian intelligence specializing in disinformation, mentioned this little anecdote in his book The KGB and Soviet Disinformation: in the summer of 1965, KGB Colonel Ivan Agayants came to Prague to check personally on active measures operations. He was impressed. Some 25 operatives were able to conduct more than one hundred operations around the world. Looking through newspaper clippings related to a recent operation, he commented, "Sometimes I am amazed how easy it is to play these games. If they [the West] did not have freedom of the press we would have to invent it for them."[2] Bittman pointed out that one of the major KGB objectives is to confuse and demoralize its American counterpart and warned that the most dangerous tools of the KGB are agents of influence. According to him, some KGB operatives among Soviet diplomats work as regular researchers and lobbyists in the United States. Soviet bloc countries finance large numbers of newspapers and magazines, as well as various press services. In most cases, these mass media outlets show no official connection to Eastern Europe.

The defection of General Jan Sejna was like Golitsyn's "bad dream" coming again for the CIA. Thanks to information Jan Sejna provided to the DIA during his debriefings, the Soviet involvement and support of international terrorism was finally proven and made public. It was only then that the CIA admitted that the KGB is in fact involved in the training and support of terrorism worldwide.

In 1971, Soviet diplomat Vladimir Sakharov[3] defected, claiming that as a student in Moscow's Institute of International Relations he was a member of the first graduating class of Arabists in the 1960s. The institute gave the Middle East top priority, as a key to breaking the back of Western imperialism. The KGB flooded the Arabic world with agents and built a vast intelligence network among all strata of Iranian society, including the Islamic clergy and radical students. He stressed that these revolutionaries need not be Marxist. "They can be Islamic or nationalist so long as they are strongly anti-American and, above all, show promise of being winners."[4]

In 1978, two-star Romanian Secretariate General Ion Mihai Pacepa defected. Having worked for the KGB for 27 years, he handled Yasser Arafat and Muhammar al-Gaddafi for the KGB and was privy to priceless insider information about the PLO and Libyan terrorism, which he brought to the West. His personal experience with Yuri Andropov, and knowledge of the 13th Department, also called "wet affairs", was invaluable.

In July 1982, defector Stanislav Levchenko[5] testified before the Permanent Select Committee on Intelligence, and the House of Representatives, that "the KGB gives major attention to foreign journalists by classifying them as permanent targets" raising the question of to what degree the KGB influences the American media. He also pointed out that the long-term Soviet goals in the Middle East are to erode the position of the United States in the Islamic world and destabilize the area.[6]

Most recently Sergei Tretyakov, who defected in October 2000, reminds us in the book Comrade J written by Pete Early: "I want to warn Americans. As a people, you are very naïve about Russia and its intentions. You believe because the Soviet Union no more exists, Russia now is your friend. It isn't, and I can show you how the SVR is trying to destroy the U.S. even today and even more than the KGB did during the Cold War."[7]

British security forces are saying that MI5 has been stretched to the limit lately. One in five Moscow Government officials in Great Britain are likely to be SVR agents. FBI counterintelligence chief David Szady[8] told Bill Gertz that "Russians are up to Cold War levels in both intelligence presence and activity."[9] There is no question, the Russian threat remains and is growing more severe every day. In the spring of 2006 the U.S. government finally admitted what it had long denied: that "Russia was not moving in a positive direction under ex-KGB officer Putin." What a surprise! Even Boris Yeltsin himself admitted in 1993 that all attempts to reorganize the KGB were "superficial and cosmetic," that the KGB couldn't be reformed and, in fact, it could be resurrected. Over the time of Putin's presidency, the FSB consolidated its power and today controls the government, the media, the economy, as well as military and security forces. Vladimir Putin continued what Yuri Andropov started a long time ago. And indeed, early in his presidency, he unveiled a plaque at KGB Lubyanka headquarters paying tribute to Andropov as an "outstanding political figure." Twenty five percent of senior government officials are so-called "silovniky." These "power guys" are a group of people loyal to the principles of the Cheka, the first Bolshevik political police. As Mr. Putin said many times, "There is no such thing as a former Chekist." They really believe they are the only ones who see and understand the world correctly. Back in the Soviet days, the KGB had to operate within Soviet laws and was under the control of the Communist Party Central Committee. Today it has become the state itself. All decision-making processes are in the hands of a small group of Putin's buddies from the KGB. Ion Pacepa explained, "This is like 'democratizing' Germany by putting the old, supposedly defeated Gestapo officers in charge." The anti-American, anti-Western mentality of the silovniky, that was always a part of KGB culture, has now increased in Russia. From their perspective, anyone who supports the West in Russia is automatically an internal enemy of the state. This kind of thing never makes any headlines in the media. The media doesn't pay attention to it and politicians pretend to be blind and deaf. This information has become an inconvenient truth that does not fit the overall political agenda. But let's look at it from another perspective.

Senator Jesse Helms said in the U.S. Senate, according to the Congressional Record, on December 15, 1987: "the State Department, Trade Department, and banking and financial institutions, as tax-exempt foundations, are effectively controlled by CFR,[10] the Trilateral Commission, as well as the Dartmouth and Bilderberg[11] groups . . . using them to spread and coordinate plans for a so-called New World Order. They are plotting to join forces with Kremlin leaders."

How much do you know about these organizations? Did you ever hear the media mention them? I doubt it. Not too much is known about them and absolutely nothing is known about their activities. This topic specifically is labeled as a "conspiracy theory" and you will probably be ridiculed just bringing it up. Only a few books were published on this topic. One of the Soviet Politburo documents records a meeting between Gorbachev and key members of the Trilateral Commission taking place on January 1989 in Moscow. However, this interesting news reached the public in 1991 and it didn't even make it into the mainstream media. Here is what David Rockefeller said at the annual meeting of the Bilderberg Group[11] on June 8th, 1991, in Baden Baden, Germany: "We are grateful to the Washington Post, the New York Times, Time Magazine and other great publications whose directors have attended our meetings and respected their promises of discretion for almost forty years. It would have been quite impossible for us to develop our plan for the world if we had been subjected to the lights of publicity during those years. But, now that the world is more sophisticated, it is prepared to march toward a world government and accept the supranational sovereignty of an intellectual and financial elite, which is surely preferable to the national auto determination practiced in past centuries . . . ."[12] It shouldn't be much of a surprise for those who followed this topic over time, but if you think of it, it's pretty wicked and the consequences are far-reaching. But, after all, it explains the direction that we are going.

Zbigniew Brezezinski, in his book The Grand Chessboard wrote: "In brief, the U.S. policy goal must be unapologetically twofold: to perpetuate America's own dominant position for at least a generation and preferably longer still; and to create a geopolitical framework that can absorb the inevitable shocks and strains of social-political change while evolving into the geopolitical core of shared responsibility for peaceful global management."[13] Henry Kissinger is still peddling this concept to this day.

Since I finished these interviews, other things have happened. Alexander Litvinenko was assassinated in November 2006 in London. There was an assassination attempt on Oleg Gordievsky in November 2007[14], and Anna Politkovskaya[15] was murdered. Only 21 cases from over 260 journalists murdered in Russia, since the collapse of the Soviet Union, were solved. Russia invaded Georgia on August 8, 2008, and closed the gas supply pipeline to Europe in January 2009. Two weeks later, Russian Prime Minister and Ex-KGB officer Vladimir Putin returned to Dresden, Germany, to receive the Dresden Medal of Honor from the hand of Saxony's governor Stanislaw Tillich, a former communist functionary himself! It finally became clear to the world that the rise of Russian imperial power is real. Oil and natural gas have replaced nukes. Is the West going to be neutered? Are we going to witness the suicide of the West?

It looks like the Kremlin's strategy of deception has been effective, and there is no danger that the West is willing to figure it out. The West has accepted former communists as business partners and the media doesn't have the determination or knowledge to bring the facts together and analyze the situation. After all, the truth is economically inconvenient. Secretary of State Hillary Clinton, during her visit to Mexico in April 2009, proclaimed, "Ideology is so yesterday." This weakness, lack of resolve, stupidity, and incompetence will only add up to our defeat.

The death of communism seems to be wishful thinking and democracy may be on the road to self-destruction. The situation today is the result of strategic blindness and the unwillingness to admit problems due to the primacy of economics. Or is the political interest overriding national security interest? For Westerners, it is hard to realize that, in Russia, Vladimir Putin is genuinely popular and that there is no way to change the public perception. Russia still thinks that it was betrayed. What is even worse is that Western democracies are refusing to see it, and Americans make no effort to understand people in the rest of the world.

In the meantime, Russian foreign and domestic policy will create a more and more unstable international situation. The old KGB strategy didn't go away. The objective remains the same: turning world opinion against U.S. foreign policy, isolating the United States from its allies and friends in Europe, and expanding traditional mistrust in Third World countries. The SVR continues to build up a network of agents of influence inside Western governments to manipulate the decision-making process, to penetrate the American press, to conduct smear campaigns against presidential and congressional candidates as well as politicians considered to be hostile or dangerous by Russian leaders, and to conduct operations that increase racial tension within American society. In the long term, the objective of Russian economic warfare and disinformation is to influence American economic relations with the outside world to benefit Russia by manipulating the international markets to the advantage of the Russian economy.

Where does all this leave us? In the movie, the puzzle is always solved at the end. The good guys win and the bad guys get punished. But in real life, it's quite different. Information is distorted and destroyed, politicians put spin on the issues, and the public is massaged to death by the media. The prosecution can never collect evidence to make a court case out of it and the villains can never be identified beyond a reasonable doubt. So, in this case, we may never know for sure who framed Roger Rabbit.

Discussion Participants

Tennent H. ("Pete") Bagley

Former CIA chief of Soviet block counterintelligence. He served twenty-two years in the CIA, handling spies and defectors in Clandestine Services.

The author of: *Spy Wars; moles, mysteries, and deadly games*

John Bok

He was Vaclav Havel's (President of Czechoslovakia) first bodyguard and later became one of the first FBIS (Czechoslovak Intelligence Service) officers.

Co-author of: *Jan 'Kato' Kavan-A Story of the Bona Fide Man*

Vladimir Bukovsky

Soviet Dissident and survivor of Gulag. He was hired by President Boris Yeltsin to build defense for the trial the Communist Party filed against Yeltsin. Bukovsky agreed under one condition: he would get access to the KGB archives. He spent one year in the archives scanning thousands of classified documents into his laptop computer.

The author of: *To Build a Castle, Judgment in Moscow*

Petr Cibulka

Former Czech dissident and political prisoner. The Chairman of the Right Block Party. In 1992 he acquired and published data from the Secret Police files disclosing over 200,000 names of STB officers and collaborators in Czechoslovakia.

Angelo Codevilla

He is a professor of international relations at Boston University and Vice Chairman of the U.S. Army War College Board of Visitors. He received his B.A. from Rutgers University, an M.A. from Notre Dame University, and his Ph.D. in Security Studies, U.S. Foreign Policy, and Political Theory from the Claremont Graduate School. Professor Codevilla has been a U.S. Naval Officer, an Assistant Professor at the Grove City College and North Dakota State College, a U.S. Foreign Service Officer, and a member of President-Elect Reagan's Transition Team within the U.S. Department of State. He dealt with matters affecting the U.S. Intelligence Community and served as a U.S. Senate Staff member dealing with oversight of the intelligence services.

Author of: *The Character of Nations: How Politics Makes and Breaks Prosperity, Family, and Civility, Between The Alps and a Hard Place, Informing Statecraft: Intelligence for a New Century, Arms Control Delusion, While Others Build: The Commonsense Approach to the Strategic Defense Initiative, War: Ends and Means, Modern France*

Frantisek Doskocil

A Communist Central Committee member and CIA agent. He was recruited as a sleeper in 1968 and activated in 1975. He was arrested in 1990 by STB and jailed without a trial. He was pardoned by President Vaclav Havel seven months later only after signing an agreement that he would keep silent for 10 years.

Author of: *Breaking Through: To be a CIA Agent in the Czechoslovak Communist Party*

Joseph D.Douglass, Jr., PhD

Former national security affair consultant with 30 years experience in defense policy, technology, and intelligence. He served as the Assistant Director of Arms Control and Disarmament Agency during Reagan's administration. He is a recognized authority on U.S. and Soviet nuclear strategy, communist decision-making, and Soviet strategic intelligence operations.

The author of: *Soviet Strategy for Nuclear War, America the Vulnerable: The Treat of Chemical and Biological Warfare, Communist Decision-Making: An Inside View, Why the Soviet Union Violates Arms Control Treaties, Communist Decision-making: An Inside View, Soviet Military Strategy in Europe, Red Cocaine: Drugging of America, Betrayed*

Edward Jay Epstein

Political analyst, author, and a specialist on Soviet disinformation and deception. He studied government at Cornell and Harvard and received a PhD from Harvard in 1973. He taught political science at MIT and UCLA.

The author of: *Inquest: The Warren Commission and the Establishment of Truth, Legend: The Secret World of Lee Harvey Oswald, News From Nowhere, Deception: The Invisible War Between the KGB and the CIA, Agency of Fear, Dossier: The Secret History of Armand Hammer, The Big Picture: The New Logic of Money and Power in Hollywood*

Robert M. Gates

The U.S. Secretary of Defense. He served as Deputy Director of the CIA from 1986 until 1989, Deputy National Security Adviser at the White House from 1989-1991, and Director of CIA from 1991 until 1993.

The author of: *From the Shadows: The Ultimate Insider's Story of Five Presidents and How They Won the Cold War*

Bill Gertz

A journalist and the defense and national security reporter for The Washington Times.

Author of: *Betrayal: How the Clinton Administration Undermined American Security, The China Threat: How the People's Republic Targets America, Breakdown: How America's Intelligence Failures Led to September 11, Treachery: How America's Friends And Foes Are Secretly Arming Our Enemies, Enemies: How Americas Foes Steel Our Vital Secrets–And How We Let It Happen, The Failure Factory: How Unelected Bureaucrats, Liberal Democrats, and Big Government Republicans Are Undermining America's Security and Leading Us to War*

Oleg Gordievsky

KGB Colonel and resident in London, double agent working for British MI6, and adviser to Mikhail Gorbachev and Margaret Thatcher.

The author of: *KGB–The Inside Story*

Vladimir Hucin

Anti-communist activist and political prisoner in Czechoslovakia. After the revolution in 1989 he was nominated by the Alliance of Political Prisoners to the newly formed BIS (Czech Intelligence Service) and became a counter-intelligence officer specialized in leftist extremism. When he threatened to expose hidden communist structures and plans for the return to totalitarian methods, he was arrested in 2001 and jailed for over a year. The trial that followed took almost five years. In the fall of 2006 he was acquitted of all charges.

Author of: *It's Not About Me, It's About You, Heroes Get No Gratitude*

Stanislav Milota

Czech cinematographer, dissident, signatory of Charter 77, and personal friend of Vaclav Havel. He became the first Chief of Staff for President Vaclav Havel in December 1989 and he resigned from this position four months later. Since 1997 he served on The Council for Radio and Television Broadcasting. He resigned from this position in 2001.

Jeff R. Nyquist

The Geo-political analyst and a renowned expert on America's fatal illusion of a balance of power, as well as diplomatic and Cold War history.

The author of: *Origins of the Fourth World War*

Ion Mihai Pacepa

Lt. General of Romanian Intelligence–the highest ranking defector ever from the Eastern bloc. A former chief of the Romanian Espionage Service and national security adviser to the country's President Nicolas Ceausescu. He was the handler of Yasser Arafat and Omar Kadafi for the KGB.

The author of: *Red Horizons, Programmed to Kill: Lee Harvey Oswald, the Soviet KGB, and the Kennedy Assassination*

Jaromir Stetina

A member of the Czech Senate, and a former journalist specialized in war conflicts in Europe, Asia, and Africa. He is the author of many books and television documentaries. In 1990 he moved to Moscow as a foreign correspondent, where he covered numerous conflicts in the former Soviet Union, including Chechnya.

Pavel Zacek

Director of the Institute for Studies of Totalitarian Regimes and former Director of the Interior Ministry Archives in Prague, Czech Republic. He was also Deputy Chairman of the Office for the Documentation and Investigation of Crimes of Communism. According to his research, the Czech StB trained 134 terrorists between 1981-1990. In 1985, the StB files contained 4000 terrorists from 190 groups around the world. The StB directly controlled 378 of them.

Author of: *In Charge of the STB: The Collapse of the Regime According to the Diary of a Secret Police Officer*

Ludvik Zifcak

Former Czech Secret Police (StB) officer of the 2nd Division/2nd Directorate working undercover as Milan Ruzicka. He was in charge of establishing the Independent Students Alliance and leading the students' demonstration in November 1989 that triggered the Velvet Revolution. He played the role of "dead student" Martin Smid, "killed" by the brutal riot police.

The author of: *Zabili jsme Kennedyho*

Footnotes

PART 1

1. Yuri Vladimirovich Andropov (1914-1984)—head of the KGB and the general secretary of the Communist Party's Central Committee. The turning point in Andropov's career was his transfer to Moscow (1951), where he was assigned to the party's Secretariat staff, considered a training ground for promising young officials. As ambassador to Hungary (July 1954–March 1957), he played a major role in coordinating the Soviet invasion of that country. Andropov then returned to Moscow, rising rapidly through the Communist hierarchy and, in 1967, becoming head of the KGB. Andropov's policies as head of the KGB were repressive; his tenure was noted for its suppression of political dissidents. Andropov was elected to the Politburo, and, as Soviet leader Leonid Brezhnev's health declined, Andropov began to position himself for succession, resigning his KGB post in 1982. Andropov was chosen by the Communist Party Central Committee to succeed Brezhnev as general secretary on November 12, scarcely two days after Brezhnev's death. He consolidated his power by becoming chairman of the Presidium of the Supreme Soviet (president) on June 16, 1983. Ill health overtook him by August 1983, and thereafter he was never seen again in public. In the West, if Andropov is remembered at all, it is for his brutal suppression of political dissidence at home and for his role in planning the 1968 invasion of Czechoslovakia. He was the godfather of Russia's new era of deception operations aimed at improving the badly damaged image of Soviet rulers in the West. In 1961, he was elected full member of the CPSU Central Committee and was promoted to the Secretariat of the CPSU Central Committee in 1962. In 1967, he was relieved of his work in the Central Committee apparatus and appointed head of the KGB on recommendation of Mikhail Suslov. For Hungarians Andropov is a symbol of the terror that followed the Soviet intrusion. He deported thousands of Hungarians into Russia and executed hundreds. The destruction of the dissident movement is Andropov's deed as well. He quietly, calmly and as if without sensibility incinerated the dissident movement. The deportation of Alexander Solzjenitsyn from the country, Andrei Sakharov's exile to Gorky town, the wide-spread use of psychiatric clinics for dissidents, open-and-closed investigations–all of this is Andropov's work. When it turned out that the CIA and the State Department had few details about Andropov—not even the name or fate of his wife—the press took whatever it could find. The press

couldn't admit that virtually nothing is known about this man: not the names of his parents, ethnic background, education, war service, preferences in music and literature, linguistic abilities, his ideas. We don't even know how tall he was. The myth about Andropov as a reformer, progressive politician and humanist was created by Andropov himself with the help of his numerous loyal followers. Harrison Salisbury in The New York Times described him as "a witty conversationalist," and "a bibliophile" and "connoisseur of modern art." Charles Fenyvesi in The Washington Post passed along a rumor that he was partly Jewish. Soon there were reports that Andropov was a man of extraordinary accomplishment, with some interests and proclivities that are unusual in a former head of the KGB. According to an article in The Washington Post, Andropov "is fond of cynical political jokes, collects abstract art, likes jazz and Gypsy music," and "has a record of stepping out of his high party official's cocoon to contact dissidents." Also, he swims, plays tennis, and wears clothes that are "sharply tailored in a West European style." Besides the Viennese waltz and the Hungarian czarda, he "dances the tango gracefully." The Wall Street journal added that Andropov "likes Glenn Miller records, good scotch whisky, Oriental rugs, and American books." To the list of his musical favorites, Time added "Chubby Checker, Frank Sinatra, Peggy Lee, and Bob Eberly," and, asserting that he had once worked as a Volga boatman, said that he enjoyed singing "hearty renditions of Russian songs" at after-theater parties. The Christian Science Monitor suggested that he has "tried his hand at writing verse-in Russian, as it happens, and of a comic variety."

2. Mikhail Sergeyevich Gorbachev (*1931)—the last General Secretary of the Communist Party of the Soviet Union, serving from 1985 until 1991, and also the last head of state of the USSR, serving from 1988 until its collapse in 1991. Gorbachev owed his steady rise to power to the patronage of Mikhail Suslov, the powerful chief ideologist of the CPSU. During Yuri Andropov's tenure as General Secretary (1982–1984), Gorbachev became one of the Politburo's most visible and active members. With responsibility over personnel, working together with Andropov, 20 percent of the top echelon of government ministers and regional governors were replaced, often with younger men. Gorbachev was elected General Secretary by Politburo in 1985. His attempts at reform as well as summit conferences with United States President Ronald Reagan contributed to the end of the Cold War, ended the political supremacy of the Communist Party of the Soviet Union and led to the dissolution of the Soviet Union. In 1990, Gorbachev was awarded the Nobel Peace Prize for "his leading role in the peace process which today characterizes important parts of the international community."

3. KGB—the Soviet Union's premier security agency, secret police, and intelligence agency, from 1954 to 1991. The name of the largest of the Russian successors to the KGB is the FSB. The KGB was an organization with a military hierarchy aimed at providing national defense, and the defense of the Communist Party of the Soviet Union. Most of the information about the KGB remains secret. The first of the forerunners of the KGB, the Cheka, was established on December 19, 1917. It replaced the Tsarist Okhrana. The Cheka underwent several names and organizational changes over the years, becoming in succession the State Politi-

cal Directorate (OGPU), People's Commissariat for State Security (NKGB), and Ministry for State Security (MGB), among others. In March 1953, Lavrentiy Beria consolidated the Russian Ministry of Internal Affairs (MVD) and the MGB into one body—the MVD; within a year, Beria was executed and MVD was split. The reformed MVD retained its police and law enforcement powers, while the second, new agency, the KGB, assumed internal and external security and intelligence functions, and was subordinate to the Council of Ministers. On July 5, 1978 the KGB was re-christened as the "KGB of the Soviet Union," with its chairman holding a ministerial council seat. On November 6, 1991, the KGB officially ceased to exist. Its services were divided into two separate organizations—the FSB for Internal Security and the Foreign Intelligence Service (SVR) for Foreign Intelligence Gathering. The KGB achieved a remarkable string of successes in the early stages of its history. The then-comparatively lax security of foreign powers such as the United States and the United Kingdom allowed the KGB unprecedented opportunities to penetrate the foreign intelligence agencies and governments with its own ideologically motivated agents such as the Cambridge Five. Arguably, the Soviet Union's most important intelligence coup, the Cambridge Five, detailed information concerning the building of the atomic bomb (the Manhattan Project), which occurred due to well-placed KGB agents within that project such as Klaus Fuchs and Theodore Hall. The KGB also pursued enemies of the Soviet Union and of Joseph Stalin. These include people such as Leon Trotsky and groups like the counter-revolutionary White Guards, eventually achieving Trotsky's assassination. Occasionally, the KGB conducted assassinations abroad, mainly of Soviet Bloc defectors, and often helped other Communist country security services with their assassinations. An infamous example is the September 1978 killing of Bulgarian emigrant Georgi Markov in London, where Bulgarian secret agents used a KGB-designed umbrella gun to shoot Markov dead with a ricin-poisoned pellet. There are also allegations that the KGB was behind the assassination attempt against Pope John Paul II in 1981 and the death of Dag Hammarskjöld in an air crash in 1961. The highest-ranking Soviet Bloc intelligence defector, Lt. Gen. Ion Mihai Pacepa, described his conversation with the head of the Romanian Communist Party Nicolae Ceausescu who told him about "ten international leaders the Kremlin killed or tried to kill:" "Laszlo Rajk and Imre Nagy of Hungary; Lucretiu Patrascanu and Gheorghiu-Dej in Romania; Rudolf Slansky the head of Czechoslovakia, and Jan Masaryk, that country's chief diplomat; the shah of Iran; Palmiro Togliatti of Italy; American President John F. Kennedy; and China's Mao Zedong." Pacepa provided some additional details, such as a plot to kill Mao Zedong with the help of Lin Biao organized by KGB and noted that among the leaders of Moscow's satellite intelligence services there was unanimous agreement that the KGB had been involved in the assassination of President Kennedy. Ludvik Zifcak in his book published in 2008 Zabili jsme Kennedyho co-incidentally supports Pacepa's thesis quoting from KGB archives that Oswald's wife Marina was indeed the KGB agent and to her credit the FBI was unable to prove Oswald's connection with KGB.

4. Vladimir Vladimirovich Putin (*1952)–spy in the old USSR who has become the leader of modern Russia. He was the second President of Russia and currently

serves as the Prime Minister of Russia and Chairman of United Russia and the Council of Ministers of the Union of Russia and Belarus. He became acting President on December 31, 1999, when President Boris Yeltsin resigned. Putin won the 2000 presidential election and in 2004 was re-elected for the second term lasting until May 7, 2008. An official biography released by the Kremlin gave just four lines of chronological information and included a gap of 21 years, from 1975 to 1996. Prior to his appointment, Putin was one of the most powerful men in the Kremlin — in a quiet, behind-the-scenes way. He was simultaneously head of the KGB's main successor service, the FSB, and secretary of the presidential Security Council, the powerful advisory body that coordinates the activities of Russia's armed forces, security agencies, and police. In his own biography, *First Person,* translated into English in 2000 and paid for by his election campaign, he speaks of humble beginnings. His father was a conscript in the Soviet Navy, where he served in the submarine fleet in the early 1930s, subsequently serving with the NKVD in a sabotage group during World War II. His paternal grandfather, Spiridon Ivanovich Putin (1879 – 1965) was employed at Vladimir Lenin's dacha (Gorki) as a cook, and after Lenin's death in 1924, he continued to work for Lenin's wife, Nadezhda Krupskaya. He would later cook for Joseph Stalin when the Soviet leader visited one of his dachas in the Moscow region. Spiridon later was employed at a dacha belonging to the Moscow City Committee of the Communist Party of the Soviet Union, at which the young Putin would visit him. Putin joined the KGB in 1975 upon graduation from university, and underwent a year's training at the KGB school in Okhta, Leningrad. He served at the Fifth Directorate of the KGB, which combated political dissent in the Soviet Union. He then received an offer to transfer to foreign intelligence First Chief Directorate of the KGB and was sent for additional year long training to the Dzerzhinsky KGB Higher School in Moscow and then in the early eighties—the Red Banner Yuri Andropov KGB Institute in Moscow (now the Academy of Foreign Intelligence). From 1985 to 1990 the KGB stationed Putin in Dresden, East Germany. Following the collapse of the East German regime, Putin was recalled to the Soviet Union and returned to Leningrad. Putin was also on the advisory board of the German real estate holding Saint Petersburg Immobilien und Beteiligungs AG (SPAG), which has been investigated by German prosecutors for money laundering. He was called to Moscow and in June 1996 assumed position of a Deputy Chief of the Presidential Property Management Department headed by Pavel Borodin. He occupied this position until March 1997. On March 26, 1997 President Boris Yeltsin appointed Putin deputy chief of Presidential Staff, which he remained until May 1998, and chief of the Main Control Directorate of the Presidential Property Management Department (until June 1998). On June 27, 1997, at the Saint Petersburg Mining Institute, Putin defended his Candidate of Science dissertation in economics titled "The Strategic Planning of Regional Resources Under the Formation of Market Relations." According to Clifford G.Gaddy, a senior fellow at The Brookings Institution, 16 of the 20 pages that open a key section of Putin's work were copied either word for word or with minute alterations from a management study, Strategic Planning and Policy, written by US professors William King and David Cleland and translated into Russian by a KGB-related institute in the early 1990s. Six diagrams and tables were also copied. The first Decree that Putin signed December 31, 1999, was the one "On guarantees for former president of the Russian Federation and members of his family." This ensured that "corruption charges against the outgoing president and his relatives" would not be pursued. In December 2007, the Russian sociologist Igor Eidman (VCIOM) qualified the regime that had solidified under Putin as "the power of bureaucratic oligarchy" which had "the traits of extreme right-wing dictatorship — the dominance of state-monopoly capital in the economy, silovniki structures in governance, clericalism and statism in ideology." Putin was Time Magazine's Person of the Year for 2007, given the title for his "extraordinary feat of leadership in taking a country that was in chaos and bringing it stability."

5. Boris Nikolayevich Yeltsin (1931-2007)—the first President of the Russian Federation, serving from 1991 to 1999. He was elected president with 57 percent of the vote. By the time he left office, Yeltsin had an approval rating of 2 percent. The Yeltsin era was marked by widespread corruption, economic collapse, and enormous political and social problems. His confrontations with parliament climaxed in the October 1993 Russian constitutional crisis, when Yeltsin called up tanks to shell the Russian White House, blasting out his opponents in parliament. Later in 1993, Yeltsin imposed a new constitution with strong presidential powers, which was approved by referendum in December. Just hours before the first day of 2000, Yeltsin made a surprise announcement of his resignation, leaving the presidency in the hands of Vladimir Putin.
6. The Palestine Liberation Organization (PLO)—political and paramilitary organization regarded by the Arab League since October 1974 as the "sole legitimate representative of the Palestinian people." In 1964 the first PLO Council, consisting of 422 Palestinian representatives handpicked by the KGB, approved the Palestinian National Charteróa document that had been drafted in Moscow. The Palestinian National Covenant and the Palestinian Constitution were also born in Moscow, with the help of Ahmed Shuqairy, a KGB influence agent who became the first PLO chairman. The Romanian espionage service (DIE) was responsible for providing the PLO with logistical support. Except for the arms, which were supplied by the KGB and the East German Stasi, everything else came from Bucharest. Even the PLO uniforms and the PLO stationery were manufactured in Romania. The PLO was considered by the USA and Israel to be a terrorist organization until the Madrid Conference in 1991. Most of the rest of the world recognized the PLO as the legitimate representatives of the Palestinian people from 1974 onwards (after the PLO's admission to the UN). The most notable of what were considered terrorist acts committed by member organizations of the PLO were:
   - The 1970 Avivim school bus massacre by the Democratic Front for the Liberation of Palestine (DFLP) killed nine children, three adults and crippled 19.
   - In the late 1960s and early 1970s, the Popular Front for the Liberation of Palestine, the second-largest PLO faction after al-Fatah, carried out a number of attacks and plane hijackings mostly directed at Israel, most infamously the Dawson's Field hijackings, which precipitated the Black September in Jordan crisis.

- In 1972 the Black September Organization carried out the Munich Massacre of Israeli Olympic athletes.
- In 1974 members of the DFLP seized a school in Israel and killed a total of 26 students and adults and wounded over 70 in the Ma'alot massacre.
- The 1975 Savoy Hotel hostage situation killing 8 civilians and 3 soldiers, carried out by Fatah.
- The 1978 Coastal Road massacre killing 37 Israeli civilians and wounding 76, also carried out by Fatah.
- According to a 1993 report by the British National Criminal Intelligence Service, the PLO was "the richest of all terrorist organizations," with $8-$10 billion in assets and an annual income of $1.5-$2 billion from "donations, extortion, payoffs, illegal arms dealing, drug trafficking, money laundering, fraud, etc." The Daily Telegraph reported in 1999 that the PLO had $50 billion in secret investments around the world.

7. The Lubyanka is the popular name for the headquarters of the KGB and affiliated prison on Lubyanka Square in Moscow. It is a large building with a facade of yellow brick, designed by Alexander V. Ivanov in 1897. Although the Soviet secret police changed its name many times, its headquarters remained in this building. Secret police chiefs from Lavrentiy Beria to Yuri Andropov used the same office on the third floor, which looked down on the statue of Cheka founder Felix Dzerzhinsky.
8. Alexander Mikhailovich Sakharovsky—head for KGB from 1956 till 1971. He personally ordered the assassination of several KGB defectors and Soviet dissidents overseas.
9. Anatoliy Mikhaylovich Golitsyn—Soviet KGB defector. Golitsyn worked in the strategic planning department of the KGB in the rank of Major. In 1961 under the name "Anatole Klimov" he was assigned to the Soviet embassy in Helsinki, Finland as vice consular and attaché. He defected with his wife and daughter to the Central Intelligence Agency (CIA) via Helsinki on December 15, 1961. As a defector, he provided "a wide range of intelligence to the CIA on the operations of most of the 'Lines' (departments) at the Helsinki and other residencies, as well as KGB methods of recruiting and running agents." He is an Honorary Commander of the Order of the British Empire and, as late as 1984, was an American citizen. In November 1962, KGB head Vladimir Semichastny approved a plan for assassination of Golitsyn and other "particularly dangerous traitors." KGB made significant efforts to discredit Golitsyn by promoting disinformation that he was involved in illegal smuggling operations. Golitsyn provided information about many famous Soviet agents including Kim Philby, Donald Duart Maclean, Guy Burgess, John Vassall, double agent Aleksandr Kopatzky who worked in Germany, and others. It was only with the defection of Anatoliy Golitsyn in 1961 that Philby was confirmed as a Soviet mole. Golitsyn was a figure of significant controversy in the Western intelligence community. Military writer, the British General John Hackett and CIA counter-intelligence director James Angleton identified Golitsyn as "The most valuable defector ever to reach the West." However, the official historian for Britain's MI5 Christopher Andrew described him as an "unreliable conspiracy theorist." Andrew believes

that although intelligence data provided by Golitsyn were reliable, some of his global political assessments of the Soviet and KGB strategy are questionable. Golitsyn's claims of widespread KGB double agent infiltration in the CIA also contributed to Angleton's growing paranoia, which ultimately led to Angleton's dismissal from the CIA. In 1984, Golitsyn published the book New Lies For Old, wherein he predicted the collapse of the communist bloc orchestrated from above. He warned about a long-term deception strategy designed to lull the West into a false sense of security, and finally economically cripple and diplomatically isolate the United States. Author Mark Riebling stated that of 194 predictions made in New Lies For Old, 139 had been fulfilled by 1993, 9 seemed 'clearly wrong,' and the other 46 were 'not soon falsifiable.

10. Perestroika—the term for the political and economic reforms introduced in June 1987 by the Soviet leader Mikhail Gorbachev. Its literal meaning is "restructuring," referring to the restructuring of the Soviet economy. Perestroika is often argued to be one reason for the fall of communist political forces in the Soviet Union and Eastern Europe, and as the end of the Cold War.

PART 2

1. Georgi Arbatov—one of the icons of world political affairs. For decades, he was one of the most influential people in Moscow. He gave advice to Soviet and Russian statesmen, from Khrushchev to Yeltsin. He had the license to talk with western politicians in Moscow or in western capitals. He is a 1973 graduate of the Moscow State Institute for International Relations and has done postgraduate work at the Institute for World Economy and International Relations of the Academy of Sciences of the Union of Soviet Socialist Republics. Six months after Andropov's appointment to the KGB, the USSR Academy of Science announced the creation of the new Institute for the Study of the USA headed by Georgi Arbatov, an expert in ideological warfare. Arbatov has become the darling of the U.S. press. With American journalists starved for any contact with Moscow insiders Arbatov was able to supply a menu of deception and disinformation. His Institute was created solely to serve Soviet intelligence. He and his Institute have been involved in so-called Active Measures activities that include overt and covert propaganda, manipulation of American and Canadian front organizations, forgeries, and other means of deliberate deception. Immediately after the creation of the Institute, he started to provide cover jobs to the KGB and GRU officers. He personally began traveling abroad several times a year as a member of scientific groups, delegations or Soviet public organizations. By the early 1970s Arbatov forged contacts and friendly relations with many prominent American and European scholars and political figures. With the help of the KGB specialists in disinformation he created the myth that he is the "chief spokes man of the Kremlin on Soviet-American relations on problems of disarmament and so on. Arbatov has played a leading role in the politics of post-Soviet Russia, as a member of the Russian Parliament (Duma) from 1994 to 2003, and as vice chairman of the liberal YABLOKO Party from 2001. While in Parliament, he was deputy chairman of the Duma Defense Committee. He was a participant in the START I negotiations in 1990 and was a special adviser to the Russian

Minister of Defense from 1997 to 2001. He currently serves on advisory boards for the Russian Ministry of Foreign Affairs and the Russian Security Council.

2. Richard Edgar Pipes (*1923)—American historian who specializes in Russian history, particularly with respect to the history of the Soviet Union. During the Cold War era he headed Team B, a team of analysts that analyzed the strategic capacities and goals of the Soviet military and political leadership.
3. George Robert Ackworth Conquest (*1917)—British historian, became a well-known writer and researcher on the Soviet Union with the publication The Great Terror. He is also an adjunct fellow of the Center for Strategic and International Studies in Washington, D.C., and a former research associate of Harvard University's Ukrainian Research Institute. He is a member of the board of the Institute for European Defense and Strategic Studies.
4. Joseph Stalin (1878–1953)—General Secretary of the Communist Party of the Soviet Union's Central Committee from 1922 until his death in 1953. In the years following Lenin's death in 1924, he rose to become the leader of the Soviet Union and launched a command economy, replacing the New Economic Policy of the 1920s with Five-Year Plans and launching a period of rapid industrialization and economic collectivization. During the late 1930s, Stalin launched the Great Purge (also known as the "Great Terror"), a campaign to purge the Communist Party of people accused of corruption or treachery. In light of revelations from the Soviet archives, historians now estimate that nearly 700,000 people were executed. Stalin vastly increased the scope and power of the state's secret police and intelligence agencies. Under his guiding hand, Soviet intelligence forces began to set up intelligence networks in most of the major nations of the world, including Germany, Great Britain, France, Japan, and the United States. Stalin saw no difference between espionage, communist political propaganda actions, and state-sanctioned violence, and he began to integrate all of these activities within the NKVD. Stalin made considerable use of the Communist International movement in order to infiltrate agents and to ensure that foreign Communist parties remained pro-Soviet and pro-Stalin.
5. Vladimir Ilyich Lenin (1870-1924)—Russian revolutionary, Bolshevik communist politician, principal leader of the October Revolution and the first head of the Union of Soviet Socialist Republics, better known as the Soviet Union. His contributions to Marxist theory are commonly referred to as Leninism. On November 8, 1917 Lenin was elected the Chairman of the Council of People's Commissars by the Russian Congress of Soviets. To protect the newly established Bolshevik government from counterrevolutionaries and other political opponents, the Bolsheviks created a Soviet state security organization, the Cheka, in December 1917. Lenin had appointed Felix Dzerzhinsky to head the Cheka and instructed him to commence the "Red Terror".
6. The Strategic Defense Initiative (SDI)—proposal by U.S. President Ronald Reagan on March 23, 1983 to use ground and space-based systems to protect the United States from attack by strategic nuclear ballistic missiles. The initiative focused on strategic defense rather than the prior strategic offense doctrine of mutual assured destruction. It gained the popular name Star Wars after the 1977 film by George Lucas. The concept for the space-based portion was to use

lasers to shoot down incoming Soviet intercontinental ballistic missiles (ICBMs) armed with nuclear warheads.

7. Velvet Revolution refers to a non-violent revolution in Czechoslovakia that saw the overthrow of the Communist government in November 1989.
8. Ion Iliescu (*1930)—Romanian politician. He joined the Communist Party in 1953, and became a member of the Central Committee in 1965, serving in various positions until Nicolae Ceausescu was overthrown in 1989. Iliescu was the elected President of Romania for eleven years (three terms), from 1990 to 1992, 1992 to 1996, and 2000 to 2004. His first and second terms were separated from the third term by the presidency of Emil Constantinescu. In 2005, investigations began that could eventually lead to Iliescu's trial on a number of charges, including crimes against humanity, related to considerable abuses of power he allegedly committed during the years 1989-1990, especially during the Romanian Revolution.
9. Vaclav Havel (*1936)—Czech writer, former dissident, politician, President of the Czech Republic. He comes from a prominent entrepreneurial/intellectual family in Prague. His grandfather Hugo Vavrecka — a former ambassador to Hungry and Minister of Propaganda in 1938—was a Nazi sympathizer and one of the Bata's managers during the WW II. Vaclav's uncle, Ivan Vavrecka, was allowed to legally immigrate to Argentina in 1949. Vaclav's other uncle, Milos Havel (1899-1968), the former owner of Barrandov Studios traveled to Western Germany in 1951 and opened a restaurant in Munich. The place became a popular hang out for the employees of Radio Free Europe. All this didn't create any trouble for Vaclav. He studied at Economics Faculty in Prague in 1955-57 and in 1962-66 dramaturgy at DAMU (Theater Academy). In 1964 he married Olga Šplíchalová and in May 1968 he traveled to Western Europe and the USA where he met Jiri Voskovec, Frantisek Peroutka, and Pavel Tigrid. In 1969 he wrote the Ten Points proclamation addressed to the government and UV KSC as a protest against the current trend in the politics. In 1975 he wrote an open letter to the President Gustav Husak analyzing the state of the society and politics in Czechoslovakia. Vaclav Havel was one of the inciters of the Charter 77 proclamation, which he signed on January 1, 1977 and one of its first spokesmen (together with J.Patocka and J.Hajek). He was jailed between January 14–May 20, 1977 and then again January 28–March 13, 1978. In May 1979 he was arrested and then sentenced to four and half years in prison. He was released from prison in May 1983 for health reasons and latter arrested twice again in 1988. On January 16, 1989 he was arrested and sentenced to nine months in prison but released on May 17, 1989. Then he was arrested for a couple of days in October 1989. He negotiated a smooth transfer of the government by promising communists they would not be punished and in December of 1989 he became the President of Czechoslovakia. When the Czech Republic was formed on January 26, 1993 he was elected its first president. After his wife Olga died in 1996, he married in 1997 in a secret ceremony actress Dagmar Veskrnova. In 1998 presidential election Vaclav Havel was re-elected by margin of one vote in the second round of voting. The presidential vote was conducted in the absence of the Republican Party Chairman Miroslav Sladek who was stripped his parliamentary immunity

and arrested on charges of inciting racial hatred. The election took place on January 20 and Sladek was acquitted and released on January 23. However many Czechs were not bothered by the legitimacy of Havel's one-vote victory. In 1990 Vaclav Havel said he knows how to bite (addressing the communists), but later he choose the road of forgetting the communists' criminal past. He also didn't do anything against policies discriminating against emigrants. Restitution of emigrants' properties and their return to the Czech Republic would definitely affect political development in the country. This way he became the guarantor of continuity between former communist and new post-communist power.

10. Mikhail Andreyevich Suslov (1902-1982)—Soviet statesman, ideologist, and a member of the Politburo and Secretariat of the Communist Party of the Soviet Union. He became the most prominent intellectual in the Soviet leadership under Joseph Stalin and held considerable sway over political decision making in the Soviet Union and beyond during the post-Stalin era. Suslov was known both as the Soviet "Red Eminence" for his loyalty to hard-line communism and as the Soviet "Grey Eminence" for his behind-the-scenes importance and asceticism. Suslov led the October 1964 coup d'état that replaced Nikita Khrushchev with Leonid Brezhnev and is credited for promoting future Soviet leaders Yuri Andropov and Mikhail Gorbachev to top positions in the party and KGB.
11. Solidarity—Polish trade union federation founded in September 1980 at the Gdansk Shipyard, and originally led by Lech Walesa. Solidarity was the first non-communist trade union in a communist country. In the 1980s it constituted a broad anti-communist social movement.
12. Détente—French term, meaning a relaxing or easing. The term has been used in international politics since the early 1970s. Generally, it may be applied to any international situation where previously hostile nations not involved in an open war de-escalate tensions through diplomacy and confidence-building measures. However, it is primarily used in reference to the general reduction in the tension between the Soviet Union and the United States and a thawing of the Cold War, occurring from the late 1960s until the start of the 1980s. The main problem with détente is that there was no clear definition of how friendly and co-operative these two nations were to become. Some historians and politicians have argued that this lack of clarity in the détente relationship was mainly to blame for the collapse of American-Soviet relations at the end of the 1970s.
13. Socialism—refers to a broad set of economic theories of social organization advocating public or state ownership and administration of the means of production and distribution of goods, and a society characterized by equality for all individuals, with an egalitarian method of compensation. Modern socialism originated in the late 19th-century intellectual and working class political movement that criticized the effects of industrialization and private ownership on society. Though often conflated with the thought of Karl Marx, Marx merely saw socialism as a stage in the ineluctable transition from capitalism to communism.
14. Mao Zedong (also Mao Tse-Tung) (1893–1976)—Chinese Communist leader. Mao led the Communist Party of China to victory against the Kuomintang in the Chinese Civil War, and was the leader of the People's Republic of China from its establishment in 1949 until his death in 1976. Chairman Mao has been regarded

as an important figure in modern world history, and is officially held in high regard in China where he is known as a great revolutionary, political strategist, and military mastermind who defeated Generalissimo Chiang Kai-shek in the Chinese Civil War, and then through his policies transformed the country into a major world power. However, Mao remains a controversial figure to this day, with a contentious and ever-evolving legacy. Critics blame many of Mao's socio-political programs, such as the Great Leap Forward and the Cultural Revolution, for causing severe damage to the culture, society, economy, and foreign relations of China, as well as a possible death toll in the tens of millions.

15. Nikita Sergeyevich Khrushchev (1894–1971)—leader of the Soviet Union, serving as General Secretary of the Communist Party of the Soviet Union from 1953 to 1964, following the death of Joseph Stalin, and Chairman of the Council of Ministers from 1958 to 1964. Khrushchev was responsible for the partial de-Stalinization of the Soviet Union, for backing the progress of the world's early space program, as well as for several relatively liberal reforms ranging from agriculture to foreign policy. After Joseph Stalin's death on March 5, 1953 there was a power struggle between different factions within the party. Initially Lavrentiy Beria controlled much of the political realm by merging the Ministry of Internal Affairs and State security. Fearing that Beria would eventually kill them, Georgy Malenkov, Lazar Kaganovich, Vyacheslav Molotov, Nikolai Bulganin and others united under Khrushchev to denounce Beria and remove him from power. Beria was executed in December. Khrushchev was not nearly as powerful as he would eventually become even after his promotion. Becoming party leader on September 7 of that year, and eventually rising above his rivals, Khrushchev's leadership marked a crucial transition for the Soviet Union. In 1958 Khrushchev replaced Bulganin as prime minister and established himself as the undisputed dictator of both state and party. He became Premier of the Soviet Union on 27 March 1958. In 1961, Khrushchev approved plans proposed by East German leader Walter Ulbricht to build the Berlin Wall, thereby reinforcing the Cold War division of Germany and Europe as a whole. His downfall came as a result of a conspiracy among the Party bosses, irritated by his erratic policies and cantankerous behavior. The Communist Party accused Khrushchev of making political mistakes, such as mishandling the 1962 Cuban missile crisis, the cold war with China and disorganizing the Soviet economy, especially in the agricultural sector. The conspirators, led by Leonid Brezhnev, Aleksandr Shelepin and the KGB chief Vladimir Semichastny, struck in October 1964, when Khrushchev was on vacation in Pitsunda, Abkhazia. On 15 October 1964, the Presidium of the USSR Supreme Soviet accepted Khrushchev's resignation as the Premier of the Soviet Union. He was replaced by Leonid Brezhnev.
16. Leonid Ilyich Brezhnev (1906–1982)—General Secretary of the Communist Party of the Soviet Union from 1964 to 1982, serving in that position longer than anyone other than Joseph Stalin. He was twice Chairman of the Presidium of the Supreme Soviet (head of state), from 7 May 1960 to 15 July 1964 and from 16 June 1977 to his death on 10 November 1982. Brezhnev became Khrushchev's protégé as he continued his rise through the ranks but, in 1963, he became involved in the plot to remove the leader from power. Alexey Kosygin, Nikolay Podgorny, Alexander Shelepin and some other high officials were also involved

in the plan. On October 14, 1964, while Khrushchev was on holiday, Politburo members voted to remove Khrushchev from office. The high point of the Brezhnev "détente" era was the signing of the Helsinki Final Act in 1975, which recognized the postwar frontiers in eastern and central Europe and, in effect, legitimized Soviet hegemony over the region.

17. Glasnost—the policy of maximal publicity, openness, and transparency in the activities of all government institutions in the Soviet Union, together with freedom of information, introduced by Mikhail Gorbachev in the second half of 1980s. Glasnost can also refer to the specific period in the history of the USSR during the 1980s when there was less censorship and greater freedom of information.
18. Communism is either a hypothetical egalitarian society based on common ownership and control of the means of production or a political ideology that promotes the establishment of such a society. Moreover the word communism is used for communist regimes, the states ruled by a Communist party, even if the party does not actually claim that it has already developed the final perfect egalitarian society of communism.
19. Charles Milles Manson (*1934)—American criminal who led what became known as the Manson Family, a quasi-commune that arose in California in the late 1960s. He was convicted of conspiracy to commit the Tate/LaBianca murders, carried out by members of the group at his instruction. He was found guilty of the murders themselves through the joint-responsibility rule, which makes each member of a conspiracy guilty of crimes his fellow conspirators commit in furtherance of the conspiracy's object. His inmate number at Corcoran State Prison is #B33920.
20. The Persian Gulf War, also known as the First Gulf War (August 2, 1990 – February 28, 1991) was a United Nations-authorized military conflict between Iraq and a coalition force from 34 nations commissioned with expelling Iraqi forces from Kuwait after Iraq's occupation and annexation of Kuwait in August 1990.
21. Saddam Hussein Abd al-Majid al-Tikriti (1937–2006)—President of Iraq from 16 July 1979 until 9 April 2003. A leading member of the revolutionary Ba'ath Party, which espoused secular pan-Arabism, economic modernization, and Arab socialism, Saddam played a key role in the 1968 coup that brought the party to long-term power. Through the 1970s, Saddam cemented his authority over the apparatuses of government as Iraq's economy grew at a rapid pace. As president, Saddam maintained power during the Iran–Iraq War (1980–1988) and the first Persian Gulf War (1991). Whereas some Arabs looked upon him as a hero for his aggressive stance against foreign intervention and for his support for the Palestinians, many Arabs and western leaders vilified him for his murdering of the Kurdish people of the north and his invasion of Kuwait. He was deposed by the U.S. and its allies during the 2003 invasion of Iraq. Captured by U.S. forces on 13 December 2003, Saddam was brought to trial under the Iraqi interim government set up by U.S.-led forces. On 5 November 2006, he was convicted of charges related to the executions of 148 Iraqi Shi'ites suspected of planning an assassination attempt against him, and was sentenced to death by hanging. He was executed on 30 December 2006.

22. Condoleezza Rice (*1954)—professor, diplomat, author, and national security expert. Rice studied at the University of Denver where she attended a course on international politics taught by Josef Korbel, a former Czech diplomat and the father of future Secretary of State Madeleine Albright. This experience sparked her interest in the Soviet Union and international relations and made her call Korbel "one of the most central figures in my life." She served as the United States Secretary of State, in the administration of President George W. Bush. President Bush was "captivated" by Rice, and relied heavily on her advice in his dealings with Mikhail Gorbachev and Boris Yeltsin. During the administration of George H.W. Bush, Rice served as the Soviet and East European Affairs Advisor during the dissolution of the Soviet Union and German reunification.
23. The Central Intelligence Agency (CIA)—civilian intelligence agency of the United States government. It is the successor of the Office of Strategic Services (OSS) formed, during World War II, to coordinate espionage activities between the branches of the US military services. Today, the CIA's primary function is collecting, analyzing information about foreign governments, corporations, and persons in order to advise public policymakers and to conduct Covert Action paramilitary and political influence operations.
24. Vladimir Alexandrovich Kryuchkov (1924-2007)—former Soviet politician and Communist Party member from 1944 till 1991. Kryuchkov joined the Soviet diplomatic service, stationed in Hungary until 1959. He then worked for the Communist Party Central Committee for eight years, before joining the KGB in 1967. His patron was Yuri Andropov. Kryuchkov was appointed head of the First Chief Directorate (FCD) in 1974 (the KGB Foreign Operations) and Deputy Chairman in 1978. In 1988 he was promoted to the rank of General of the Army and became KGB Chairman. In 1989-1990, he was a member of the Politburo. During the August Coup of 1991, Kryuchkov was among the gang of eight that led the State Emergency Committee that temporarily ousted Gorbachev. Following the failed coup attempt, Kryuchkov was imprisoned for his participation. However, in 1994 the State Duma freed him in an amnesty.
25. George Herbert Walker Bush (*1924)—the 41st President of the United States from 1989 to 1993. Bush held a variety of political positions prior to his presidency, including Vice President of the United States in the administration of Ronald Reagan (1981–1989), Director of Central Intelligence (DCI) under Gerald R. Ford, Ambassador to the United Nations (1971-1972), and Envoy to China.
26. James Addison Baker, III (*1930)—the Chief of Staff in President Ronald Reagan's first administration and on Reagan's National Security Council during Reagan's second administration 1985-1988, and Secretary of State in the George H. W. Bush administration.
27. Central Committee most commonly refers to the central executive unit of a Leninist (commonly also Trotskyist) or Communist party, whether ruling or non-ruling. In a Communist party, the Central Committee is made up of delegates elected at a Party Congress. In those Communist parties historically ruling around a Marxist-Leninist state, the Central Committee makes decisions for the party between congresses, and usually is responsible for electing the Politburo.

28. Alexander Dubcek (1921-1992)—Slovak politician and briefly leader of Czechoslovakia (1968-1969), famous for his attempt to reform the Communist regime (Prague Spring). Later, after the overthrow of the Communist government in 1989, he was Speaker of the federal Czechoslovak parliament. His parents met as emigrants in the United States but they were deported to Europe after his father refused to serve in the US Army during World War I. Alexander was born in Slovakia but the family moved to the Soviet Union where his father joined the communist party and became active in politics. Dubcek joined party in 1936 and moved back to Slovakia in 1938. He was appointed to the Central Committee of the Slovak Communist Party, became a full time politician and studied politics in Moscow. In 1964 he became the Chairman of Slovak Communist Party and replaced Antonin Novotny as the leader of the Czechoslovak Communist Party in 1968. His attempt to create "socialism with a human face" ended with the Soviet invasion in September 1968. After the revolution in November 1989 he became a leader of Social Democratic Party (CSSD) and served as a Speaker in the Czechoslovak Parliament. He was one of the key witnesses against Jakes, Lenart, and others charged with treason after the Velvet Revolution. His career ended abruptly in November 1992 when he was killed in a car accident.
29. Andrei Andreyevich Gromyko (1909-1989)—Soviet politician and diplomat. He served as Minister for Foreign Affairs for the Soviet Union (1957-1985) and Chairman of the Presidium of the Supreme Soviet (1985-1988). Gromyko entered the department of the foreign affairs in 1939 after Joseph Stalin's purges in the section responsible for the Americas. He was soon sent to the United States and worked in the Soviet embassy there until 1943, when he was appointed the Soviet ambassador to the United States. He became known as an expert negotiator. In the West, Mr. Gromyko received a nickname "Mr. Nyet" (Mr. No).
30. Richard Bruce "Dick" Cheney (*1941)—the 46th Vice President of the United States from 2001 to 2009 in the administration of George W. Bush. He represented Wyoming in the U.S. House of Representatives from 1978-1989. Cheney was selected to be the Secretary of Defense during the presidency of George H. W. Bush, holding the position for the majority of Bush's term. During this time, Cheney oversaw the 1991 Operation Desert Storm.
31. Lawrence Sidney Eagleburger (*1930)—American statesman and former career diplomat, who served briefly as the United States Secretary of State under President George H. W. Bush. Previously, he had served in lesser capacities under Presidents Richard Nixon, Jimmy Carter, Ronald Reagan, and George H. W. Bush.
32. Nicolae Ceausescu (1918–1989)—Secretary General of the Romanian Workers' Party, later the Romanian Communist Party from 1965 until 1989, President of the Council of State from 1967 and President of Romania from 1974 until 1989. His rule was marked in the first decade by an open policy towards Western Europe and the United States of America, which deviated from that of the other Warsaw Pact states during the Cold War. Ceausescu's government was overthrown in December 1989 and he was shot, following a two-hour session by a military court.

33. William Joseph Casey (1913–1987)—the Director of Central Intelligence from 1981 to 1987. During his tenure at the CIA, Casey played a large part in the shaping of Reagan's foreign policy, particularly Reagan's approach to Soviet international activity. Casey believed that the Soviet Union was the source of most worldwide, terrorist activity in spite of CIA analysts.
34. AFL-CIO—The American Federation of Labor and Congress of Industrial Organizations, is a national trade union center, the largest federation of unions in the United States, made up of 56 national and international unions.
35. Malta Summit consisted of a meeting between U.S. President George H. W. Bush and U.S.S.R. leader Mikhail Gorbachev, taking place between December 2-3 1989, just a few weeks after the fall of the Berlin Wall. No agreements were signed at the Malta Summit. Its main purpose was to provide the two superpowers—the United States and the Soviet Union—with an opportunity to discuss the rapid changes taking place in Europe. During the summit, President Bush expressed his support for Gorbachev's perestroika initiative, and other reforms in the Eastern bloc.
36. The Yalta Conference was the wartime meeting from February 4, 1945 to February 11, 1945 among the heads of government of the United States, the United Kingdom, and the Soviet Union—President Franklin D. Roosevelt, Prime Minister Winston Churchill, and Premier Josef Stalin—for the purpose of discussing Europe's postwar reorganization. Mainly, it was intended to discuss the re-establishment of the nations of war-torn Europe.
37. Wojciech Witold Jaruzelski (*1923)—former Polish communist political and military leader. He served as Prime Minister from 1981 to 1985, head of the Polish Council of State from 1985 to 1989, and President from 1989 to 1990. On December 13, 1981, Jaruzelski imposed martial law in Poland. In 1939 Jaruzelski and his family were captured by the Soviet Army, and deported to Republic of Kazakhstan-where he performed forced labor. He was later selected for enrollment into the Soviet Officer Training School by the Soviet authorities.
38. Lech Walesa (*1943)—Polish politician and a former trade union and human rights activist. He co-founded Solidarity, the Soviet bloc's first independent trade union, won the Nobel Peace Prize in 1983, and served as President of Poland from 1990 to 1995.

PART 3

1. Charter 77 (Charta 77) was officially born on January 1, 1977 as an informal group of people concerned about human rights in Czechoslovakia. When the first 217 people signed the Charter 77 declaration, 156 of them were former communists. Authors of the proclamation, Jiri Hajek, Vaclav Havel, and Jan Patocka appealed in this document to the leaders of the nation to comply with the Helsinki Human Rights Agreement. The document was never published in the media. The Interior Minister Jaromir Obzina said in 1979: "The Charter was written by the best brains of the 'opposition.' It has been written in such a clever way that if we were to make it public, 90 percent of people would not understand what it was about. This represents a danger that some 2 million

additional people could sign it." Later in November 1989 the Charter 77 group became the base of the Civic Forum (OF) and joined with representatives of the communist government to achieve the monopoly of power. The intelligence analysis of the KSC (Communist Party) screenings during 1969-1970 stated that approximately 800 communist party officials were expelled and transferred to so call reserves for future needs later—like Charter 77 and other variations for future development. The report also states that approximately 1,120 communists emigrated—were sent abroad—to work in opposition movements there and collect intelligence data. The whole operation was partially under KGB control. At the end of 1977 it was decided in the meeting between KGB and StB that some members of UV KSC (Communist Party Central Committee) will be kept out of the picture. Only 12 select members of UV KSC in Czechoslovakia were partially informed about these actions. During the period 1980-1989 Charter Foundation paid $376,000 to finance Charter 77 activities in Czechoslovakia and $1,341 million for personal expenses of Charter 77 members. This amount doesn't include individual awards dissidents received abroad. An additional $6 million was transferred to the personal accounts of Charter 77 leaders. The Charter's account—Charta Foundation—was managed by professor Janouch in Sweden. Janouch came from a prominent communist family and his wife had Soviet citizenship. When the account reached millions of dollars and some investment strategy was necessary money was transferred to Kommerzbank in Hamburg, Germany. Charter 77 was operating all the time with the blessing and under the control of StB and KGB. The system of managing Charter's activity was quite complex. Acceptance of new Charter 77 members ended November 17, 1989 when membership reached approximately 1,900. The majority of them had no idea about the function and goals of this organization. The management of Charter was in the hands of 70–85 people, mostly former communists. At the present time some 180 of their family members are holding high positions in the government and economy. This group was selected and approved in the beginning by both, Soviets and American sides. During the 13 years of its existence Charter 77 never achieved any political influence. It was not anticipated. The purpose was to make Czechoslovak citizens familiar with people that otherwise nobody would know anything about in November 1989. The danger of being the dissident depended on who was one before. The opinion of general public was, more or less, that Chartists were just a bunch of nuts. Overall 43 StB officers were involved overseeing Charter's activities. Each of them supervised 5–7 field agents. When new interior minister Dr.Richard Sacher discovered in March 1990 that some materials regarding activities of Charter 77 and personal files of some of its leaders were compromised, a danger that the connection between Charter and the former communist government could leak out arose. On April 2, 1990 he ordered, on request of President Vaclav Havel, to remove from archives all documents about: the president, members of the cabinet, and members of the Parliament. It was ordered to put these documents in metal containers, seal it, and to inform the Interior Ministry immediately whenever anyone would make an attempt to seek information about these people. He also appointed Jan Ruml to the position of deputy director at the Interior Ministry. Within six weeks after his arrival 15 thousand personal files disappeared. For example, audio recordings from Charter representatives meetings with foreign diplomats that Charter routinely passed on StB vanished. Also disappeared personal files of Charter 77 leaders: Vaclav Havel, J.Dienstbier, Zuzana Dienstbierova, Petr Uhl, Jaroslav Sabata, A.Sabatova, L.Hejdanek, Vaclav Benda, J.Gruntorad, M.Palous, Kanturek, Eva Kanturkova, Vlasta Chramostova, Marta Kubisova, Z.Jicinsky, M.Motejl, Dr. Danisz, Zdenek Richetsky, Peter Pithart, J.Urban, P.Kucera, I.Fiser, Jiri Hajek, A.Marvanova, P.Sustrova Jan Ruml, R.Slansky, W.Komarek, Milos Zeman, Vaclav Klaus, V.Dlouhy and others. Also all documents from negotiations about the transfer of power in December 1989 disappeared as well as files about intelligence organizations activities abroad.

2. GRU, or Glavnoje Razvedyvatel'noje Upravlenije, is the acronym for the foreign military intelligence directorate of the General Staff of the Armed Forces of the Russian Federation, (formerly the Red Army General Staff of the Soviet Union). The GRU is Russia's largest intelligence agency. It deploys six times as many agents in foreign countries as the SVR, which is the KGB intelligence successor. It also commanded 25,000 Spetsnaz troops in 1997.
3. Civic Forum (OF)—political movement in the Czech part of Czechoslovakia set up during the Velvet Revolution in 1989. Civic Forum's purpose was to unify all anti-authoritarian forces in Czechoslovakia and to overthrow the communist regime. They succeeded and Vaclav Havel, its leader and founder, was elected president on December 29, 1989. It didn't have a clear political strategy much beyond the June 1990 elections. However, in March and April 1990 Civic Forum did campaign successfully and they managed to get more than 80 percent of the votes in the first free elections in Czechoslovakia since 1946. In the elections of 1992 Civic Movement failed to reach the 5 percent threshold and eventually disappeared.
4. StB—State Security in former Czechoslovakia, was a plainclothes Secret police force from 1945 to its dissolution in 1990. Serving as an intelligence and counter-intelligence agency, any activity that could possibly be considered anti-communist fell under the purview of StB. From its establishment in June 30, 1945, the StB was bound to and controlled by the Communist Party of Czechoslovakia. The communists used the StB as an instrument of power and repression: the StB spied on and intimidated political opponents of the Party and forged false criminal evidence against them, facilitating the Communists rise to power in 1948. Even then, before Czechoslovakia became a communist state, the StB used forcing confessions by means of torture, including the use of drugs, blackmail and kidnapping. After the coup, these practices developed under the tutelage of Soviet advisors. Its purpose was to defend and reinforce the unlimited power of the communist party. To achieve these goals this organization created and maintained an atmosphere of fear and permanent danger within society using physical terror, torture, murder, unlawful imprisonment and threat. Between 1948-89 248 people were executed, 4,500 died in the prison, 327 were killed when attempting to cross the border, 205 486 were sentenced to jail, and almost 200,000 defected. No number can reveal how many people were interrogated, barred from jobs, high schools, and colleges. StB was dissolved on February 1, 1990. At 2006 there was 1,100 former members of the StB still working for the

Interior Ministry. The Ministry does not dispute this figure, but says there is no cause for concern. Many ex-StB officers now hold important posts in civilian life and politics.

5. Confederation of Political Prisoners—association of former political prisoners in Czech Republic.
6. KAN—Club of Committed Non-Party Members, was a group formed by 144 leading Czechoslovak intellectuals and prominent social figures during the Prague Spring movement. The group proclaimed commitment to human rights and civil equality, political pluralism and the principles embodied in the UN Declaration on human rights. The KAN was crushed and abolished in August 1968 when the Warsaw Pact army seized Czechoslovakia. During KAN's peak they claimed to have almost 15,000 members.
7. FBIS—Czech Federal Security Intelligence Service was the intelligence agency from 1991 till the brake-up of Czechoslovakia in 1993.
8. The publication known as "Cibulka's Files" listing StB agents (the communist secret police) in Czechoslovakia was published by Petr Cibulka in 1992. The file wasn't complete, containing only 80 percent of documents from 2nd Division StB. David Eleder, a member of Civic Committee at the Interior Ministry after the revolution in November 1989, originally acquired the files by unknown means. He later died in Croatia under suspicious circumstances; a sportsman and a good swimmer was found drowned in a creek two feet of water deep. Petr Cibulka himself today believes that files were doctored and released on purpose as a deception to distract the public.
9. People's Militia (Lidove milice) was a militia organization of Communist Party of Czechoslovakia during 1948–1989. The predecessors of militia were armed groups of factory workers (Factory Militias) formed in June 1945 to protect the factories during post-war chaos. The militias were hastily equipped and set on alert during communist takeover of power at the end of February 1948. The task of the militias was to protect against guerrillas expected to appear after the take-over, against undercover agents sent to Czechoslovakia and to cooperate with the police and the army. During February 1948 the militias obtained 10,000 rifles and 2,000 submachine guns. The equipment was continually modernized with sniper rifles, machine guns, mortars, anti-aircraft machine guns and transport vehicles. Non-communists were slowly removed from the militias. The control over the militias went to Ministry of Interior. In 1952 the official status of the militias changed to be the armed part of Communist Party of Czechoslovakia and the control was moved to the newly established departments at the central committee of communist party. Toward the end of 1980s political tensions in Czechoslovakia grew up and the militias, equipped with batons, were frequently deployed to disperse demonstrations against the regime. In 1989 38,985 militia-men participated in this activity. After the communist party fell from power the militias were dissolved on December 21, 1989. In January 1988 militia in Czechoslovakia had 86,494 members.
10. Aldrich Hazen Ames (*1941)—former Central Intelligence Agency counter-intelligence officer and analyst convicted in 1994 of spying for the Soviet Union and later Russia. Ames began working for the CIA in 1962 and began spying for

the Soviet Union during 1985. He was assigned to the CIA's Europe Division/ Counterintelligence branch, where he was responsible for directing the analysis of Soviet intelligence operations. He had access to the identities of U.S. sources in the KGB and Soviet military. The information Ames provided led to the compromise of at least 100 U.S. intelligence operations. During the nine years that he worked for the KGB as a mole, Ames single handily shut down the CIA's eyes and ears in the Soviet Union by telling the Russians in 1985 the names of every "human asset" that the U.S. had there. In all, he sold the KGB the names of twenty-five "sources." All, but one (Oleg Gordievsky), all Russians, were arrested and executed. Altogether, the Soviets paid Ames approximately $4.6 million for his services making him the highest paid spy in the world. Ames and his wife were arrested on February 21, 1994 and he is serving his life sentence in the federal prison system.

11. Richard Sacher—Czechoslovak post-communist interior minister for six months, from December 1989 to June 1990.
12. Civic Democratic Party (ODS)-neoconservative, neoliberal and eurosceptic party in Czech Republic.
13. Social Democratic Party (CSSD)—major left-wing party in Czech Republic, it regards itself as centre-left.
14. Obroda (Revival)—Club founded in early 1989 by reform communists who had been expelled from the party after the Prague Spring in 1968.
15. General Aloiz Lorenc, CSc. (*1939)—After the war he joined armed forces; he graduated from Officers Institute in Poprad and studied in the artillery technical school in Prague and Kosice before he became a professional officer. In 1970 he was admitted to the service of the SNB and in special department of Interior Ministry, which was the central authority cryptanalysis services in Czechoslovakia. On the basis of Soviet specialists evaluation and the executives of Federal Ministry of the Interior Lorenc was promoted in 1977 to the rank lieutenant and became the youngest chief of the central administration of the Interior Ministry of Czechoslovakia. Two years later he was promoted to the rank of General. This is probably due to his appointment in Moscow, where he spent the entire month in April 1983 completing the course at the university for the KGB nomenclatura cadres. According to the KGB representatives he showed deep knowledge of scientific communism, as well as special legal subjects and scientific organization of work. On November 1, 1985 GenMjr. Lorenc became the first deputy Interior Minister of Czechoslovakia. He also managed reorganization of the counterintelligence administration in the second half of 1988 and some other departments of Federal Interior Ministry. In short, Lorenc was primarily responsible for all activities counter intelligence bodies of state security, internal intelligence, and the economy.
16. Marian Calfa (*1946)—Prime Minister of Czechoslovakia during and after the Velvet Revolution, and a key facilitator of smooth power transfer from the Communists to a new democratic representation. Calfa assumed the power of Acting President following Gustav Husak's resignation until the election of Vaclav Havel on December 29. He was the last Communist Prime Minister, on January 18, 1990 leaving the KSC to join the Public Against Violence (VPN) party and,

when it dissolved in April 1991, became a leading member of the Civic Democratic Union (ODU-VPN). Historians consider him as a Power behind the throne, who greatly contributed to the smoothness and speed of Velvet Revolution and election of Vaclav Havel as President.

17. Ladislav Adamec (*1926)—Czech politician. He joined the Communist Party in 1946 and the party's central committee in 1966. He served as deputy premier (1969-87) and premier (1987-88) in the Czech Socialist Republic before being named head of the national government on October 11, 1988. During the 1989 Velvet Revolution, Adamec opened the country's borders and refused to authorize military intervention, but his offer of limited multiparty government was rebuffed by Vaclav Havel and other pro-democracy leaders. Adamec resigned on December 7, 1989, stepped down as Communist Party leader the next year, but he remained a member of the new Czech parliament until 1992.
18. Martin Mejstrik (*1962)—politician and former Senator (2002-2008). In 1986 he joined Socialist Union of Youth. He was one of the prominent organizers of student uprising in 1989.
19. Anytime StB tried to investigate suspicious activities of some people (Kavan, Janouch, Pelikan...) the order from KGB came to stop all activities and destroy all documentation to the case. The only proof of that today is the note in the files: "The files closed on the request of our soviet friends."
20. Jan Patocka (1907-1977) is considered one of the most important contributors to Czech philosophical phenomenology, as well as one of the most influential central European philosophers of the 20th century. In 1977 he became one of the founders and the main spokesperson for the Charter 77 (Charta 77) human rights movement in Czechoslovakia. In the days just before his death, he was subjected to long interrogations by the Czechoslovak secret police due to his involvement with the movement. He died at the age of 69 of apoplexy, after an 11 hours interrogation.
21. Jiri Dienstbier (*1937)—Czech dissident and politician. Czechoslovak Foreign Minister 1989-192 and the Vice Chairman of the federal government. Since 2008 he is a Senator for the electoral district of Kladno. Dienstbier studied journalism at the Philosophical Faculty of Charles University between 1955-1960. At the University of Burgundy in France, Dijon gained the title Doctor Honoris Causa. As a student Dienstbier joined the Communist Party in 1958. During the 1950's and 1960's as communist journalist he was able to travel around the World during the communist era in Czechoslovakia. Between 1958-69 he worked as foreign political commentator and editor for Czechoslovak [communist] Radio, between 1964-67 Dienstbier was the CZ Radio correspondent for the Far East and was in Jakarta, Indonesia at the time when there was unsuccessful communist coup. He participated in the democratization process "Prague Spring in 1968. In 1977 he became one of the first 250 signatories of Charter 77 and in the years 1979 and 1985 and was its spokesman. After the birth of the Civic Forum (OF) in November 1989, he became the speaker of the coordination center and in December of the same year he was appointed foreign minister. While in his post as Foreign Minister, Dienstbier was involved in various scandals regarding

appointing various "former" communists and StB agents [StB foreign espionage section mostly] as Czechoslovak Ambassadors around the World.

22. Tomas Hradilek—communist party member 1966-1969, signed Charter 77 in 1977, spokesman of Charter 77 1989-1990. Founder of Civic Forum. Interior Minister in 1990.
23. Jan Princ—BIS Colonel and the director of Olomouc BIS subsidiary. Husband of Kveta Princova, spokeswoman for the dissident organization Charter 77. Jan Princ owned a communist passport with number, which was affixed only to StB cooperators.
24. Privatization—the coupon privatization was a great rip-off on Czech citizens. Masterminded and executed by fellows from the Institute of Prognosis under leadership of Vaclav Klaus and Dusan Triska it allowed transformation of the national property to hands of former communists, Stb and KGB agents, and swindlers. The bill for privatization between 1990-2000 reached 2,385 billion KC ($75 billion), 460,000 KC for each taxpayer!
25. Dusan Triska (*1946)—is considered the architect of Czechoslovakia's privatization.
26. Prognostic Institute—special division of the Czech Academy of Science, was created in 1984 to find a way to switch from socialist economy system to market economy. It was a direct copy of the institute of the same name in Moscow founded by KGB General Michail Ljubimov on the order from Yuri Andropov. The Institute under the leadership of Valtr Komarek worked under KGB supervision and employed many later successful politicians: Vaclav Klaus, Josef Tosovsky, Vladimir Dlouhy, Milos Zeman, Tomas Jezek, Jan Mladek, Karel Dyba, Vladimir Rudlovcak, Miloslav Randsdorf and Karel Köecher, the famous spy arrested in USA and exchanged later for Soviet dissident Natan Sharansky.
27. Valtr Komarek (*1930)—His parents were founding members of the Czechoslovak Communist Party. Komarek joined the party in the age of 16 and studied in Moscow State Institute of Economy where he was appointed to the Moscow administration of the Communist Party Soviet Union as a director of the Czechoslovak Communist Party group in the USSR. Also Komarek was appointed as a secretary for ideology in the national [Soviet] Committee and worked also in public posts on the Moscow Institute of Economics. After his return to Czechoslovakia he was put in charge of the new economic strategy at The Czechoslovak Central Planning Committee. Between 1964-67 Valtr Komarek was ordered to Cuba and became economics advisor for then Cuban Industry Minister Enrique Che-Guevara. Latter in 1984 he was appointed to head the new Prognostic Institute at the Academy of Sciences. After the revolution Komarek, a Communist Party member, but backed by Civic Forum, was appointed First Deputy Premier.
28. Milos Zeman (*1944)—well-known Czech politician. He was a member and leader of the Czech Social Democratic Party. Former speaker of the chamber of deputies (lower house of the Czech parliament) from 1996 until 1998, and the prime minister of the Czech Republic from 1998 until 2002.

29. Vaclav Klaus (*1941)—President of Czech Republic since 2003. He studied economy at Prague and later received scholarships in Italy (1966) and the USA (1969). Until 1970 he also worked in the economics section at the Academy of Science and at the State Bank 1971-86. He also worked for The Prognostic Institute and during that period frequently lectured at Universities abroad. In December 1989 immediately after the revolution he became the Minister of Finance. He was the chairman of the Civic Forum (OF) October 1990–February 1991 and the co-founder and the chairman of Civic Democratic Party (ODS) since April 1991. Since October 1991 he served as the Vice-Premier of Czechoslovak government and in June 1992 he became the Premier of the Czech government. He resigned from this post in November 1997 due to complicity in a political funding and corruption scandal stemming from a secret Swiss bank account in his name containing $5 million—exposed at the time as secret donations in exchange for special favors. A year later, Mr. Klaus began a series of secret meetings with the SVR's Resident in Prague. SVR opened an operational file on Klaus under the codename 'Kolesnikov'. In 2002 he resigned from the post of chairman of ODS. Running for the presidency in 2003 he failed to get majority of votes in his run in January elections but he got 142 out of 280 votes in the third runoff and he became the president on March 7, 2003.
30. Fond Z—What actually happened with the StB archives in 1990 came out only when in the court regarding the operation "Decontamination" (Asanace)—the StB operation to force dissidents out of Czechoslovakia in the late seventies, and early eighties. During the hearings Sacher admitted that he created a Fund "Z" where all files of legislators, members of the government, and officials from the State Attorney's office were compiled. He also requested a compilation of all StB files on Charter 77 members. In April 1990 he passed all the materials to representatives of Charter 77. (They are not identified till today.) He said: "They promised to return the materials to the State Archives after reading them over. I have no knowledge if they returned these files or not." Viliam Ciklamini was the First Secretary of the first Federal Interior Minister Richard Sacher. He insists that he was fired by Sacher because he didn't agree with the plundering of StB archives and with illegal lustrations. He claims that President Vaclav Havel personally participated in "wild" lustrations, which had to cover connections of some of the top politicians and dissidents with StB. Mr. Ciklamini stated later: "Sacher and Havel privately ran a lustration of politicians. In the process they found out that half of the Parliament and the federal government are communist agents. Then they created a special Fund "Z" where they put all those selected for important posts, mostly dissidents. They wanted to control the situation. Zdenek Formanek, director of intelligence then, first found out that Sacher was checking files and pulling files of some of the individuals out. He went immediately to the President's Office to inform Havel. He told his secretary he wanted to report an illegal lustration. Havel immediately called Sacher telling him that there was a leak. Then Sacher blamed the whole affair on Formanek. Formanek discovered that 20 people in the interior ministry were going through the files, day and night. They were doing it on Sacher's and Havel's request. But not everybody was sheltered in this special fund. Only those who were considered

potential politicians. Those selected to participate in politics in the future. In any case, it was illegal.

It was a struggle for power. If I would compare it to something, it would be a situation I experienced during my intelligence work in the mid-eighties in Africa. We treated democracy here like we did in developing countries."

31. Jan Ruml (*1953)—Deputy Interior Minister of the Czech and Slovak Federative Republic in April 1990. In 1992 he was elected to the House of the Nations of the Federal Assembly on behalf of the Civic Democratic Party (ODS). From July 1992 to September 1996 he served as the Minister of the Interior of the Czech Republic and after he stepped down, he became a Member of the Parliament. He was a son of a high-ranking communist, Stalinist enthusiast, and a former foreign correspondent for Rude Pravo newspaper. His StB file was closed and sealed in 1987!
32. Jan Langos (1946-2006)—former anti-communist dissident who served as Czechoslovak Interior Minister from early 1990 until July 1992. In 1993 he was instrumental in establishing the Slovak Institute of National Memory in Bratislava where he served as director since 2003. He was also a key source of support for Czech politicians lobbying for a similar institute in the Czech Republic. Mr.Langos was the person who moved so called "Fund Z," created by Richard Sacher, to an undisclosed location. He died in a freak car accident on the strait highway in the middle of nowhere on June 15, 2006.
33. Uncensored News—the independent newspaper Petr Cibulka started to publish in 1991.
34. Pavel Landovsky (*1936)—actor, former dissident, one of the key figures in Czechoslovakia's Charter 77 protest movement and close friend of Vaclav Havel. He became the victim of the infamous Asanace campaign masterminded StB that used intimidation, mental and physical abuse, even torture to force selected "unwanted" dissidents to flee the country. Landovsky was forced to immigrate to Vienna, Austria in 1978.
35. Michael Kocab (*1954)—Czech pop star, entrepreneur, and politician. Currently minister for Human Rights. He was the Chairman of the Parliamentary Committee for departure of Red Army from Czechoslovakia in 1990. His code name in StB files was "Muk", file number 37868. His supervising officer was Josef Sasek. In 1989 together with Michal Horacek they started, with the help of StB resident Oskar Krejci, the Bridge Initiative–the dialog between OV and the government, respective between Vaclav Havel and Jiri Adamec. Michal Horacek and Michal Kocab served as a contact between Vaclav Havel and KGB.
36. Michal Horacek (*1954)—one of the Czech Republic's most prominent lyricists, a man who has worked with so many top musicians. By the summer of 1989, Michal Horacek and the local rock star of the time, Michael Kocab, established a civic initiative called MOST (Bridge). It had a sole objective was to provide grounds for future talks between the Communist government and the dissidents. This dialogue helped to shape the Czechoslovak transition of political power as peaceful. It was eventually even dubbed the Velvet Revolution.

37. Frantisek Janouch (*1931)—nuclear physicist. He studied in Leningrad where he joined the communist party in 1948 and at Lomonosov University in Moscow. After his return to Czechoslovakia he worked at the Institute of Nuclear Physics where he was also the Chairman of the communist party organization. In 1970 he was expelled from the communist party and in 1974 he was allowed to move to Sweden. He is claiming to be a professor but he never obtained such a title. He also claims to be a founder of Charter 77 Foundation in Sweden. In fact the Foundation was created by Peter Larson and Jiri Pallas. Janouch took over the Foundation later and accepted "former" communist agents as members of the Charter 77 Foundation Board of Directors, among them StB agent Jan Muhlfeit (*1962), StB file # 165511 as a computer specialist. The Foundation sought support for the movement in Czechoslovakia. Janouch claims that George Soros was the biggest contributor to Havel's Charter 77 [according to sources Soros supplied all together $7 million to Charter 77 and Solidarity in Poland], but Janouch also stated that Soros only supplied one third of the total amount. After the "collapse of communism" in Czechoslovakia in November 1989 Janouch moved Foundation to Prague. The database of the Foundation disappeared and Muhlfeit became the director of Eastern European section of Microsoft Central.
38. Frantisek Bublan (*1951)—former Czech dissident. He studied at Charles University, faculty of Catholic Theology. He served as the Minister of the Interior (2004-2006). His tenure there was highly controversial and was remarked by many affairs.
39. Jan Kavan (*1946)—the Czech Representative in EU Parliament. Born in London into the family of Czech diplomat Pavel Kavan and British teacher Rosemary Kavan. The family returned to Czechoslovakia in 1950. His father was later arrested and became one of the key witnesses in the process with Rudolf Slansky (who was accused of treason and executed). Kavan studied in the sixties at the Charles University and was active in politics. After the Soviet invasion in 1968 he immigrated to Great Britain. He studied at the London School of Economics, Oxford, and Reading. He started the Palach Press Agency, which published information about dissidents' activities and illegally shipped forbidden literature to Czechoslovakia. In 1976 he was arrested in Belgium for drug smuggling. In 1979 he was stripped of Czech citizenship. He returned to Czechoslovakia in November 1989, joined the Civic Forum and in 1990 he became chairman of the parliamentary committee for foreign affairs. In 1991 he was indicted on collaborating with StB during the 1969-70 period. The file documenting Jan Kavan's relationship with StB (code name Kato, file # 11777/307 and # 12402/332) was first discovered by the interim director of BIS Stanislav Devaty. Kavan admitted to have connections in England with Mr. Zajicek, code name "Zachystal," from the First Department of StB–foreign espionage. In 1996 the court came to the conclusion that Jan Kavan, regardless of his contacts with StB, was unaware whom he was dealing with and all charges against him were dismissed. In the other words he didn't know whom he was working for. After his acquittal he became a senator and the vice-chairman of the Helsinki Committee for human rights in Czech Republic. In 1998 Kavan became a Vice-Premier and Minister of foreign affairs. But the whole affair didn't go away thanks to the book Kato–The Case of The Real Man (Kato–Pribeh opravdoveho cloveka) by John Block and Premysl Vachalovsky published by J.W.Hill in

the year 2000. The BIS agents were buying the book in bulk from the bookstores to keep it for reaching readers. Kavan's career in the Ministry of Foreign Affairs was full of scandals. From a driving accident under the influence of alcohol, leaking to the press information about an Iraqi agent, secret trips of his officers to Iraq, and cheating of the lustration law (all in 1998) to the large amount of cash found accidentally in his office's vault and the arrest of his deputy Karel Srba indicted on corruption charges and the murder for hire charges to cover some illegal activities. At the end of his term Kavan managed to convince his colleagues in the cabinet to put aside 118 million crowns ($4 million) to finance his UN office in New York. On July 8, 2002 he became a Chairman of the UN General Assembly. At the same time he also served as a deputy in the Czech Parliament. According to documents discovered in StB archives by researchers from the Committee for Investigation and Documentation of Communist Crimes, Jan Kavan was smuggling books and flyers from England to Czechoslovakia in specially modified car. In every run they also carried $6,000 in the special compartment. The "perfect" false documents for trips were made in Germany by person from one leftist organization with close ties to Carlos the Jackal (Ilich Ramírez Sánchez). The contact with Palach Press was John Trenor. After downloading the cargo in Czechoslovakia the car continued driving to the Soviet Union. StB started to investigate this suspicious activity of Jan Kavan but they were ordered by KGB to stop the investigation and destroy all documentation to the case. Another case investigated by FBIS happened during the dissolution of Czechoslovakia (separation into Czech and Slovak Republics in January 1, 1993). Stamps to temporarily mark the old currency were printed in a print shop in Columbia by the company owned by Jan Kavan's relative. One of the shipments of stamps was tracked by FBIS to Syria where four pallets of 500 Czechoslovak crown bills were marked with these "runaway" stamps. FBIS asked CIA to put a GPS tracking on the shipment and followed the container traveling by the boat through Hamburg, Germany and arriving to The National Bank in Prague, Czech Republic, four days after official closure of all financial transactions of the old currency.

40. Jiri Lang (*1957)—BIS director, working in counter-intelligence since 1990. Before that he was employed for 14 years in Energoproject.
41. "Letters to Olga" is a book of letters by Vaclav Havel to his wife Olga Havlova during his stay in prison from June 1979 to September 1982.
42. Minkovice—the toughest prison for political prisoners in the communist Czechoslovakia. Inmates called it the concentration camp Minkau.
43. Petr Uhl—former Trockist, leading human rights activist who later became Deputy Vice-Prime-Minister for Human Rights. He released to media fabricated news that Charles University student Martin Smid was beaten to death during the Friday November 17, 1989 night demonstration by red-bereted paratroopers of the Czech military. The news was first broadcasted on Radio Free Europe and was quickly picked up by all media. This was the catalyst that energized the public and jump-started the revolution. Hearing the news the crowds in the streets multiplied. One week later on November 24 a one half million people came out to protest and hear Alexander Dubcek to speak.

PART 4

1. Spy Wars; moles, mysteries, and deadly games by Pete Bagley
2. Sun Tzu (pronounced Soon-zuh) was born in 400 BC and died in 320 BC. He is traditionally believed to be the author of The Art of War, sometimes called the Sun Tzu, an influential ancient Chinese book on military strategy considered to be a prime example of Taoist strategy. During the 19th and 20th centuries, Sun's The Art of War grew in popularity and saw practical use in Western society, and his work has continued to influence both Asian and Western culture and politics.
3. Lt. Col. Yuri Ivanovich Nosenko (1927-2008)—KGB defector and a figure of significant controversy within the U.S. intelligence community, since his claims contradicted Anatoliy Golitsyn. Nosenko contacted the CIA in Geneva, when he accompanied a diplomatic mission to that city in 1962. He offered his services for a small amount of money, claiming that a prostitute had robbed him of $900. He claimed to be deputy chief of the Seventh Department of the KGB, and provided some information that would only be known by someone connected to the KGB. He was given the money he requested and told $25,000 a year would be deposited in an account in his name in the West. Then, at a meeting set up in 1964 he unexpectedly claimed that he had been discovered by the KGB and needed to defect immediately. Nosenko claimed that the Geneva KGB residency had received a cable recalling him to Moscow and he was fearful that he had been found out. NSA was later, but not at the time, able to determine that no such cable had been sent, and Nosenko subsequently admitted making this up to persuade the CIA to accept his defection, which the CIA did. Nosenko claimed that he could provide important information about the assassination of President John F. Kennedy, affirming that he had personally handled a review of the case of Lee Harvey Oswald, who had lived in the Soviet Union prior to the Kennedy assassination. Later Nosenko said that, while the KGB had conducted surveillance of Oswald, it had never tried to recruit him. This issue was critical because KGB involvement with Oswald might suggest Soviet involvement in the Kennedy assassination–a prospect that could have propelled the Cold War into a nuclear war. Two lie detector tests conducted by the CIA suggested that Nosenko was lying about Oswald. Moreover, Nosenko confessed that he had lied to the CIA about his military rank. He was interrogated for 1,277 days. On March 1, 1969 he was formally acknowledged to be a genuine defector, and released, with financial compensation from the CIA. Nosenko's case officer when met in Geneva initially in 1962 and subsequently when he defected in 1964 was Tennent H. "Pete" Bagley. Bagley, subsequently chief of counterintelligence for the Soviet Russia ("SR") Division and Division Deputy Director, wrote a book about the Nosenko case. (Bagley, Tennent H., Spy Wars: Moles, Mysteries, and Deadly Games, Yale University Press, 2007). Ion Mihai Pacepa in his latest book Programmed to Kill supports the theory that Oswald was indeed hired by KGB to assassinate President Kennedy (Programmed to Kill: Lee Harwey Oswald, the Soviet KGB, and the Kennedy assassination (Ivan R. Dee Publishing, 2007). Coincidently Ludvik Zifcak in his book Zabili jsme Kennedyho (We Killed Kennedy) supports Pacepa's thesis, providing evidence from KGB archives in

Moscow, that Oswald's Russian wife Marina was in fact the KGB agent and to her credit the CIA was not able to accuse KGB from plotting the assassination.

4. Stephen de Mowbray—junior officer in MI-6 who served in Washington in the mid-1960s.
5. James Jesus Angleton—CIA's counter-intelligence chief from the 1950s to the 1970s. Acting on information provided by KGB defector Anatoliy Golitsyn, he feared that the KGB had moles in two key places: in the CIA's counter-intelligence section, and in the FBI's counter-intelligence department. With those moles in place, the KGB would be aware of and therefore could control US counter-spy efforts to detect, capture, and arrest their spies. It could protect their moles by safely redirecting investigations that might uncover them, or provide them sufficient advance warning to allow their escape. Moreover, KGB counter-intelligence vetted foreign sources of intelligence, so that moles in that area were positioned to stamp their approval of double agents sent against the CIA. In retrospect, in the context of the capture of the Soviet moles Aldrich Ames and Robert Hanssen, it appears Angleton's fears—then deemed excessively paranoid—were well grounded, although both Ames and Hanssen operated and were exposed long after Angleton left the CIA in 1974. Still, his officially disbelieved assertions cost him his counter-intelligence post in the CIA.
6. Arthur Martin—the senior counterespionage officer in MI-5.
7. Newton "Scott" Miler—CIA Deputy Director of Plans, former Chief of Operations.
8. Harold Adrian Russell "Kim" Philby (1912–1988)—high-ranking member of British intelligence. A socialist, he served as an NKVD and KGB operative. In 1963, Philby was revealed as a member of the spy ring now known as the Cambridge Five, along with Donald Maclean, Guy Burgess, Anthony Blunt and John Cairncross. Of the five, Philby is believed to have been most successful in providing classified information to the Soviet Union. His activities were moderated only by Stalin's paranoia that Philby was a triple agent.
9. William Egan Colby (1920–1996)—spent a career in intelligence for the United States. During World War II he served with the OSS and after the war he joined the newly created CIA. He served as Director of CIA from 1973 to 1976.
10. ULTRA was the name used by the British for intelligence resulting from decryption of encrypted German radio communications in World War II. The term eventually became the standard designation in both Britain and the United States for all intelligence from high-level cryptanalytic sources. The name arose because the code-breaking success was considered more important than the highest security classification available at the time (Most Secret) and so was regarded as being Ultra secret. Those few people with clearance for Ultra information were given the code word "bigot." This allowed those with the clearance to discreetly identify that status of others with a question such as, "Are you a bigot?" or "Are there any bigots in the room?" Much of the German cipher traffic was encrypted on the Enigma machine, hence the term "Ultra" has often been used almost synonymously with "Enigma decrypts."

11. Gustave Bertrand, (1896–1976)—French military intelligence officer who made a vital contribution to the decryption, by Poland's Cipher Bureau, of German Enigma ciphers, beginning in December 1932. This achievement would in turn lead to Britain's celebrated World War II Ultra operation. In 1973, the Paris publishing house Plon published his book, Enigma ou la plus grande énigme de la guerre 1939-1945 ("Enigma or the Greatest Enigma of the War of 1939-1945"). The book, one of the principal primary sources on the history of Enigma decryption, for the first time gave a detailed account of the some eleven years of Franco-Polish collaboration in breaking and reading Enigma before and during World War II.
12. Robert Philip Hanssen (*1944)—former FBI agent who spied for Soviet and Russian intelligence services against the United States for more than 20 years. Despite the fact that he revealed highly sensitive security information to the Soviet Union, federal prosecutors agreed to not seek the death penalty in exchange for his guilty pleas to 15 espionage and conspiracy charges. Hanssen was arrested on February 18, 2001, charged with selling American secrets to Moscow for more than $1.4 million in cash and diamonds over a 22-year period. He was subsequently sentenced to life in prison without parole. His activities have been described as "possibly the worst intelligence disaster in US history." In 1983, Hanssen transferred to the Soviet analytical unit, which was directly responsible for studying, identifying, and capturing Soviet spies and intelligence operatives in the United States. Hanssen's section was in charge of evaluating Soviet agents who volunteered to give intelligence to the U.S., to determine if they were genuine or double agents. In 1985, he was transferred to the FBI's field office in New York, where he continued to work in counterintelligence against the Soviets. On two occasions, Hanssen gave the Soviets a complete list of American double agents. Hanssen expressed interest in a transfer to the new National Counterintelligence Center, founded in 1994 and charged with coordinating counterintelligence activities. But when a superior told him that he would have to take a lie detector test to join, Hanssen changed his mind. Hanssen is federal prisoner #48551-083 and is currently serving his sentence at ADX Florence, a Supermax federal penitentiary in Florence, Colorado, where he spends 23 hours per day in solitary confinement.
13. The Federal Bureau of Investigation (FBI) is the primary unit in the United States Department of Justice, serving as both a federal criminal investigative body and a domestic intelligence agency.
14. The National Security Agency/Central Security Service (NSA/CSS)—cryptology intelligence agency of the United States government, administered as part of the United States Department of Defense. Created on November 4, 1952 by President Harry S. Truman, it is responsible for the collection and analysis of foreign communications and foreign signals intelligence, which involves a significant amount of cryptanalysis. It is also responsible for protecting U.S. government communications and information systems from similar agencies elsewhere, which involves a significant amount of cryptography. NSA has recently been directed to help monitor U.S. federal agency computer networks to protect them against attacks.

15. Richard McGarrah Helms (1913–2002)—Director of Central Intelligence (DCI) from 1966 to 1973. In 1972, Helms ordered the destruction of most records from the huge MKULTRA project, over 150 CIA-funded research projects designed to explore any possibilities of mind control. The project became public knowledge two years later, after a New York Times report. Its full extent may never be known. He was the only director to have been convicted of lying to Congress over CIA undercover activities. In 1977, he was sentenced to the maximum fine and received a suspended two-year prison sentence. Despite this, Helms remained a revered figure in the intelligence profession. In 1983, President Ronald Reagan awarded Helms the National Security Medal.
16. Michelle Van Cleave—National Counterintelligence Executive, an interagency director.
17. Jan Sejna (1927-1997)—General of the Czechoslovak Army in communist Czechoslovakia. In 1956, he became Chief of the Secretariat of the MNO, in 1963 the Chief Secretary of the Main Committee of the Communist Party of Czechoslovakia (KSC) at the MNO. In October 1967 he was promoted to the rank of General. After losing political power and influence at the beginning of the Prague Spring, he defected and was granted asylum in the United States, much to the dismay of Soviet authorities. In the following three decades in the United States, Sejna worked as a counterintelligence analyst for the CIA and later as a consultant to the DIA until his death in 1997. On September 17, 1996 Sejna testified in Congress on U.S. POWs in the USSR and their use for various nuclear, biological, chemical and mind-control drugs experiments. This testimony was postponed many times. In the morning of September 17 CIA agents were trying to find Sejna on the Capitol and take him away before he could appear before the U.S. House Subcommittee on Military Personnel [Sen. John Kerry presiding]. DIA agents were hiding him till the last minute and brought him in. Sejna has in fact received death threats directly before he testified and was dead 10 months later under more than suspicious circumstances. Czech Military Intelligence website even today is maintaining a large section dedicated to discredit Jan Sejna.
18. The CIA systematically denied any connection between terrorism and the Soviet Union till DIA agents debriefing Sejna used his information to cross-referenced it with CIA's own files. Only then, unable to discredit their own sources, the true about the Soviet support of terrorism was publicly acknowledged.
19. The Defense Intelligence Agency, or DIA, is a major producer and manager of military intelligence for the United States Department of Defense, employing over 16,500 military and civilian employees worldwide. The DIA and DIC provide military intelligence to war fighters, defense policymakers and force planners within the Department of Defense and the United States Intelligence Community, in support of U.S. military planning and operations and weapon systems acquisition. DIA, designated in 1986 as a Defense Department combat support agency, was established in 1961 as a result of a decision by Secretary of Defense Robert S. McNamara, under President John F. Kennedy.
20. National Intelligence Estimates (NIEs) are United States federal government documents that are the authoritative assessment of the Director of National Intel-

ligence (DNI) on intelligence related to a particular national security issue. NIEs are produced by the National Intelligence Council and express the coordinated judgments of the United States Intelligence Community, the group of 16 U.S. intelligence agencies. NIEs are classified documents prepared for policymakers.

21. The Vietnam War occurred in Vietnam, Laos and Cambodia from 1959 to 1975. The war was fought between the communist North Vietnam, supported by its communist allies, and the government of South Vietnam, supported by the United States and other member nations of the Southeast Asia Treaty Organization (SEATO).
22. Manuel Antonio Noriega (*1934)—former Panamanian general and the military dictator of Panama from 1983 to 1989. He was never officially the president of Panama, but held the post of "chief executive officer" for a brief period in 1989. The 1989 invasion of Panama by the United States removed him from power. He was captured, detained as a prisoner of war, and flown to the U.S. Noriega was tried on eight counts of drug trafficking, racketeering, and money laundering in April 1992. His US prison sentence ended in September 2007. Pending the outcome of extradition requests by both Panama and France, he remains in prison as of April 2009.
23. Michael Levine—former senior United States law enforcement agent, as 25 years veteran of the Drug Enforcement Administration (DEA). He has gained much attention for his criticisms of the CIA and the influence it has played on DEA operations. He has even gone as far as claiming the CIA was instrumental in the creation La Corporation, the "General Motors of cocaine." In "Deep Cover" now in the top fifty "Project Censored" archives of Bill Moyers, Levine revealed that Edwin Meese, the then Attorney General of the United States, had blown the cover of a DEA undercover team, posing as a Mafia family, that had penetrated the Office of the President of Mexico and was "buying" Mexican military protection for the transportation of 15 tons of cocaine through Mexico into the United States. Levine has testified as an expert witness in 500 civil and criminal trials internationally and domestically and has lectured on Undercover Operations and Human Intelligence for a wide range of professional audiences ranging from the Defense Intelligence Agency and the FBI advanced undercover seminar to the New York State Department of Justice Services and the Royal Canadian Mounted Police.
24. Vladimir Bogdanovich Rezun—writes under the name Viktor Suvorov (*1947). He made his name writing books about Soviet history, the Soviet Army, GRU, and Spetsnaz. His testimony about the capabilities of the Soviet Special Forces created concern in the West. Suvorov began his service in the Soviet Army's 41st Guards Tank Division, and worked in Soviet military intelligence (GRU) before defecting to the United Kingdom in 1978, where he worked as an intelligence analyst and lecturer. At the time he was working in Geneva, Switzerland under United Nations cover. Rezun was smuggled out of the country to England with his wife and two young children. A career soldier, he had participated in the invasion of Czechoslovakia in 1968 and had later supervised the training of the elite Spetsnaz special forces. He had also undertaken missions in Munich, Rome, Basel, Amsterdam, Vienna and Hamburg.

25. Russian special purpose regiments or Spetsnaz. These Russian special forces can specifically refer to any élite or special purpose units under subordination of the Federal Security Service (FSB) or Internal Troops of Russian Ministry of Internal Affairs, and the units controlled by the military intelligence service GRU. Spetsnaz has trained the Republican Guard of Syria, Iraq and Iran and they have been involved in training other Special Forces units across the world. These internal troop units originally were raised for internal use against counter-revolutionaries and other undesirables. Spetsnaz carry out reconnaissance and social warfare missions in "peacetime" as well as in war. According to Vladimir Rezun, a GRU defector who used the pseudonym "Viktor Suvorov," there were 20 Spetsnaz brigades plus 41 separate companies. Total strength of Spetsnaz forces was around 30,000 troops at the time but their numbers are unknown today. Spetsnaz GRU, or Russian army special forces, are the original SPETSNAZ and are generally considered the best-trained units of the Armed Forces of the Russian Federation. The units of Spetsnaz GRU have no official names. They are generally referred to by unit numbers, for example,"16th Separate Brigade of Spetsnaz," much like any other military unit, and are sometimes deployed under VDV command aegis. Few details are actually known about the operations of Spetsnaz GRU, but it is known that the units were heavily involved in operations in Afghanistan and Chechnya. Spetnaz GRU teams usually wear standard-issue VDV uniforms, light blue VDV berets and unit patches in order to avoid identification. However, they can also wear different uniforms, for instance, they would wear the uniform of a unit which is stationed nearby, in order to blend in.
26. Stanislav Lunev (*1946)—former Soviet military officer, the highest-ranking GRU officer to defect from Russia to the United States. He worked as a GRU intelligence officer in Singapore in 1978, in China from 1980, and in the United States from 1988. He defected to U.S. authorities in 1992. Since then he has worked as a consultant to the FBI, CIA and other agencies and private corporations. He remains in the FBI's Witness Protection Program. Lunev is mostly known for his description of nuclear sabotage operations that have allegedly been prepared by the KGB and GRU against the western countries. It was known from other sources that large arms caches were hidden by the KGB in many countries for the planned terrorism acts. They were booby-trapped with "Lightning" explosive devices. One of such cache, which was identified by Vasili Mitrokhin, exploded when Swiss authorities tried to remove it from woods near Berne. Several others caches were removed successfully. Lunev asserted that some of the hidden caches could contain portable tactical nuclear weapons known as RA-115 "suitcase bombs". Such bombs have been prepared to assassinate US leaders in the event of war. Lunev states that he had personally looked for hiding places for weapons caches in the Shenandoah Valley area and that "it is surprisingly easy to smuggle nuclear weapons into the US" either across the Mexican border or using a small transport missile that can slip undetected when launched from a Russian airplane.

    According to Lunev, a probable scenario in the event of war would be poisoning of Potomac River with chemical or biological weapons, "targeting the residents of Washington DC." He also noted that it is "likely" that GRU operatives have placed already "poison supplies near the tributaries to major

US reservoirs." These allegations have been confirmed by former SVR officer Kouzminov who was responsible for transporting dangerous pathogens from around the world for Russian program of biological weapons in the 1980s and the beginning of 1990s. He described a variety of biological terrorism acts that would be carried out on the order of the Russian president in the event of hostilities, including poisoning public drinking-water supplies and food processing plants.

27. Alexander Valterovich Litvinenko (1962–2006)—officer who served in the Soviet KGB and latter FSB. In 1988 he was officially transferred to the Third Chief Directorate of the KGB, Military Counter Intelligence. Later that year, after studying for a year at the Novosibirsk Military Counter Intelligence School, he became an operational officer and served in KGB military counterintelligence until 1991. In 1991, he was promoted to the Central Staff of the Federal Counterintelligence Service, specializing in counter-terrorist activities and infiltration of organized crime. In November 1998, Litvinenko and several other FSB officers publicly accused their superiors of ordering the assassination of Russian tycoon and oligarch, Boris Berezovsky. Litvinenko was arrested the following March on charges of exceeding his authority at work. He was acquitted in November 1999 but re-arrested before the charges were again dismissed in 2000. In October 2000 Litvinenko and his family travelled to Turkey where he applied for asylum at the United States Embassy in Ankara, but his application was denied. He was granted asylum in the United Kingdom, where he became a journalist and writer. During his time in London Litvinenko authored two books, "Blowing up Russia: Terror from within" and "Lubyanka Criminal Group" where he accused Russian secret services of staging the Russian apartment bombings and other terrorism acts in an effort to bring Vladimir Putin to power. He also accused Putin of ordering the murder of Russian journalist Anna Politkovskaya. Litvinenko alleged that Ayman al-Zawahiri, a prominent leader of al-Qaeda, was trained for half of a year by the FSB in Dagestan in 1997 and called him "an old agent of the FSB" Litvinenko said that after this training, Ayman al-Zawahiri "was transferred to Afghanistan, where he had never been before and where, following the recommendation of his Lubyanka chiefs, he at once . . . penetrated the milieu of bin Laden and soon became his assistant in al Qaeda." Former KGB officer and writer Konstantin Preobrazhenskiy supported this claim and said that Litvinenko "was responsible for securing the secrecy of Al-Zawahiri's arrival in Russia, who was trained by FSB instructors in Dagestan, Northern Caucasus, in 1996-1997". On 1 November 2006 Litvinenko suddenly fell ill and was hospitalized in what was established as a case of poisoning by radioactive polonium-210 and resulted in his death on 26 November. The British investigation into his death resulted in a failed request to Russia for the extradition of Andrey Lugovoy whom they accused of Litvinenko's murder, contributing to the further cooling of Russia–United Kingdom relations.
28. Dr. Ayman Muhammad Rabaie al-Zawahiri (*1951)—prominent leader of al-Qaeda, and was the second and last "emir" of Egyptian Islamic Jihad, having succeeded Abbud al-Zummar in the latter role when Egyptian authorities sentenced al-Zummar to life imprisonment. Al-Zawahiri is a qualified surgeon, and is an author of works including numerous al-Qaeda statements. In 1998 al-Zawa-

hiri formally merged Egyptian Islamic Jihad into al-Qaeda. According to reports by a former al-Qaeda member, he has worked in the al-Qaeda organization since its inception and was a senior member of the group's shura council. He is often described as a "lieutenant" to Osama bin Laden, though bin Laden's chosen biographer has referred to him as the "real brains" of al-Qaeda. On December 1 1996, Ahmad Salama Mabruk and Mahmud Hisham al-Hennawi—both carrying false passports—accompanied al-Zawahiri on a trip to Chechnya. Their leader was traveling under the name Abdullah Imam Mohammed Amin, and trading on his medical credentials for legitimacy. The group was arrested within hours of entering Russian territory and spent five months in a Makhachkala prison awaiting trial. Assassinated former FSB agent Alexander Litvinenko alleged that during this time al-Zawahiri was indeed being trained by the FSB, and that he was not the only link between al-Qaeda and the FSB. Former KGB officer and writer Konstantin Preobrazhenskiy supported Litvinenko's claim and said that Litvinenko "was responsible for securing the secrecy of Al-Zawahiri's arrival in Russia, who was trained by FSB instructors in Dagestan, Northern Caucasus, in 1996-1997." Ayman al-Zawahiri is under indictment in the United States for this role in the 1998 U.S. embassy bombings in Dar es Salaam, Tanzania, and Nairobi, Kenya. The Rewards for Justice Program of the U.S. Department of State is offering a reward of up to US $25 million for information about his location.

PART 5

1. Adolf Hitler (1889-1945)—Austrian born German politician and the leader of the National Socialist German Workers Party (NSDAP), popularly known as the Nazi Party. He was the ruler of Germany from 1933 to 1945, serving as chancellor from 1933 to 1945 and as head of state (Führer und Reichskanzler) from 1934 to 1945.
2. Jeane Jordan Kirkpatrick (1926-2006)—American ambassador and an ardent anticommunist. After serving as Ronald Reagan's foreign policy adviser in his 1980 campaign and later in his Cabinet, the longtime Democrat-turned-Republican was nominated as the U.S. ambassador to the United Nations and became the first woman to hold this position. She is famous for her "Kirkpatrick Doctrine," which advocated U.S. support of anticommunist governments around the world, including authoritarian dictatorships, if they went along with Washington's aims—believing they could be led into democracy by example. Kirkpatrick served on Reagan's Cabinet on the National Security Council, Foreign Intelligence Advisory Board, Defense Policy Review Board, and chaired the Secretary of Defense Commission on Fail Safe and Risk reduction of the Nuclear Command and Control System.
3. The antiwar movement against Vietnam in the US from 1965-1971 was the most significant movement of its kind in the nation's history. Deep-rooted in early Sixties' student radicalism protesting political repression on college campuses, the Antiwar Movement is considered to be a direct outgrowth of the Free Speech Movement, led by the likes of Mario Savio at U.C. Berkeley. At the outbreak of the Vietnam War, student radicalism inspired by the Free Speech Movement later grew to represent a national voice protesting United States involvement

in the war, as Americans started to question the relevance of U.S. presence in a conflicts taking place halfway around the world.

4. John Forbes Kerry (*1943)—the junior United States Senator from Massachusetts and chairman of the Senate Foreign Relations Committee. As the presidential nominee of the Democratic Party, he was defeated by 34 electoral votes in the 2004 presidential election by the Republican incumbent President George W. Bush. Senator Kerry is currently the Chairman of the United States Senate Committee on Foreign Relations. He is a Vietnam veteran, and was a spokesman for Vietnam Veterans Against the War when he returned home from service. Before entering the Senate, he served as an Assistant District Attorney and Lieutenant Governor of Massachusetts under Michael Dukakis, who would also become a future democratic presidential nominee.
5. Thomas Jefferson (1743–1826)—the third President of the United States (1801–1809), the principal author of the Declaration of Independence (1776), and one of the most influential Founding Fathers for his promotion of the ideals of republicanism in the United States. Major events during his presidency include the Louisiana Purchase (1803) and the Lewis and Clark Expedition (1804–1806). As a political philosopher, Jefferson was a man of the Enlightenment and knew many intellectual leaders in Britain and France. He idealized the independent yeoman farmer as exemplar of republican virtues, distrusted cities and financiers, and favored states' rights and a strictly limited federal government.
6. James Earl "Jimmy" Carter, Jr. (*1924) served as the 39th President of the United States from 1977 to 1981 and was the recipient of the 2002 Nobel Peace Prize. Carter served two terms in the Georgia Senate and as the 76th Governor of Georgia, from 1971 to 1975. The final year of his presidential tenure was marked by several major crises, including the 1979 takeover of the American embassy in Iran and holding of hostages by Iranian students, a failed rescue attempt of the hostages, serious fuel shortages, and the Soviet invasion of Afghanistan.
7. George Walker Bush (*1946)—former President of the United States. Bush is the eldest son of the 41st U.S. President George H. W. Bush and Barbara Bush. He served as the 43rd President from 2001 to 2009. He was the 46th Governor of Texas from 1995 to 2000 before being sworn in as President on January 20, 2001.

PART 6

1. Pyotr Semyonovich Popov (died 1960)—major in the Soviet military intelligence (GRU). He was the first GRU official successfully recruited by the CIA. Between 1952 and 1958, he provided the United States with large amounts of information concerning military capabilities and espionage operations. Popov described the organization of the Soviet military command, provided the names of Russian intelligence agents in Europe and gave insight into the 'illegals' network run by the Soviets. He was arrested in 1958 and executed by Soviet authorities in 1960.
2. The Office of Strategic Services (OSS) was a United States intelligence agency formed during World War II. It was the wartime intelligence agency, and it was the predecessor of the Central Intelligence Agency (CIA). The OSS was estab-

lished by a Presidential military order issued by President Roosevelt on June 13, 1942. While the OSS produced a lot of information, its reliability was increasingly questioned by the British Intelligence. Eventually by May 1944 through collaboration between OSS, British Intelligence, Cairo and Washington the entire "Dogwood-chain" was found to be unreliable and dangerous. According to Venona intercepts program, which was declassified in 1995, the OSS housed at one time or another between fifteen and twenty Soviet spies. Duncan Lee, Donald Wheeler, Jane Foster Zlatowski, and Maurice Halperin passed information to Moscow. The War Production Board, the Board of Economic Warfare, the Office of the Coordinator of Inter-American Affairs and the Office of War Information, included at least half a dozen Soviet sources each among their employees. In the opinion of some, almost every American military and diplomatic agency of any importance was compromised to some extent by Soviet espionage. Some 349 persons identified had an intentional "covert relationship" with Soviet intelligence. A number of spies within the Manhattan Project have never been positively identified. Most are only known by their codenames, as revealed in the VENONA decrypts.

3. McCarthyism—the politically motivated practice of making accusations of disloyalty, subversion, or treason without proper regard for evidence. The term specifically describes activities associated with the period in the United States known as the Second Red Scare, lasting roughly from the late 1940s to the late 1950s and characterized by heightened fears of Communist influence on American institutions and espionage by Soviet agents. The Communist Party of the United States (CPUSA) increased its membership through the 1930s, reaching a peak of about 75,000 members in 1941. During the post–World War II era of McCarthyism, many thousands of Americans were accused of being Communists or communist sympathizers and became the subject of aggressive investigations and questioning before government or private-industry panels, committees and agencies. The primary targets of such suspicions were government employees, those in the entertainment industry, educators and union activists. In Congress, the primary bodies that investigated Communist activities were the House Committee on Un-American Activities, the Senate Internal Security Subcommittee, and the Senate Permanent Subcommittee on Investigations. Between 1949 and 1954, a total of 109 investigations were carried out by these and other committees of Congress.

4. The Venona project was a long-running and highly secret collaboration between intelligence agencies of the United States and United Kingdom that involved the cryptanalysis of messages sent by several intelligence agencies of the Soviet Union, mostly during World War II. In the early years of the Cold War, Venona would be an important source of information on Soviet intelligence activity for the Western powers. Although unknown to the public, and even to presidents Franklin D. Roosevelt and Harry Truman, the closely guarded program was of critical importance behind many famous events of the early Cold War, such as the Rosenberg spying case and the defections of Donald Maclean and Guy Burgess. Later with the release of the Mitrokhin Archives after the fall of the USSR much of Venona was corroborated. Most of the messages, which would later prove to be decipherable, were intercepted between 1942 and 1945. They were

decrypted beginning in 1946 and continuing until 1980, when Venona was cancelled. The Venona Project was initiated in 1943, under orders from the deputy Chief of Military Intelligence (G-2), Carter W. Clarke. Clarke distrusted Joseph Stalin, and feared that the Soviet Union would sign a separate peace with the Third Reich, allowing Germany to focus its military forces against Great Britain and the United States. Code-breakers of the U.S. Army's Signal Intelligence Service analyzed encrypted high-level Soviet diplomatic intelligence message intercepted in large volumes during and immediately after World War II by American, British and Australian listening posts. Approximately 2,200 of messages were decrypted and translated; some 50 percent of the 1943 GRU-Naval Washington to Moscow messages was broken. Out of some hundreds of thousands of intercepted encrypted texts, it is claimed that fewer than 3,000 have been partially or wholly decrypted. Venona makes crystal clear that the leadership of the CPUSA was not only aware of Soviet intelligence networks in the government, but also actively assisted the KGB in recruiting American communists to spy. The CPUSA even had several liaisons working with KGB spymasters. The KGB code word for members of the CPUSA was "Fellow Countrymen." Nearly every American who worked for the KGB or GRU was a member of the CPUSA. That does not mean, of course, that all communists were Soviet spies, but most assuredly, most spies were communists. The fact remained that some 200+ people who had served as Soviet spies were still unidentified. 235 spies were exposed by VENONA, highlighting the deep penetration of the OSS, and later the impact on CIA/FBI relationships. According to Venona intercepts President of Czechoslovak government-in-exile Edvard Benes was the Soviet spy codename "19."

5. Barry Morris Goldwater (1909–1998) was a five-term United States Senator from Arizona (1953–1965, 1969–1987) and the Republican Party's nominee for President in the 1964 election. He was also a Major General in the U.S. Air Force Reserve. He was known as "Mr. Conservative." Goldwater soon became most associated with labor-union reform and anti-communism; he was an active supporter of the conservative coalition in Congress.
6. Marxism-Leninism—communist ideology that emerged as the mainstream tendency among the Communist parties in the 1920s as it was adopted as the ideological foundation of the Communist International during Stalin's era. According to G. Lisichkin, Marxism-Leninism as a separate ideology was compiled by Stalin basically in his "The questions of Leninism" book. During the period of Stalin's rule in the Soviet Union, Marxism-Leninism was proclaimed the official ideology of the state. Some contemporary communist parties continue to regard Marxism-Leninism as their basic ideology, although some have modified it to adapt to new and local political circumstances.
7. Jackson Northman Anderson (1922–2005) was an American newspaper columnist and is considered one of the fathers of modern investigative journalism. Anderson won the 1972 Pulitzer Prize for National Reporting for his investigation on secret American policy decision-making between the United States and Pakistan during the Indo-Pakistan War of 1971. He discovered a CIA plot to assassinate Fidel Castro, and has also been credited for breaking the Iran-Contra affair.

8. The Watergate scandal was a political scandal during the presidency of Richard Nixon that resulted in the indictment and conviction of several of Nixon's closest advisors, and ultimately his resignation on August 9, 1974.
9. Joseph Raymond McCarthy (1908–1957) was an American politician who served as a Republican U.S. Senator from the state of Wisconsin from 1947 until his death in 1957. From 1950 onward, McCarthy continued to exploit the fear of Communism and to press his accusations that the government was failing to deal with Communism within its ranks. He was noted for making claims that there were large numbers of Communists and Soviet spies and sympathizers inside the federal government and elsewhere. He made accusations of Communist infiltration into the State Department, the administration of President Truman, Voice of America, and the United States Army. McCarthy and President Truman clashed often during the years both held office. McCarthy characterized Truman and the Democratic Party as soft on, or even in league with, Communists, and spoke of the Democrats' "twenty years of treason." It was the Truman Administration's State Department that McCarthy accused of harboring 205 (or 57 or 81) "known Communists." However, McCarthy was never able to substantiate his sensational charges. With the highly publicized Army-McCarthy hearings of 1954, McCarthy's support and popularity began to fade. Later in 1954, the Senate voted to censure Senator McCarthy by a vote of 67 to 22, making him one of the few senators ever to be disciplined in this fashion.
10. Vadim Viktorovich Bakatin (*1937) was a Soviet politician who served as the last chairman of the KGB in 1991. He was appointed to dismantle the KGB, but he was unable to control this organization and to fulfill the task.
11. Alexander Nikolaevich Yakovlev, (1923–2005) was a Russian economist who was a Soviet governmental official in the 1980s and a member of the Politburo and Secretariat of the Communist Party of the Soviet Union. The chief of party ideology, the same position as that previously held by Mikhail Suslov, he was called the "godfather of glasnost" and "God's commie" as he is considered to be the intellectual force behind Mikhail Gorbachev's reform program of glasnost and perestroika.
12. George John Tenet (*1953) was the Director of Central Intelligence for the United States Central Intelligence Agency and is Distinguished Professor in the Practice of Diplomacy at Georgetown University. Tenet held the position as the DCI from July 1997 to July 2004, making him the second-longest serving director in the agency's history — behind Allen Welsh Dulles.
13. Chekism is a term used by some historians and political scientists to emphasize the omnipotence and omnipresence of secret political police in the Soviet Union and contemporary Russia. Derived from Cheka, the name of the first Soviet secret police organization that conducted Red Terror in Russia, the word emphasizes the importance and political power of Cheka and the successor Soviet and Russian secret police services: the NKVD, KGB, and FSB. Some politologists define Chekism also as an imperial ideology that includes an aggressive anti-Americanism. Andrei Illarionov, a former advisor of Vladimir Putin, describes contemporary Chekism as a new socio-political order "distinct from any seen in our country before". In this model, members of the Corporation of Intelligence

Service Collaborators [Russian abbreviation KSSS] took over the entire body of state power, follow an omerta-like behavior code, and "are given instruments conferring power over others–membership "perks," such as the right to carry and use weapons." According to Illarionov, this "Corporation has seized key government agencies–the Tax Service, Ministry of Defense, Ministry of Foreign Affairs, Parliament, and the government-controlled mass media–which are now used to advance the interests of KSSS members. Through these agencies, every significant resource of the country–security/intelligence, political, economic, informational and financial–is being monopolized in the hands of Corporation members." The ideology of "Chekists" is "Nashism ("ours-ism"), the selective application of rights," he said. Chekists perceive themselves as a ruling class, with political powers transferred from one generation to another. According to a former FSB general, "A Chekist is a breed." "A good KGB heritage—a father or grandfather, say, who worked for the service—is highly valued by today's silovniki. Marriages between silovniki clans are also encouraged."

14. Viktor Andriyovych Yushchenko (*1954)—the third and current President of Ukraine. He took office on January 23, 2005. As an informal leader of the Ukrainian opposition coalition, he was one of the two main candidates in the October–November 2004 Ukrainian presidential election. Yushchenko won the election through a re-vote of the runoff between him and Viktor Yanukovych, the government-supported candidate. Yushchenko won in the revote (52% to 44%). Public protests prompted by the electoral fraud played a major role in that presidential election and led to Ukraine's Orange Revolution.
15. Alexander Grigoryevich Lukashenko (*1954)—served as the President of Belarus since 20 July 1994. Before his career as a politician, Lukashenko served as a military officer and worked as a director for manufacturing plants and farms. During his first two terms as President, Lukashenko restructured the Belarusian economy by introducing economic integration with the Russian Federation.
16. Vaclav Klaus—According to Robert Eringer, the former FBI counter-intelligence agent, we can reveal that Mr. Klaus, while a 21-year-old student at the University of Economics, Prague, in 1962, was recruited by Czech StB under codename "Vodicka." In 1970 Mr. Klaus starred in "Operation Rattrap," staged by StB with the assistance of Soviet KGB advisers. He was publicly named as an "anti-socialist malcontent" and "purged" from the Economic Institute. Its purpose was to pose Mr. Klaus as a "victim" of the regime so he could continue to penetrate dissident circles as a deep-cover mole. The ruse was successful and Mr. Klaus effectively monitored opposition activities and reported dissident intentions, succeeding also in establishing a personal relationship with underground leader Vaclav Havel, who would become the Czech Republic's first democratically-elected president in 1993. One of Mr. Klaus's first acts as a state official was to track down the operational file kept on him and shred it. However, a duplicate "Red File" had been dispatched to Moscow, in October 1989, for safekeeping. It remains in the archives of the Russian Foreign Intelligence Service (SVR). In December 1997 Mr. Klaus was forced to resign as prime minister due to complicity in a political funding and corruption scandal

stemming from a secret Swiss bank account in his name containing $5 million—exposed at the time as secret donations in exchange for special favors. Just over a year later, Mr. Klaus began a series of secret meetings with the SVR Resident (station chief) in Prague. An SVR officer told Mr.Eringer, "We opened an operational file on Klaus under the codename 'Kolesnikov,' and did not rule out the possibility of a recruitment attempt (on the basis of possessing his file and being privy to his darkest secret)." It is unclear whether Mr. Klaus's political career was resurrected with SVR assistance, but it's crystal clear that Mr. Klaus has since established an unusually close relationship with Vladimir Putin.

PART 7

1. Many documents Vladimir Bukovsky copied in Moscow's archives are available at http://psi.ece.jhu.edu/~kaplan/IRUSS/BUK/GBARC/buk.html
2. Mikhail Alexandrovich Bakunin (1814-1876)—well-known Russian revolutionary and theorist of collectivist anarchism. He is remembered as a major figure in the history of anarchism and an opponent of Marxism, especially of Marx's idea of dictatorship of the proletariat. He continues to be an influence on modern-day anarchists, such as Noam Chomsky.
3. The National Liberation Movement was a worldwide movement, which began between the first two world wars, growing to massive proportions after 1945, in favor of national self-determination for the colonies of the imperialist powers. The existence of the Soviet Union was the single most important factor that made national liberation achievable, because it gave a place for these nations to turn to.
4. The Tri-Continental or OSPAAAL (Organization of Solidarity with the People from Africa, Asia and Latin America) was another propaganda tool utilized to foment revolutions throughout the world and also to show Cuba's dislike of the United States through graphic image. One of the main purposes of the organization is to promote the causes of freedom fighters in the Third World. It was founded in Havana in January 1966, after the Tricontinental Conference, a meeting of leftist delegates from Guinea, the Congo, South Africa, Angola, Vietnam, Syria, North Korea, the Palestine Liberation Organization, Cuba, Puerto Rico, Chile and the Dominican Republic.
5. FARC—The Revolutionary Armed Forces of Colombia–People's Army, is a self-proclaimed Marxist-Leninist revolutionary guerrilla organization. FARC was established in the 1960s as the military wing of the Colombian Communist Party and thus originated as a guerrilla movement. The group later became involved with the cocaine trade during the 1980s to finance itself. According to the Colombian government, as of 2008, FARC have an estimated 6,000-10,000 members.
6. The International Socialist Division of Labor (June 7, 1962)—under the leadership of Nikita Khrushchev, head of both the CPSU and the Soviet government, efforts to intensify the economic integration of COMECON member states were stepped up in the 1960s. When joint economic planning foundered on Romania's resistance, a system was established that merely coordinated national economic planning.

7. The Red Brigades (often abbreviated as the BR) were a terrorist communist-inspired group located in Italy and active, mainly via political assassinations and bank robberies· The Red Brigades were founded in August 1970 by Renato Curcio, a student at the University of Trento, his girlfriend Margherita Cagol and Alberto Franceschini. According to Clarence A. Martin, the BR were credited with 14,000 acts of violence in the first ten years of the group's existence. According to Ion Pacepa, Red Brigades primary support allegedly came from the Czechoslovak StB and the Palestine Liberation Organization (PLO). Soviet and Czechoslovakia small arms and explosives would have came from the Middle East via heroin traffickers along well established smuggling routes. Logistic support and training were allegedly carried out directly by the Czechoslovak StB both in Prague and at remote PLO training camps in North Africa and Syria. According to the Mitrokhin Archives, the Italian Communist Party lodged several complaints with the Soviet ambassador in Rome regarding Czechoslovak support of the Red Brigades, but the Soviets were either unwilling or unable to stop the StB. This was one of several contributing factors in ending the covert relationship that the Italian Communist Party had with the KGB culminating with a total break in 1979.
8. The Red Army Faction or RAF (in its early stages commonly known as Baader-Meinhof Group) was postwar West Germany's most violent and prominent militant left-wing anti-capitalist group. It described itself as a communist "urban guerrilla" group engaged in armed resistance. The RAF was formally founded in 1970 by Andreas Baader, Gudrun Ensslin, Horst Mahler, Ulrike Meinhof, Irmgard Möller, and others. The RAF operated from the late 1960s to 1998, committing numerous operations, especially in the autumn of 1977, which led to a national crisis that became known as "German Autumn." It was responsible for 34 deaths, including many secondary targets—such as chauffeurs and bodyguards—and many injuries in almost 30 years of activity. After German reunification in 1990, it was confirmed that the RAF had received financial and logistic support from the Stasi, the security and intelligence organization of East Germany, which had given several members a shelter and new identities. This was already generally suspected at the time.
9. Yasser Arafat (1929-2004)—Palestinian leader. He was Chairman of the Palestine Liberation Organization, President of the Palestinian National Authority, and leader of the Fatah political party, which he founded in 1959. Arafat spent much of his life fighting against Israel in the name of Palestinian self-determination. Originally opposed to Israel's existence, he modified his position in 1988 when he accepted UN Security Council Resolution 242. He is known to many as the "father of modern terrorism." In fact, groups under Arafat's direct or indirect command–including Fatah, Black September, Tanzim and Al Aqsa Martyrs Brigade–were responsible for hundreds of bombings, hijackings, assassinations and other attacks, including the 1972 murder of 11 of Israel's Olympic athletes in Munich, the 1973 murder of the American ambassador to Sudan, Cleo Noel, and the 1985 hijacking of the Achille Lauro cruise ship (resulting in the murder of wheelchair-bound Leon Klinghoffer). In August 2002, the Israeli Military Intelligence Chief alleged that Arafat's personal wealth was in the range of USD $1.3 billion. In 2003 the International Monetary Fund (IMF) conducted an audit

of the PNA and stated that Arafat diverted $900 million in public funds to a special bank account controlled by Arafat and the PNA Chief Economic Financial adviser. Also in 2003, a team of American accountants–hired by Arafat's own finance ministry–began examining Arafat's finances. The team claimed that part of the Palestinian leader's wealth was in a secret portfolio worth close to $1 billion, with investments in companies like a Coca-Cola bottling plant in Ramallah, a Tunisian cell phone company and venture capital funds in the US and the Cayman Islands. The head of the investigation stated that "although the money for the portfolio came from public funds like Palestinian taxes, virtually none of it was used for the Palestinian people; it was all controlled by Arafat."

10. Carlos the Jackal, [Ilich Ramirez Sanchez], (*1949)—Venezuelan-born leftist terrorist. After several bungled bombings, Ramírez Sánchez achieved notoriety for a 1975 raid on the OPEC headquarters in Vienna, resulting in the death of three people. For many years he was among the most wanted international fugitives. He was given the nom de guerre Carlos when he became a member of the leftist Popular Front for Liberation of Palestine (PFLP). Carlos was given the "Jackal" moniker by the press (The Guardian) when the Frederick Forsyth novel The Day of the Jackal was reportedly found among his belongings. East European states tolerated Carlos. For over two years he lived in Hungary, in Budapest's noble quarter, the second district. His main go-between for some of his money-sources like Gaddhafi or Dr. George Habash was the friend of his sister "Dietmar C." C, a known German terrorist, was the leader of the Panther Brigade of the PFLP. Carlos was expelled from Hungary in late 1985. During his career, most of it during the Cold War, western accounts persistently claimed he was a KGB agent but the link is tenuous at best. He is now serving a life sentence in Clairvaux Prison in northeast France. He is known to have had a sporadic correspondence with Venezuelan President Hugo Chávez from his prison cell. President Chávez replied, with a letter in which he addresses Carlos as "distinguished compatriot." On June 1, 2006, Chávez referred to him as his "good friend" during a meeting of OPEC countries held in Caracas.

PART 8

1. The Mossad—Institute for Intelligence and Special Operations) is the national intelligence agency of Israel.
2. Terry Reed—businessman and long-time CIA asset, author of the book Compromised: Clinton, Bush, and the CIA. (S.P.I. Books/ Shapolsky Publishers Inc.: NY. 1994). His story feeds into the hypothesis shared by many scholars that the contra supply apparatus organized by the CIA was fused with pipelines of narcotics into the US.
3. Felix Rodriguez (born 1941 in Havana, Cuba) was a Central Intelligence Agency officer famous for his involvement in the Bay of Pigs invasion, in the interrogation and execution of the Marxist-Leninist revolutionary Che Guevara. Rodriguez was also involved in the Contra resupply operation during the Reagan Administration's war against the Nicaraguan communists. He had close ties to George H.W. Bush.

4. The Medellin Cartel was an organized network of "Drug Suppliers and Smugglers" originating in the city of Medellín, Colombia. The Cartel operated in Colombia, Bolivia, Peru, Central America, The United States, as well as Canada and even Europe throughout the 1970s and 1980s. It was founded and run by Pablo Escobar, Jorge Ochoa, along with Ochoa's brothers Juan David and Fabio. During the height of its operations, the Cartel brought in more than $60 million per month. The total amount of money made by the Cartel was in the tens of billions, and very possibly the hundreds of billions of dollars.
5. William Jefferson "Bill" Clinton (*1946)—served as the 42nd President of the United States from 1993 to 2001. He was elected Governor of Arkansas in 1978, making him the youngest governor in the country at age thirty-two and he kept his job for ten years.
6. Chasing Dirty Money by Peter Reuter and Edwin M.Truman, published by Institute For International Economics in Boston ©2004, page 14.

PART 9

1. James Baker (*1930)—served as the Chief of Staff in President Ronald Reagan's first administration and in the final year of the administration of President George H. W. Bush. Baker also served as Secretary of the Treasury from 1985-1988 in the second Reagan administration, and Secretary of State in the George H. W. Bush administration.
2. Harry Lloyd Hopkins (1890-1946)—one of Franklin Delano Roosevelt's closest advisers. He was one of the architects of the New Deal. Christopher Andrew reported in the book KGB The Inside Story based on information provided by Oleg Gordievsky that Iskhak Ahkmerov, the KGB officer who controlled the illegal Soviet agents in the U.S. during the war, had said that Hopkins was "the most important of all Soviet wartime agents in the United States." Hopkins secret meetings with Ahkmerov were not known to anyone until Gordievsky revealed them. They began before Hopkins made a trip to Moscow in July 1941, a month after the Germans invaded the Soviet Union. His insistence that aid be extended to Stalin with no strings attached justifies Ahkmerov's evaluation of his performance. There is evidence that Hopkins even went so far as to arrange for the shipment of uranium to the Soviet Union to help them develop the atomic bomb. Despite this, Andrew argued that Harry Hopkins was "an unconscious rather than a conscious agent." After Vasily Mitrokhin defected in 1992 his documents showed that Hopkins had warned the Soviet ambassador that the FBI had learned through a bug it had placed in the home of Steve Nelson, a Soviet illegal agent, that Nelson was getting money from the embassy. Ray Wannall, former FBI assistant director for counter-intelligence, says he always suspected that Hopkins was a Soviet agent and that this is proof of his treachery.
3. Armand Hammer (1898–1990)—flamboyant United States business tycoon most closely associated with Occidental Petroleum, a company he ran for decades. He was known as well for his art collection, philanthropy, and for his close ties to the Soviet Union. Thanks to business interests around the world and his "citizen diplomacy," Hammer cultivated a wide network of friends and acquaintances.

Late in life, he would brag that he had been the only man in history friendly with both Lenin and Ronald Reagan. Hammer remains a controversial figure because of his ties to the Soviet Union, which led to speculation that he was disloyal to the United States. Hammer was born in Manhattan, New York to Russian-born Jewish immigrants Julius and Rose Hammer. His father was brought to the United States from Odessa in 1875 and settled in The Bronx. According to multiple biographers, Hammer was named after the "Arm and Hammer" symbol of the Socialist Labor Party of America, in which his father, a committed socialist, had a leadership role at one time. Later in his life Hammer would admit the communist tie himself. Hammers' name was widely used in propaganda by the Soviets. The contradiction between Hammer's open sympathy for the Soviet Union and his success as a capitalist, as well as his involvement in international affairs and politics, have made Hammer a subject of suspicion and conspiracy theory for many. Further, his close relationship with former Democratic Tennessee Senator Albert Gore, Sr., despite Hammer's own party affiliations, has been the subject of especially broad scrutiny and speculation. Edward Jay Epstein in his book Dossier: The Secret History of Armand Hammer claims that James Angleton, head of counterintelligence for the CIA, said that the CIA has received evidence from the British secret service that Hammer laundered money for the Soviets.

4. Isidor Feinstein Stone—American journalist, a Soviet spy working for KGB since 1936 under code name Pancake.
5. Walter Duranty—(1884-1957), was a Liverpool-born British journalist who served as the New York Times Moscow bureau chief from 1922 to 1936. Duranty won a Pulitzer Prize in 1932 for a set of stories written in 1931 on the Soviet Union. He has since fallen into disrepute because of his denying the terror famine organized by Stalin in Ukraine.

PART 10

1. Lavrentiy Pavlovich Beria (1899-1953)—Soviet politician and chief of the Soviet security and police apparatus, Soviet chief of secret police under Joseph Stalin.

   In August 1938 Stalin brought Beria to Moscow as deputy head of the People's Commissariat for Internal Affairs (NKVD), the ministry overseeing the state security and police forces. In March 1939 Beria became a candidate member of the Communist Party's Politburo. In February 1941 he became a Deputy Chairman of the Council of People's Commissars and in June, when Nazi Germany invaded the Soviet Union, he became a member of the State Defense Committee. In 1944, as the Germans were driven from Soviet soil, Beria was in charge of dealing with the various ethnic minorities accused of collaboration with the invaders, including the Chechens, the Ingush, the Crimean Tartars and the Volga Germans. All these were deported to Soviet Central Asia, with significant loss of life. In December 1945 Beria left the post of Minister for Internal Affairs while retaining general control over national security matters from his post of Deputy Prime Minister, under Stalin. During the postwar years Beria supervised the establishment of Soviet-style systems of secret police in the countries of the Warsaw Pact, and after the Soviet Union's break with Tito he organized show trials of Communist leaders such as Laszlo Rajk in Hungary and Rudolf Slansky in Czechoslovakia. Despite Beria's history as Stalin's most ruthless henchmen, he was at the forefront of liberalization after Stalin's death, presumably as a means of winning support for his campaign to become leader. He signed a decree banning the use of torture in Soviet prisons, despite his own history of personally torturing many people. He persuaded the Presidium and the Council of Ministers to urge the Communist regime in East Germany to allow liberal economic and political reforms. Beria's past made it impossible for him to lead a liberalizing regime in the Soviet Union, a role that later fell to Khrushchev. The essential task of Soviet reformers was to bring the secret police under party control, and Beria could not do this since the police were the basis of his own power. Accounts of Beria's fall vary. According to the most recent accounts Khrushchev convened a meeting of the Presidium on June 26, where he launched an attack on Beria, accusing him of being in the pay of British intelligence. Beria was taken completely by surprise. Molotov and others then also spoke against Beria, and Khrushchev put a motion for his instant dismissal. Malenkov then pressed a button on his desk as the pre-arranged signal to Marshal Georgy Zhukov and a group of armed officers in a nearby room. They immediately burst in and arrested Beria. In December 1953 it was announced that Beria and six accomplices had been "conspiring for many years to seize power in the Soviet Union and restore capitalism." Beria was tried by a "special tribunal," and was allowed no representation and no appeal. When the death sentence was passed, he and his subordinates were immediately executed.

2. STASI—The Ministry for State Security in East Germany. Founded on February 8, 1950 it was modeled on the Soviet MGB and was regarded by the Soviet Union as an extremely loyal and effective partner. The STASI infiltrated almost every aspect of GDR life. In the mid-1980s, a network of civilian informants began growing in both German states. By the time East Germany collapsed in 1989, the STASI employed an estimated 91,000 employees and 300,000 informants. About one of every 50 East Germans collaborated with the STASI–one of the most extensive police infiltrations of a society in history.
3. Putin lived in Dresden between 1984-90 and never publicly explained what he did there. He was formally assigned to run a Soviet-German "friendship house" in Leipzig and carried out duties. This was his own cover story. His real job was discovering potential KGB agents among foreign students at the Technical University. He looked for people whose families were parts of the political elite at home, and who could become valuable informants after returning to their native countries. Putin was also involved in the secret "Lutsch" (the Beam) operation, in which the KGB observed its own friends, i.e., the East German leadership. According to German intelligence specialists who described Putin's task, the goal was stealing Western technology or NATO secrets. A newly revealed document shows Putin was trying to recruit agents to be trained in "wireless communications." But for what purpose is not clear.
4. Larry King, born as Lawrence Harvey Zeiger (*1933)—American television and radio host. He is recognized in the United States as one of the premier broadcast interviewers of modern times.

PART 11

1. The International Foundation for Socio-Economic and Political Studies (The Gorbachev Foundation) was created by Mikhail Gorbachev, former President of the USSR, in January 1992. Its inauguration took place in March 1992. The Foundation became one of the first independent think tanks in the post-Soviet Russia. The Public Affairs Center was set up as the Gorbachev Foundation's public outreach arm to study and preserve the heritage of Perestroika, as well as to discuss, support and promote the ideas and non-governmental projects which facilitate the consolidation of civil society and democratic reforms in Russia. The Public Affairs Center is working closely with the Gorbachev Foundation's Research and Information Center assisting in developing research and public activities carried out by the Gorbachev Foundation.
2. George Gordon Byron (1788–1824)—British poet and a leading figure in Romanticism.
3. Eric Arthur Blair (1903-1950)—better known by his pen name George Orwell, was an English author. His work is marked by a profound consciousness of social injustice, an intense opposition to totalitarianism, and a passion for clarity in language. His most famous works are the satirical novel Animal Farm (1945) and the dystopian novel Nineteen Eighty-Four (1949).
4. Aldous Leonard Huxley (1894-1963)—English writer. Huxley analyzed the causes of this, such as overpopulation as well as all the means by which populations can be controlled. He was particularly interested in the effects of drugs and subliminal suggestion. Best known for Brave New World a novel written in 1931 and published in 1932. Set in the London of AD 2540 the novel anticipates developments in reproductive technology and sleep-learning that combine to change society. The future society is a living embodiment of the ideals that form the basis of futurism. Huxley answers this book with a reassessment in an essay, Brave New World Revisited (1958), and with his final work, a novel titled Island (1962).
5. Sumer was a civilization and a historical region located in Southern Iraq (Mesopotamia), known as the Cradle of civilization. It lasted from the first settlement of Eridu in the Ubaid period (late 6th millennium BC) through the Uruk period (4th millennium BC) and the Dynastic periods (3rd millennium BC) until the rise of Babylon in the early 2nd millennium BC.
6. The Roman Empire was the post-Republican phase of the ancient Roman civilization, characterized by an autocratic form of government and large territorial holdings in Europe and around the Mediterranean.
7. Napoleon Bonaparte (1769-1821)—military and political leader of France whose actions shaped European politics in the early 19th century.
8. Francois Maurice Adrien Marie Mitterrand (1916-1996)—served as President of France from 1981 to 1995, elected as representative of the Socialist Party (PS). He became the first socialist president of the Fifth Republic and the first left-wing head of state since 1957. He is to date the only member of the Socialist Party to be elected President of France. He was re-elected in 1988 and held office until 1995. During each of his two terms, he dissolved the Parliament after

his election to have a majority during the first five years of his term, and then each time his party lost the next legislative elections. As of 2009 he holds the record of longest serving (almost 14 years) President of France.

9. Felipe Gonzalez Marquez (*1942)—Spanish socialist politician. He was the General Secretary of the Spanish Socialist Workers' Party (PSOE) from 1974 to 1997. To date, he remains the longest-serving Prime Minister of the Spanish government, after having served four successive mandates from 1982 to 1996.
10. Willy Brandt (1913–1992)—German politician, Chancellor of West Germany 1969–1974, and leader of the Social Democratic Party of Germany (SPD) 1964–1987. His most important legacy is the Ostpolitik, a policy aimed at improving relations with East Germany, Poland, and the Soviet Union. This policy caused considerable controversy in West Germany, but won Brandt the Nobel Peace Prize in 1971. Brandt was forced to resign as Chancellor in 1974 after it was exposed that one of his closest aides had been working for the Stasi (the East German secret police). This became one of the biggest political scandals in postwar West German history.
11. Markentalism—French economists Adam Smith (1767-1832) and Jean-Baptiste Say.
12. Nazism—officially National Socialism refers to the ideology and practices of the National Socialist German Workers' Party under Adolf Hitler, and the policies adopted by the dictatorial government of Nazi Germany from 1933 to 1945. Nazism is often considered by scholars to be a form of fascism.
13. Genghis Khan—founder and emperor of the Mongol Empire, the largest contiguous empire in history. He came to power by uniting many of the nomadic tribes of northeast Asia. After founding the Mongol Empire he started the Mongol invasions and raids of the Kara-Khitan Khanate, Caucasus, Khwarezmid Empire, Western Xia and Jin dynasties. During his life, the Mongol Empire eventually occupied a substantial portion of Central Asia.
14. Franklin Delano Roosevelt (1882-1945)—the 32nd President of the United States. He was a central figure of the 20th century during a time of worldwide economic crisis and world war. Elected to four terms in office, he served from 1933 to 1945 and is the only U.S. president to have served more than two terms. During the Great Depression of the 1930s, Roosevelt created the New Deal to provide relief for the unemployed, recovery of the economy, and reform of the economic and banking systems. He led the United States as it became the 'Arsenal of Democracy.' Roosevelt, working closely with his aide Harry Hopkins, made the United States the principal arms supplier and financier of the Allies. He and his wife, Eleanor Roosevelt, remain touchstones for modern American liberalism. Roosevelt's administration redefined American liberalism and realigned the Democratic Party.
15. Zbigniew Kazimierz Brzezinski (*1928)—Polish-born American political scientist, geostrategist, and statesman who served as United States National Security Advisor to President Jimmy Carter from 1977 to 1981. Known for his hawkish foreign policy at a time when the Democratic Party was increasingly dovish, he is a foreign policy "realist." Major foreign policy events during his term of office

included the normalization of relations with the People's Republic of China (and the severing of ties with the Republic of China), the signing of the second Strategic Arms Limitation Treaty (SALT II), the brokering of the Camp David Accords, the transition of Iran from an important US client state to an anti-Western Islamic Republic, and encouraging dissidents in Eastern Europe. He became a leading critic of the Nixon-Kissinger détente. Brzezinski co-founded the Trilateral Commission with David Rockefeller, serving as director from 1973 to 1976. He is currently professor of American foreign policy at Johns Hopkins University's School of Advanced International Studies, a scholar at the Center for Strategic and International Studies.

16. Yoshihiro Francis Fukuyama (*1952)—American philosopher, political economist, and author. Fukuyama is best known as the author of The End of History and the Last Man, in which he argued that the progression of human history as a struggle between ideologies is largely at an end, with the world settling on liberal democracy after the end of the Cold War and the fall of the Berlin Wall in 1989. Fukuyama predicted the eventual global triumph of political and economic liberalism: "What we may be witnessing is not just the end of the Cold War, or the passing of a particular period of post-war history, but the end of history as such . . . That is, the end point of mankind's ideological evolution and the universalization of Western liberal democracy as the final form of human government."
17. The Trilateral Commission is a private organization, established to foster closer cooperation between the United States, Europe and Japan. It was founded in July 1973, at the initiative of David Rockefeller who was Chairman of the Council on Foreign Relations at that time. Rockefeller proposed the creation of an International Commission of Peace and Prosperity in early 1972 (which would later become the Trilateral Commission). At the 1972 Bilderberg meeting, the idea was widely accepted, but elsewhere, it got a cool reception. According to Rockefeller, the organization could "be of help to government by providing measured judgment." In July 1972, Rockefeller called his first meeting, which was held at Rockefeller's Pocantico compound in New York's Hudson Valley. It was attended by about 250 individuals who were carefully selected and screened by Rockefeller and represented the very elite of finance and industry. The organization has come under much scrutiny and criticism by political activists and academics working in the social and political sciences. President Jimmy Carter appointed 26 former Commission members to senior positions in his Administration. Later it was revealed that Carter himself was a former Trilateral member. In the 1980 election, it was revealed that Carter and his two major opponents, John B. Anderson and George H. W. Bush, were also members, and the Commission became a campaign issue. Ronald Reagan was not a Trilateral member, but after being chosen as Republican nominee he pick Bush as his running mate. As president, he appointed a few Trilateral members to Cabinet positions and held a reception for the Commission in the White House in 1984. The John Birch Society believes that the Trilateral Commission is dedicated to the formation of one world government. In 1980, Holly Sklar released a book titled Trilateralism: the Trilateral Commission and Elite Planning for World Management. Alex Jones claims the "Commission constitutes a conspiracy seeking to gain control of the U.S. Government to create a new world order." Sen. Barry Goldwater wrote in

his book With No Apologies "In my view, the Trilateral Commission represents a skillful, coordinated effort to seize control and consolidate the four centers of power: political, monetary, intellectual, and ecclesiastical. All this is to be done in the interest of creating a more peaceful, more productive world community. What the Trilateralists truly intend is the creation of a worldwide economic power superior to the political governments of the nation-states involved. They believe the abundant materialism they propose to create will overwhelm existing differences. As managers and creators of the system they will rule the future."

18. David Rockefeller Sr. (*1915)—American banker, statesman, globalist, and the current patriarch of the Rockefeller family. He is founder, honorary chairman, and lifetime trustee of the Trilateral Commission. Mr. Rockefeller serves as honorary chairman of the Americas Society, the Council on Foreign Relations and Rockefeller University. He is also former chairman of the Rockefeller University Council, and chairman emeritus of the Museum of Modern Art in New York City. A graduate of Harvard College and the University of Chicago (Ph.D.), Mr. Rockefeller served as an officer of the Chase Manhattan Bank from 1946 to 1981. He was chairman and chief executive officer from 1969 until 1980, and continued as chairman until his retirement in 1981. He served as chairman of the bank's international advisory committee from 1981 to 1999 and remained a member of the international council of J.P. Morgan Chase until 2005. Mr. Rockefeller has also been involved in numerous other businesses, cultural and educational organizations. A lifelong globalist, due to the strong influence of his father, he had at an early age further spread his connections when he was invited to attend the inaugural elitist Bilderberg Group meetings, starting with the Holland gathering in 1954. He has been a consistent attendee through the decades and has been a member of the "steering committee," which determines the invitation list for the upcoming annual meetings. These have frequently included prominent national figures that have gone on to be elected as political leaders of their respective countries. David Rockefeller joined the Council on Foreign Relations as its youngest-ever director in 1949 and subsequently became chairman of the board from 1970 to 1985; today he serves as honorary chairman. In 2002 Rockefeller authored his autobiography "Memoirs" wherein, on page 405, Mr. Rockefeller writes: "For more than a century ideological extremists at either end of the political spectrum have seized upon well-publicized incidents such as my encounter with Castro to attack the Rockefeller family for the inordinate influence they claim we wield over American political and economic institutions. Some even believe we are part of a secret cabal working against the best interests of the United States, characterizing my family and me as "internationalists" and of conspiring with others around the world to build a more integrated global political and economic structure—one world, if you will. If that's the charge, I stand guilty, and I am proud of it."

19. Valery Giscard d'Estaing (*1926)—French centre-right politician who was President of the French Republic from 1974 until 1981. He is a proponent of the United States of Europe and, having limited his involvement in national politics after his defeat, he became involved with the European Union. He notably presided over the Convention on the Future of the European Union that drafted

the ill-fated Treaty establishing a Constitution for Europe. He took part, with a prominent role, to the annually held Bilderberg private conference.

20. Henry Alfred Kissinger (*1923)—German-born American political scientist, diplomat, and winner of the Nobel Peace Prize. A proponent of Realpolitik, Kissinger played a dominant role in United States foreign policy between 1969 and 1977. During this period, he pioneered the policy of détente and the formation of a new strategic anti-Soviet Sino-American alliance. He negotiated a settlement ending the Vietnam war, but the cease-fire proved unstable and no lasting peace resulted beyond the retreat of US troops. Kissinger served as National Security Advisor and Secretary of State under President Richard Nixon, and continued as Secretary of State under Nixon's successor Gerald Ford. He was the "most frequent visitor" to the George W. Bush White House as an unofficial political advisor on Israel and the Middle East—including the invasion and occupation of Iraq. In 1977 Kissinger was appointed to Georgetown University's Center for Strategic and International Studies. He is known to be member of the Bilderberg Group, Bohemian Grove, Trilateral Commission, Council on Foreign Relations, and Aspen Institute.
21. Yasuhiro Nakasone (*1918)—Japanese politician who served as Prime Minister of Japan from November 27, 1982 to November 6, 1987. A contemporary of Ronald Reagan, Helmut Kohl, François Mitterrand, Margaret Thatcher, and Mikhail Gorbachev, he is best known for pushing through the privatization of state-owned companies, and for helping to revitalize Japanese nationalism during and after his term as prime minister.
22. Fascism—comprises a radical and authoritarian nationalist political ideology and a corporatist economic ideology. Fascists advocate the creation of a single-party state. Fascist governments forbid and suppress criticism and opposition to the government and the fascist movement. Fascism opposes class conflict, blames capitalist liberal democracies for its creation and communists for exploiting the concept. Fascism is much defined by what it opposes, what scholars call the fascist negations—its opposition to individualism, rationalism, liberalism, conservatism and communism. In the economic sphere, many fascist leaders have claimed to support a "Third Way" in economic policy, which they believed superior to both the rampant individualism of unrestrained capitalism and the severe control of state communism. This was to be achieved by a form of government control over business and labor. No common and concise definition exists for fascism and historians and political scientists disagree on what should be in any concise definition.
23. Betrayal: How the Clinton Administration Undermined American Security, by Bill Gertz, 1999.
24. John Fitzgerald "Jack" Kennedy (1917-1963)—35th President of the United States; established the Peace Corps; assassinated on November 22, 1963, in Dallas, Texas.
25. Lyndon Baines Johnson (1908–1973)—often referred to as LBJ, served as the 36th President of the United States from 1963 to 1969 after serving as the Vice President of the United States from 1961 to 1963. He succeeded to the presidency following the assassination of President John F. Kennedy, completed

Kennedy's term and was elected President in his own right in a landslide victory in the 1964 Presidential election. As President was responsible for designing the "Great Society" legislation that included civil rights laws, Medicare, Medicaid, aid to education, and the "War on Poverty." Simultaneously, he escalated the American involvement in the Vietnam War from 16,000 American soldiers in 1963 to 500,000 in early 1968.

26. Peter Maurice Wright (1916-1995)—English scientist and former MI5 counterintelligence officer noted for writing the controversial book Spycatcher, which became an international bestseller with sales of over two million copies. Spycatcher was part memoir, part exposé of what Wright claimed to be serious institutional failings in MI5 and his subsequent investigations into it. He was a friend of the CIA counterintelligence chief James Angleton.
27. The African National Congress (ANC) has been South Africa's governing party, supported by its tripartite alliance with the Congress of South African Trade Unions (COSATU) and the South African Communist Party (SACP), since the establishment of non-racial democracy in April 1994. It defines itself as a "disciplined force of the left." The organization became the ANC in 1923 and formed a military wing, the Umkhonto we Sizwe (Spear of the Nation) in 1961. The ANC was often criticized by western governments who shared the South African government's characterization of the group as a terrorist organization. Several high-profile anti-Apartheid activists such as Archbishop Desmond Tutu criticized the ANC for its willingness to resort to violence. The ANC's willingness to ally with Communists was also the subject of both foreign and domestic criticism. A Pentagon report of the late 1980s described the ANC as "a major terrorist organization."
28. Hugo Rafael Chavez Frias (*1954) is the President of Venezuela. As the leader of the Bolivarian Revolution, Chávez promotes a political doctrine of participatory democracy, socialism and Latin American and Caribbean cooperation. He is also a critic of neoliberalism, globalization, and United States foreign policy. A career military officer, Chavez founded the left-wing Fifth Republic Movement after orchestrating a failed 1992 coup d'état against former President Carlos Andres Perez. He was elected President of Venezuela in 1998 and re-elected in 2000 and 2006. Supporters view him as a socialist liberator, hailing him for promoting Latin American integration, an enemy of imperialism and neoliberalism, empowering Venezuela's poor and indigenous communities, and reducing poverty and unemployment. Critics of Chavez in Venezuela and the United States claim that the Chavez government is leading Venezuela in an authoritarian direction, with Chavez himself becoming a dictator, abandoning democratic tradition, extending state control over the economy, eliminating dissent, and carrying out "social programs that will set Venezuela back." Inter-American Commission on Human Rights, human rights watch, and European parliament express concern about human rights Situation in Venezuela under Chavez governing.
29. Fidel Alejandro Castro Ruz (*1926)—former Head of State of Cuba, a position he held for nearly 50 years, and a leader of the Cuban Revolution. Fidel Castro, as he is widely known, was the Prime Minister of Cuba from February 1959 to December 1976 and then President of the Council of State of Cuba

until he transferred power to his brother Raúl Castro in February 2008. He was born to a millionaire Spanish father and went to the most elite schools. He started a political career at early age and was a recognized figure in politics. Castro came to power as a result of the Cuban revolution that overthrew the U.S-backed dictator Fulgencio Batista, and shortly became Prime Minister of Cuba. Instead of filling his initial promise, to have democratic elections "within months," he delayed them and eventually abolished them. Castro purged labor unions, moderates, took control of the media, and loyalty to him became the primary criteria for all appointments. In 1965 he became First Secretary of the Communist Party of Cuba and led the transformation of Cuba into a one-party socialist republic.

30. Georg Wilhelm Friedrich Hegel (1770-1831)—German philosopher, and with Johann Gottlieb Fichte and Friedrich Wilhelm Joseph Schelling, one of the creators of German Idealism. In particular, he developed a concept of mind or spirit that manifested itself in a set of contradictions and oppositions that it ultimately integrated and united, such as those between nature and freedom, and immanence and transcendence, without eliminating either pole or reducing it to the other.
31. Vilfredo Federico Damaso Pareto (1848-1923)—Italian industrialist, sociologist, economist, and philosopher. He made several important contributions to economics, particularly in the study of income distribution and in the analysis of individuals' choices.
32. Carl Jacob Christoph Burckhardt (1818-1897)—Swiss historian of art and culture, and an influential figure in the historiography of each field. He is known as one of the major progenitors of cultural history, albeit in a form very different from how cultural history is conceived and studied in academia today.

PART 12

1. Ladislav Bittman (*1930)—STB agent since 1954. In 1956 he became the deputy chief of Czechoslovakia's department of disinformation, running propaganda campaigns against the United States and other countries. After the Soviet invasion of Czechoslovakia in 1968 he defected to the United States and became a US citizen in 1979.
2. The KGB and Soviet Disinformation by Ladislav Bittman, page 70.
3. Vladimir Sakharov—Soviet diplomat, Middle Eastern specialist, and KGB agent who defected to the U.S. in 1972.
4. The KGB and Soviet Disinformation by Ladislav Bittman, pages 110-112.
5. Stanislav Alexandrovich Levchenko (*1941)—KGB defector. He started working for GRU in 1966 and switched to KGB in 1968. In 1975, he was sent undercover abroad, as journalist in Tokyo, Japan. From 1975 to 1979, he posed as a Soviet journalist in Japan working for the Russian magazine New Times (Novoye Vremya) and directing Soviet covert operations in Japan and East Asia, helping influence and recruit Japanese officials and journalists. In 1979, he was promoted to the rank of KGB Major and appointed Acting Chief of the Active Measures (Covert Action) Group of the Tokyo Residency of the KGB. He

defected to the United States in 1979 and obtained U.S. citizenship in 1989. He was instrumental in detailing the KGB's Japanese spy network to the U.S government, including Congressional testimony in the early 1980s. After his defection, Levchenko supplied the names of about 200 Japanese agents who had been used by the KGB. Included in his list were a former labour minister for the Liberal Democratic Party, Hirohide Ishida and Socialist Party leader Seiichi Katsumata. Takuji Yamane of the newspaper Sankei Shimbun was also mentioned. A Soviet court condemned Levchenko to death in 1981. Svetlana and Nikolai Ogorodnikov tried to hunt him down in the United States, but they were exposed in the Richard Miller spy case.

6. The KGB and Soviet Disinformation by Ladislav Bittman, page 109.
7. Comrade J, by Pete Earley, page 8.
8. David Szady—currently serves as the National Counterintelligence Executive, a position created by Presidential Decision Directive in December 2000. Mr. Szady was appointed by the Counterintelligence Board of Directors and was affirmed by the Director of Central Intelligence, the Secretary of Defense, and the Attorney General in March 2001. He has more than 28 years of service in the FBI, with 25 years experience in espionage and foreign counterintelligence investigations.
9. Enemies: How America's Foes Steal Our Vital Secrets-And How We Let It Happen, by Bill Gertz, 2006, page 127.
10. The Council on Foreign Relations (CFR)—American nonpartisan foreign policy membership organization founded in 1921 and based in New York City, with an additional office in Washington, D.C. Some international journalists and American paleoconservatives believe it to be the most powerful private organization to influence United States foreign policy. It publishes the bi-monthly journal Foreign Affairs and has an extensive website. The Council's mission is promoting understanding of foreign policy and the United States' role in the world. It has a think tank that employs prominent scholars in international affairs and it commissions subsequent books and reports. A central aim of the Council, it states, is to "find and nurture the next generation of foreign policy leaders." It established "Independent Task Forces" in 1995, which encourage policy debate. Comprising experts with diverse backgrounds and expertise, these task forces seek consensus in making policy recommendations on critical issues. The internal think tank is The David Rockefeller Studies Program, which grants fellowships and programs are described as being integral to the goal of contributing to the ongoing debate on foreign policy. At the outset of the organization, founding member Elihu Root said the group's mission should be to "guide" American public opinion. In the early 1970s, the CFR changed the mission, saying that it wished instead to "inform" public opinion. Today it has about 4,300 members, which over its history have included senior serving politicians, more than a dozen Secretaries of State, former national security officers, bankers, lawyers, professors, former CIA members and senior media figures. Journalist Joseph Kraft, a former member of both the CFR and the Trilateral Commission, said the Council "comes close to being an organ of what C. Wright Mills has called the Power Elite–a group of men, similar in interest and outlook, shaping events from invulnerable positions behind the scenes." The Council has been the subject of many conspiracy theories. This is partly due to

the number of high-ranking government officials in its membership, among with world business leaders, its secrecy clauses, and the large number of aspects of American foreign policy that its members have been involved with. Some believes that the CFR plans a one-world government.

11. The Bilderberg Group—unofficial annual invitation-only conference of around 130 guests, most of whom are persons of influence in the fields of politics, business, and banking. Although the group has no official name, the "Bilderberg Group" title comes from what is generally recognized to be the location of its first official meeting in 1954: the Bilderberg Hotel in Arnhem, the Netherlands. It has an office in Leiden in the Netherlands. The steering committee does not publish a list of attendees, though some participants have publicly discussed their attendance. Historically, attendee lists have been weighted towards politicians, bankers, and directors of large businesses. Because of its secrecy and refusal to issue news releases, the group is frequently accused of secretive and nefarious world plots. This thinking has progressively found acceptance within both elements of the populist movement and fringe politics. The radio host Alex Jones claims the Bilderberg Group intends to dissolve the sovereignty of the United States and other countries into a supra-national structure called the North American Union.
12. THE SPOTLIGHT: The Media Protects Bilderberg Group by James P. Tucker Jr.
13. The Grand Chessboard by Zbigniew Brzezinski, page 215.
14. Oleg Gordievsky was transported to the hospital on November 2, 2007 and remained unconscious for 34 hours. He claims being poisoned with thallium by a Russian assassin who visited him in his house. MI6 refused to investigate the case.
15. Anna Politkovskaya—Russian journalist, was an outspoken critic of the war in Chechnya. She was found shot dead in Moscow in October 7, 2006.

Index

LaVergne, TN USA
09 September 2010
196491LV00008B/37/P